I0124531

Marketing Dreams,
Manufacturing Heroes

Marketing Dreams, Manufacturing Heroes

THE TRANSNATIONAL LABOR BROKERING OF FILIPINO WORKERS

ANNA ROMINA GUEVARRA

RUTGERS UNIVERSITY PRESS
New Brunswick, New Jersey, and London

Library of Congress Cataloging-in-Publication Data

Guevarra, Anna Romina, 1973–
    Marketing dreams, manufacturing heroes : the transnational labor brokering
of Filipino workers / Anna Romina Guevarra.
        p. cm.
    Includes bibliographical references and index.
    ISBN 978–0–8135–4633–9 (hardcover : alk. paper)
    ISBN 978–0–8135–4634–6 (pbk. : alk. paper)
    1. Filipinos—Employment—Foreign countries.   2. Alien labor, Philippine.
I. Title.
    HD8714.G83   2009
    331.6′2599—dc22   2009008094

A British Cataloging-in-Publication record for this book is available
from the British Library.

Copyright © 2010 by Anna Romina Guevarra

All rights reserved

No part of this book may be reproduced or utilized in any form or by any means,
electronic or mechanical, or by any information storage and retrieval system,
without written permission from the publisher. Please contact Rutgers University
Press, 100 Joyce Kilmer Avenue, Piscataway, NJ 08854–8099. The only exception
to this prohibition is "fair use" as defined by U.S. copyright law.

Visit our Web site: http://rutgerspress.rutgers.edu

Manufactured in the United States of America

Marketing Dreams, Manufacturing Heroes

THE TRANSNATIONAL LABOR BROKERING OF FILIPINO WORKERS

ANNA ROMINA GUEVARRA

RUTGERS UNIVERSITY PRESS

New Brunswick, New Jersey, and London

LIBRARY OF CONGRESS CATALOGING-IN-PUBLICATION DATA

Guevarra, Anna Romina, 1973–
    Marketing dreams, manufacturing heroes : the transnational labor brokering
of Filipino workers / Anna Romina Guevarra.
        p. cm.
    Includes bibliographical references and index.
    ISBN 978–0–8135–4633–9 (hardcover : alk. paper)
    ISBN 978–0–8135–4634–6 (pbk. : alk. paper)
    1. Filipinos—Employment—Foreign countries.   2. Alien labor, Philippine.
I. Title.
    HD8714.G83   2009
    331.6′2599—dc22   2009008094

A British Cataloging-in-Publication record for this book is available
from the British Library.

Copyright © 2010 by Anna Romina Guevarra

All rights reserved

No part of this book may be reproduced or utilized in any form or by any means,
electronic or mechanical, or by any information storage and retrieval system,
without written permission from the publisher. Please contact Rutgers University
Press, 100 Joyce Kilmer Avenue, Piscataway, NJ 08854–8099. The only exception
to this prohibition is "fair use" as defined by U.S. copyright law.

Visit our Web site: http://rutgerspress.rutgers.edu

Manufactured in the United States of America

For my parents, Leila and Cornelius,
and for my life partner, Robert

CONTENTS

Preface

These are some of the terraces made by our men here. They certainly enhance the exquisite landscape and panoramic view of Wadi Derna. I intend to plant a huge billboard on the flat ground proclaiming "HANDIWORK OF FILIPINO CRUSADERS FOR LIBYAN PROGRESS AND DEVELOPMENT."

—Cornelius Guevarra, migrant worker, November 24, 1982

I ARRIVED IN MANILA on September 2, 2001, with an overwhelming sense that I was entering a strangely familiar place. After sitting on a plane filled with a group of boisterous and animated Filipina workers who were returning home from Japan and then being immediately greeted at the Ninoy Aquino International Airport with a cardboard cutout of President Gloria Macapagal Arroyo bearing a welcome sign hailing overseas Filipino workers as *bagong bayani* (modern-day heroes), I felt a momentary sense of validation that I was in the right place. While I was aware of the ways in which the Philippine state has imbued its overseas employment program with social value by recognizing Filipinos' participation in it as a form of social heroism, I was ill prepared to embrace fully the degree to which the pursuit of overseas work directed people's life goals to the extent that their hope of a "better" livelihood resides outside the Philippines.

Mag abroad na lang tayo (let us go/work abroad). This sentiment echoed the everyday conversations of people I met, befriended, or observed while studying the Philippines and its culture of labor migration; it was a place engulfed with the notion of overseas migration as Filipinos' ultimate "opportunity." Whether standing in a grocery checkout line, viewing television programs interrupted by news reports of overseas recruitment fairs, passing through the overseas remittance centers mushrooming throughout Manila's crowded streets, or waiting in the lobbies of recruitment agencies, I sensed Filipinos' hopelessness and desperation. I was astonished to hear Filipinos proclaim their pride in being Filipinos while in the same breath lamenting their dissatisfaction with the country's economic progress and envisioning the promise of a golden future outside the Philippines.

Perhaps this is the same kind of lament my late father, Cornelius Guevarra, faced as he pursued overseas work. He left the Philippines in 1982 for a two-year contract in Libya, which did not have the workforce to carry out its infrastructure development. During that period, the labor recruitment industry was unregulated, so employment agencies engaged freely in unscrupulous business practices such as withholding workers' wages or not providing overseas workers adequate means to contact their families back home. My memory of these years was colored by the many times my mother and I, as a child of nine, waited in lines outside the agency that arranged my father's overseas employment, along with a mass of other families, to demand the release of his wages, and by hours spent outside the airport awaiting his return because this same agency could not provide the exact date and time of his arrival back in the Philippines.

During that period, as a transnational family, long before the ready availability of e-mail or phone cards, we communicated through letters and photographs exchanged and sent through workers who were going to the same work site as my father's or through his friends who were returning home to the Philippines. A couple of years after his death in 1995, I uncovered one of the many photos he had sent. It bore the inscription I quoted above. At first glance, the photo seems to capture nothing but a desolate, red rocky land with a few scattered trees. But this seemingly empty space is now paved and developed, a suitable foundation for the country's development projects. For me, this photograph is emblematic of not just the changes in the global economy that labor migrants like my father help to enable but also the economic and social transformations that migrants themselves hope to obtain in exchange for their labor. This paved and developed land may seem insignificant to passersby. But for labor migrants like my father, this is the "handiwork of Filipino crusaders" that he proudly proclaimed and made visible, and it represents the sacrifices that serve as foundation and inspiration for this book.

Acknowledgments

THIS BOOK HAS BEEN my hardest and longest marathon. From San Francisco, Los Angeles, Phoenix, and now Chicago, writing this book is probably one of the most solitary, exhausting, and humbling activities in which I have ever engaged in my life. I am indebted to a community of support that sustained me in this journey.

First, I thank all the men and women who participated in this project in the Philippines, Arizona, and Texas for giving life to the transnational process that I try to uncover in this book. I grew up in a migrant family, but the knowledge I possessed prior to entering the field was not even close to what I learned in my research. The labor-brokering process is much more intricate and complicated than I'd known, as brokers showed me, and the struggles and sacrifices of workers much deeper, as I came to see as nurses shared with me their work, dreams, and disappointments. I hope that I have done some justice to representing their perspectives and experiences, although I realize that my representation is partial and my analysis likely to be in disagreement with theirs. Special thanks go to the Philippine Nursing Association of Arizona for opening their doors and introducing me to a vibrant community of Filipino nurses.

At Rutgers University Press, I am grateful to my editor, Adi Hovav, whose enthusiasm for this project has meant the world to me. As this is my first book, I did not know what having an editor meant. Adi not only walked me through the book publishing process, but, much to my amazement, also read through each chapter and worked closely with me on my writing. Adi guided me to find, and in some ways resurrect, my voice. She reminded me about the importance of representation and clarity to engage a wider audience. For this and her patience and understanding of the various life circumstances that affected the production of the book, I am grateful. I appreciate the support that Leslie Mitchner provided to shepherd my book through its final stages. I also thank the supportive and patient staff members at the press—in particular, Marilyn Campbell, Allyson Fields, Suzanne Kellam, Katie Keeran, Beth Kressel, Alicia Nadkarni, Karen Baliff Ornstein, and Michael Tomolonis—who shepherded my book through the copyediting, production, marketing, and advertising processes. I am also very grateful to Romaine Perin for her careful, thorough, and expert copyediting.

I also owe my survival of this process to the mentorship that I received along the way. The project began during my graduate studies at the University of California, San Francisco, and I am indebted to Howard Pinderhughes, Adele Clarke, Virginia Olesen, and Aihwa Ong for believing in and supporting it. Howard, my advisor, gave me the intellectual autonomy to pursue this project but also taught me how to survive graduate school. I appreciate his confidence in my ability to craft a project that extended beyond the intellectual confines of the department. I thank Ginnie for her generous feedback as I began working through the process of writing and Adele for her unrelenting support and "you go, girl" sentiments that continue to sustain me beyond graduate school. I thank Aihwa Ong for her enthusiasm about the project and for her often firm, yet gentle, encouragement to get the book out.

As a postdoctoral fellow at the Institute of Labor and Employment at the University of California, Los Angeles, I was fortunate to be under the wings of Ruth Milkman, who provided me the mentorship, intellectual space, and resources to complete the second phase of the project. I especially thank Ruth for helping me shape the book during its initial stages and for her unyielding support in the career transitions that fundamentally enabled me to complete the book.

At Arizona State University (ASU) at the West Campus, where I landed my first job and where the actual writing began, I am grateful to several people. First and foremost I want to acknowledge my Ethnic Studies Manuscript Group—Shari Collins Chobanian, Gloria Cuádraz, C. Alejandra Elenes, and Michelle Telléz. I thank them for reading various incarnations of the manuscript and for their honest and incisive comments throughout as we met weekly and even during the summer months in Phoenix when the heat made it difficult to be outdoors. This community of women acted much like an intellectual boot camp of sorts where many healthy disagreements and debates occurred, but it was also a place of refuge and inspiration. The book is better not only because of the feedback they provided but also because of what I learned from their work. I thank Shari for sharing her passion about environmental refugees. I am grateful to Alejandra for bringing me into the world of La Llorona, La Virgen de Guadalupe, and La Malinche and look forward to seeing her book. I was happy to have a glimpse of Gloria's oral history project and her valiant efforts to recuperate the long-forgotten contributions of Mexican American migrant workers to the economy of Litchfield Park as they toiled and lived in its labor camps. I am inspired by the work that Michelle has done with the community of Maclovio Rojas and her commitment to give voice to their struggles. Her work will, undoubtedly be a brilliant book. I am honored to have been part of this community and am indebted for their friendships and ongoing support.

Second, I appreciate the time with my ASU colleagues at Social and Behavioral Sciences—an eclectic interdisciplinary group. Special thanks to Mary Burleson, Luis Cabrera, David Coon, Julie Murphy Erfani, Sonya Glavac, Sara Gutierrez, Jeff Juris, Tom Keil, Kristin Koptiuch, Dawn McQuiston-Surrett, Jose Nañez, Luis Plascencia, William Simmons, Barbara Tinsley, and Suzanne Vaughan. Mary and David's sense of humor especially came in handy during those long nights where we competed to see who could stay in their offices the latest. Bill Simmons offered welcoming distractions to the book through the Border Justice events. Luis Cabrera's weekly check-ins about my "progress" kept me on my toes, as did Suzanne's gentle reminders to keep my eyes on my research when times got tough. I appreciate the conversations with Luis Plascencia—a fellow Sun Valley Junior High School graduate—whose interests in migration and theoretical insights provided a much needed intellectual support. I am indebted to Kristin Koptiuch for her faith in my work, for showing me the excitement of teaching, and for letting me be an anthropologist. Barbara Tinsley gave me the time I needed work on the manuscript at a crucial time and for that I am grateful. A special mention goes to Lisa Kammerlocher, the Social and Behavioral Sciences Department's liaison librarian extraordinaire, whose friendship, humor, and sense of social justice also made ASU so welcoming.

At the University of Illinois at Chicago (UIC), I am fortunate to have found a supportive home in sociology with colleagues who have made this transition easy and helped provide a space where I can finish the last leg of this marathon. I especially thank Maria Krysan and Tony Orum for being my mentoring team and Tony for reading portions of the manuscript. Nilda Flores Gonzalez has been a superb role model and has gone through great lengths to welcome me to the sociology department. I thank Laurie Schaffner for her critical "interventions," kindness, and faith in me and my work. I appreciate the encouragement and insights that Richard Barrett, Cedric Herring, and Pamela Popielarz have extended to me with regard to my scholarship and possible ways of pursuing further some of the ideas that stem from this book. I am thankful for Barbara Risman's mentorship, enthusiasm, and ability to create an intellectual community with a research culture firmly in place. I deeply appreciate her enthusiasm toward my work and for helping to bring me to UIC. I am glad to have picked the office I did because it put me in close proximity with Lorena Garcia, who has also been instrumental in my ability to complete the book. Apart from our sharing many late nights in the office and moments of insanity, the writing accountability group she formed with Rooshey Hasnain kept me on track and saved my life. This book could not have been completed without Lorena and Rooshey's encouragement and inspiration. I am very much indebted to one of our graduate students, Michael Rodriguez Muñiz, who generously provided his time, skill, and creativity in generating the amazing image for the book cover. I also thank the sociology staff—Candace Hoover, Olga Padilla, Amanda Stewart, and Teri Williams—whose daily support allows me to do the work that I do.

My colleagues in Asian American studies and gender and women's studies have also provided numerous types of support in this journey. Special thanks to Jennie Brier, Mark Chiang, Judith Gardiner, John D'Emilio, Elena Gutierrez, Helen Jun, Norma Moruzzi, and Barbara Ransby for extending their support to me and welcoming me to their communities. I am especially thankful to Gayatri Reddy and Kevin Kumashiro for their guidance, protection, and friendship; their generosity of spirit, leadership, and sense of fairness never cease to amaze me. I am also glad to know that we have a shared passion for food and bubble tea. I am fortunate to be at a campus with a vibrant Asian American community and grateful for the support I have received from Karen Su, Elvin Chan, Corinne Kodama, and the Asian American Resource and Cultural Center. Beyond UIC, I am lucky to have colleagues and friends like Rick Bonus, Grace Chang, Emily Ignacio, Belinda Lum, Martin Manalansan, and Robyn Rodriguez—all of whom have cheered me on and offered invaluable words of wisdom along the way, especially during moments of crisis and challenges.

My ability to do this work is made possible by various funding sources. I'm indebted to the Fulbright 2001–2002 grant I received to conduct fieldwork in the Philippines and extend my gratitude to the Philippine-American Educational Foundation, which provided a support system that eased the process for doing research in a country that was then foreign to me: Dr. Calata, Gigi, EC, Mila, Marjorie, Susie, Yolly, and Fred. It is through this grant that I met an incredibly talented cohort of Fulbright grantees who provided welcoming diversions to work: Dalisay Estrada, Michelle Favis, Robert Ingenito, Jane Pater, Rona-Kathleen Reodica, and Annie Senner. I only regret that I have lost touch with them and hope that this book will help us reconnect. The Social Development Research Center of De La Salle University hosted and welcomed me as a visiting researcher. I especially thank Dr. "Tata" Lamberte for her guidance and the enthusiasm and support she has shown and Yoyie, Weng, and Rommel for their sense of humor and for helping me adjust to the Philippine way of life. At the University of California, San Francisco, the Eugena-Cota Robles Fellowship, the NIGMS training grant, the UCSF School of Nursing Century Club, and the University of California's President's Fellowship also provided invaluable financial support. The research funds provided by the University of California Institute of Labor and Employment postdoctoral fellowship in 2003–2004 allowed me to conduct fieldwork interviewing Filipino nurses in Texas . At ASU, the New College of Interdisciplinary Arts and Sciences Scholarship, Research, and Creative Activities grant of 2005–2006 provided the financial support to carry out the last phase of this project.

Most important, I thank my family and friends for their patience, forgiveness, and understanding for the times when I couldn't always return e-mail or phone calls, for the late birthday presents, and my for turning down several family gatherings. In the Philippines, I thank my aunt, Belen Bahia, who made me feel at home and helped ease my homesickness for being away from my family. I thank her for forgiving the times I often disappeared to do my fieldwork and for insisting I take the time to enjoy the company of family. Her joyful spirit is contagious and I only regret that I couldn't spend more time with her. My longtime friends William Duncan, Everardo Gutierrez, Victoria Manyarrows, and Teresa Scherzer have been avid supporters who, at different points in this journey, have given me the encouragement I needed.

I am lucky to have a family who has kept me grounded and thank them for inspiring me every day. My mom understood my decision to become a different kind of doctor and her everyday generosity, patience, and determined sense of survival are humbling. My late father's intellectual legacies and experiences as a migrant worker laid the foundation for this work. My sister, Corinne (Anne), whose strength and independence make her one of the most amazing woman warriors I know, and my brother, John—who has sacrificed much to provide for his daughter—are a source of strength.

I am also grateful to have wonderful in-laws—Roberta, Jim, Bob, and Ilene, who have always shown interest in my work and cheered me on through this process. I thank my ten-year-old niece, Adree, and my two-year-old nephew, Brody, who both give me immense joy and inspiration and who provided welcome diversions from writing. I only hope that this book can be as captivating to them as reading *Twilight* or watching Elmo.

Most of all, I thank Robert Meyers Jr., my husband and partner of fifteen years, who undertook this journey with me from beginning to end. I thank him for reading every page of this manuscript, for creating a home environment conducive to writing, and sometimes, for letting me be crazy without question or judgment. He gave me the push I needed at crucial points, helped prop me up whenever I stumbled, provided the sustenance for me to face the next hurdle. But most of all, he kept me moving forward and reminded me to always have faith.

Abbreviations

ADB	Asian Development Bank
BBA	Bagong Bayani Award
CFO	Commission on Filipinos Overseas
CGFNS	Commission on Graduates of Foreign Nursing Schools
DFA	Department of Foreign Affairs
DOLE	Department of Labor and Employment
FAME	Federated Association of Manpower Exporters
GPB	Government Placement Branch
MOFYA	Model OFW Family of the Year Award
MTPDP	Medium-Term Philippine Development Plan
NCLEX	National Council Licensure Examination
NGO	nongovernmental organization
NRCO	National Reintegration Center for OFWs
NSB	National Seamen Board
NSCB	National Statistical Coordination Board
OCW	overseas contract worker
OEDB	Overseas Employment Development Board
OFI	overseas Filipino investor
OFW	overseas Filipino worker
OPA	overseas performing artist
OWWA	Overseas Workers Welfare Administration
PDOS	Pre-departure Orientation Seminar
PEOS	Preemployment Orientation Seminar
POEA	Philippine Overseas Employment Administration
POLO	Philippine Overseas Labor Office
PRA	Provincial Recruitment Activity

TESDA	Technical Education and Skills Development Authority
TOEFL	Test of English as a Foreign Language
TSE	Test of Spoken English
WIDF	Women in Development Foundation

Marketing Dreams,
Manufacturing Heroes

CHAPTER 1

Home of the Great Filipino Worker

I know that our president and our leaders want us to believe that it is up to the individual Filipino to decide to work overseas. [But] she has to consider her financial status when making that decision. And her financial status says that *you don't have a status!* So you have to leave. There are a lot of promises about giving us some opportunities to work here but nothing really happens and Filipinos just end up going overseas.

—A former overseas Filipina nurse in Saudi Arabia

WHILE WAITING in a cramped space of a recruitment agency's reception area in Manila, a middle-aged woman sitting across from me asks, "Where are you going?" with the certainty that I was also a potential worker. She is one of the modern-day heroines of the Philippines who leave the country to join thousands of her compatriots in a crusade of hope and survival that they envision lie overseas.[1] In her tired eyes and exasperated voice, she characterizes life in the Philippines as eternally hopeless and one to which she was returning unwillingly after a three-year terminal contract as a seamstress in Taiwan. "Life has become too hard here in the Philippines and I would have rather stayed in Taiwan, even if it meant becoming a janitor," she tells me as she finds herself in this agency applying for a similar job. Her next destination: the Marshall Islands.

In retrospect, her question jarred me, not so much because she assumed that I was there to seek overseas employment but because it aptly served as a type of tagline, befitting a country whose citizens are on the move—those who willingly reconfigure their careers, their families, and their emotional beings in order to leave. They imagine (and are made to imagine) their future and their economic salvation to exist outside the Philippines. A walk through the streets of Manila alone reinforces this desire and confirms the possibility of escape.

First, there are the ubiquitous recruitment agencies clustering on street corners, offering "dream jobs," "a new life," or opportunities to become a "millionaire," all of which are backed by the agency's unsurpassed "fast deployment" guarantees. Readers of the country's major newspapers are bombarded by the same promises, which take up more than 90 percent of the classified ads every Sunday. Conveniently located around these agencies are the businesses that also profit from this industry—the travel agencies that advertise "special rates for OFWs" (overseas Filipino workers), the banks that promote themselves as official OFW Remittance Centers, the shops fashioning the latest and most cost-effective telecommunication services to "bring OFWs closer to home," or the state-accredited medical clinics that specifically cater to conducting the required medical exams for OFWs. Radio and television programs are occasionally interrupted by announcements of upcoming job fairs held by foreign employers, often conducted in fancy hotel ballrooms and facilitated by exemplary Filipinos living and working overseas who seek to show their compatriots that they, too, can become a success story.

Second, there is the state, steadfast in its claim that it does not promote overseas employment yet participating in overseas "marketing missions," parading its citizens as the hottest global labor commodity, whose education, English-language fluency, and "tender loving care" attitude are their "comparative advantage" over others. Even the Department of Tourism's Web site interestingly includes Filipino workers along with the country's "more than usual" natural wonders and tourist attractions, referring to them as "workers of worth." It features examples of trustworthy Filipinos employed at the airport, a resort, or a coffee shop, who stumbled upon and returned large sums of money or valuables to their rightful owners. These same workers of worth are also the Filipinos whom labor brokers depict as always ready to go, members of a steady stream of applicants for overseas work.

Joining them are those who pursue the unimaginable, such as teachers and nurses working as domestic workers and doctors retraining as nurses, seeking quick tickets out of the country. It is no wonder that the

woman who mistook me for an applicant asked, after realizing that I came from "America," for my phone number. I may not have been an applicant like her but I could certainly have been her potential employer. She asked, "Can I just come with you, even to mop your floor?" While I found her question amusing, the seriousness in her voice was deeply disturbing, because it underscored the privileged status that I may not have recognize but that I embodied and signified. While I knew I did not have the disposable income to hire domestic labor, in her eyes, my U.S. citizenship automatically signaled otherwise.

In the midst of its landscape of despair and desperation, the Philippine state refuses to claim that it promotes overseas employment. President Gloria Macapagal Arroyo may be proud to honor migrants as modern-day heroes and hail the Philippines as the home of the Great Filipino Worker, but she cannot take full credit for this social imaginary. The Philippines is a country on the move, but it is so as a result of a transnationally coordinated phenomenon involving both labor-sending and -receiving countries and global economic restructuring processes that have heightened the division of labor between the global North and South, putting the Philippines in this particular trajectory.

While the Philippines is just one of the many nations supplying labor to the globe, it has the most institutionalized labor-export process, enabling it to supply a range of workers. Unlike other labor-exporting economies, which tend to focus on a particular workforce deployment—Indonesia and Sri Lanka have a large share of the market in domestic work; India dominates the information technology sector—the Philippines does not focus on one skill category. Filipinos work as teachers, nurses, engineers, cooks, janitors, factory workers, dancers, hotel personnel, and seafarers, to name just a few. With its labor-exporting economy, it responds quickly to address emerging labor shortages and creatively brokers Filipinos to fill them. As President Gloria Macapagal Arroyo noted on June 7, 2002, in commemoration of Migrant Workers Day, "The Philippine economy will [in] the foreseeable future continue to be heavily dependent on overseas worker remittances. The work and reputation of the overseas Filipinos confirm to the world that indeed, the Philippines is the home of the Great Filipino Worker."

In this book, I examine these processes by highlighting the role of the state, employment agencies, and workers in constructing this social imaginary—the Philippines as the home of the Great Filipino Worker. I counter the culturally essentialist and racialized discourse of surplus that promotes the Philippines as a *natural* source of *ideal* labor. In this discourse, the country is often touted as a place of untapped labor resources because it cannot generate viable local employment as a result of an economy that is recovering from legacies of debt and trade deficits that are remnants of its colonial past and exacerbated by the administration of former president Ferdinand Marcos and his cronies. This oversimplified claim does not take into account the varied mechanisms that propel this social imaginary and, specifically, the overseas migration of Filipino workers. I argue that this transnationally coordinated phenomenon enables the production of Filipino migrant workers through a racialized and gendered labor-brokering process that ultimately represents Filipinos as ideal global labor commodities and overseas employment as their ideal opportunity.

I do not suggest that Filipinos are not ideal workers or that working overseas does not provide myriad opportunities for upward social and professional mobility. Rather, my aim is to highlight a new lens through which we can understand how the Philippines continues to be a global labor resource and unravel the cultural logic (Jameson 1991; Ong 1999) that give meaning to this phenomenon. While I underscore the globalizing economic forces that drive the migration of Filipinos overseas, I also highlight the social and cultural spheres that contribute to this social imaginary. How do Filipinos come to imagine their future outside the Philippines and how do prospective employers come to imagine them? The concept of cultural logic allows for an examination of the ways in which the economic, social, political, and cultural spheres intersect and interact to produce the Philippines' labor export economy and, in particular, shape the labor brokering of Filipino workers. I argue that the cultural logic that informs this labor-brokering process revolves around two principal elements: a Filipino ethos of labor migration and the gendered and racialized moral economy of the Filipino migrant.

First, labor brokering the Great Filipino Worker and the country's vibrant labor-export economy are enabled through an *ethos of labor migration*, a kind of sociocultural phenomenon that distinctively characterizes the Philippines and governs Filipinos' way of life and aspirations.[2] The phenomenon emerged through colonial legacies that put the Philippines into a particular economic trajectory and is intensified through a series of strategic partnerships between the state, employment agencies, and workers. In highlighting this ethos of labor migration, we can unravel the historical forces that contribute to its creation and maintenance as well as the specific mechanisms that give meaning to it and the simultaneous accommodation and resistance that Filipinos enact toward it. My work is situated specifically in the contemporary period, characterized by a persistent global division of racialized and gendered labor, a heightened demand for highly skilled and educated workers, and a perception of the so-called Third World as a lucrative source of care workers. The care workers I highlight in this book are nurses and domestic workers, who constitute a bulk of the Philippines' workforce deployment. They provide a window through which to see comparatively how such transnational labor-brokering processes differ according to the social value attached to these types of labor.

Second, the mechanisms that inform the labor-brokering process revolve around the formation of the gendered and racialized moral economy of the Filipino migrant, which links notions of family, religion, and nationalism with neoliberal capitalist ideals of economic competitiveness (Guevarra 2003, 2006b).[3] That is, the social imaginary of the home of the Great Filipino Worker operates through the ability of the state, in partnership with employment agencies, to discipline (Foucault 1979) its migrant workers. It is a kind of disciplinary power whose objective is to regulate and normalize individuals through a system that instills a particular type of racialized work ethic and ultimately creates a docile citizen who is beneficial to the state and its economic interests. In this case, the state and employment agencies exercise a kind of disciplinary power toward migrant Filipinos that aims to govern their social conduct through the notion of "empowerment" and promotion of an ethic of responsibility to their nation, families, and the image of the Great Filipino Worker. For its female workers, the state reminds them that they are not only workers but also mothers, wives, or Filipino women who must uphold a particular image of femininity (Guevarra 2003, 2006b).

Thus, the labor-brokering process reflects a neoliberal mode of governing *from a distance*, where the goal is to regulate workers' conduct and produce disciplined labor commodities that are useful to transnational capital, the Philippine state, and workers' individual families. In this book, I illustrate these dynamics through the deployment of discursive representations (for example, so-called heroes or ambassadors of goodwill) and the ways in which these strategies become disempowering to the very workers they seek to empower, and how workers themselves respond to and reconfigure this power.

STATE-LED TRANSNATIONALISM, LABOR BROKERING, AND (DIS)EMPOWERING MIGRANTS

One salient consequence of economic globalization is that transnational capital has made nation-states vulnerable to its power. That is, what we increasingly see are the demands of transnational capital for creating environments that are supported and protected, not constrained and punished, by the state. The creation of places, such as export-processing zones, that are exempt from usual state regulations is one example of this process, which Sassen (1996) refers to as the "partial denationalization of territory."[4] While some scholars characterize this vulnerability as resulting in the decline or weakening of the state and its sovereignty (see Appadurai 1996), others (Sassen 1996) note that such vulnerability has led to transformations in state power that force the state to expand its programs of government. One way this happens is through "state-led transnationalism" (Basch, Glick Schiller, and Szanton Blanc 1994; Goldring 2002). This phrase characterizes the ways that the state tries to accommodate the transnational movements of its people and the formation of deterritorialized nation-states, by trying to reincorporate its transmigrants into its nation-building projects.[5] These practices include encouraging transmigrants to make capital investments in their home countries, to send remittances regularly to their families, or to envision their home countries as ideal places for holiday vacations. The goal of the state here is to build transnational relations with its overseas migrants in the hope of finding ways that they can serve as resources for the country.

This state-led transnationalism is crucial for managing the state's vulnerability to economic globalization, specifically in terms of ensuring a profitable strategic positioning in the global economy. Such conduct shows how the state has already begun to adopt a capitalist market perspective in its program of government (see Barry, Osborne, and Rose 1996; Burchell, Gordon, and Miller 1991). Undertheorized in the literature examining instantiations of this state-led transnationalism are its implications on notions of citizenship and gender relations. That is, if the survival of the state depends on its competitiveness in the global marketplace and its ability to create deterritorialized nation-states, what are the consequences of these strategies, especially to the very subjects of these practices, and how might these strategies affect or implicate men and women and their value differently?

In exploring this theoretical gap, I present the labor-brokering practices of the state, working together with employment agencies, as a unique form of labor control and a mechanism of neoliberal capitalist discipline that informs the country's state-led transnationalism. As Robyn Rodriguez (2005, forthcoming) highlights, the Philippine state, as a labor brokerage state, is instrumental not only in defining the Philippines' role as a labor supplier but also in shaping Filipino workers' sense of belonging to the nation.[6] The labor-brokering process I illustrate captures both the perspective of the state and its partnership with other actors, including the private employment agencies and the workers themselves. The brokering process I describe is specifically focused on the production of care workers and the gendered and racialized processes embedded in this.

By *labor brokering*, I am referring to not only how Filipinos are marketed as global labor but also how the Philippine state, through its connections with the private employment agencies, enacts its ruling power through this process. This is at the core of a Foucauldian understanding of political power whereby "government" is the "domain of strategies, techniques, and procedures" (Rose and Miller 1992, 183) through which ruling bodies can fulfill their goals and interests.[7] This is especially relevant for the Philippine state, which seeks to maximize the economic returns from overseas employment as it takes the stance of simply "managing" this process. The Philippines, whose economy has been called a "celebrated failure," may not be considered a privileged node of economic activity, but it is, nevertheless, a key labor resource and a promising beneficiary of the remittances of its overseas workers.[8] With almost 10 percent of its population living overseas in 2007, and about 4 million of this number being contract workers, the state enjoys a steady flow of U.S. dollars remitted to the country annually (Commission on Filipinos Overseas 2007). In 2007 alone, the remittances of Filipino migrant workers was approximately $14.4 billion, a 13 percent increase from the previous year and approximately 10 percent of the country's gross domestic product (GDP) (Philippines Overseas Employment Administration 2008).[9]

As I describe in this book, managing labor migration and specifically the remittances garnered from overseas migrants not only exemplifies the development of a Philippine state-led transnationalism but also reflects its adoption of values based on neoliberal capitalist principles. These "free market" values promote the importance of economic competitiveness and individual responsibility, under the guise of freedom and choice. I scrutinize these processes by highlighting the labor-brokering practices of the state, acting with employment agencies, as an art of government, those practices designed to govern individuals (who have "chosen" to work overseas) by an ability to affect their conduct, underscoring a disciplinary process through which Filipinos become appropriate subjects of labor and simultaneously appropriate citizens of the Philippine state (Foucault 1991; Rose and Miller 1992; Rose 1999). The Philippine state is a governmentalized state, one that takes on a market interest, ruling its citizens from a distance and deriving its power and legitimacy from a concern for how to best affect the conduct of its population. Further, as Rose and Miller (1992) explain, the art of governing populations entails "technologies of government"—those particular technical and programmatic vehicles that ensure the exercise of power. For the Philippine state and its government of migrant workers, "empowerment" is one such technology of government that supports its labor-brokering practices and ultimately attempts to fulfill the goal of producing "responsible" (that is, economically competitive, entrepreneurial, and self-accountable) and therefore, *ideal* workers and global commodities.

In this book, I tease out the process of labor brokering as a form of labor control and neoliberal capitalist discipline that allows the state and its partners to manage the country's overseas employment program by uniquely using the language of empowerment to govern the conduct of its workers. In doing so, I address how workers—the very subjects of this disciplinary power—embrace or resist this mechanism of labor control that in fact attempts to define their sense of belonging to the Philippines and their worth as Filipino workers. I interrogate the gendered implications of this disciplinary power by illustrating how Filipinas are mobilized

differently from men to fulfill an ethic of responsibility for their families
and their nation. I analyze the implications of this program of government, a program whereby such practices enable the development of a
type of state-led transnationalism that affords the Philippines a strategic
position in the global economy as a labor provider and an economic beneficiary of overseas remittances. I show the potential of these practices to
disempower migrants through the country's inability to protect them and
by its maintaining a cycle of dependency on overseas employment as the
most economically lucrative program of development, at the expense of
nurturing the local economy.

GLOBALIZING CARE WORK AND THE "THIRD WORLD" AS THE USUAL SUSPECT

At the heart of global capital accumulation is an intensified demand
for labor that enables the process discussed above. Employers, however,
are not looking for just any type of labor. Feminist scholars have shown us
how gender matters in this process and the prominent role that the "Third
World" plays in the global division of labor.[10] They challenge the often
too narrow conceptualization of globalization processes as gender neutral
by foregrounding how gender is an invaluable resource for capital, as seen
in the creation of transnational labor markets that depend on the labor of
Third World women, particularly in production work and care work.[11]

Ideological constructions of poor and Third World women as ideal
workers illustrate the production of racialized stereotypes about the suitability of women as global labor commodities, reifying the circulation of
what Salzinger (2003, 10) refers to as the "trope of productive femininity," materializing in the icon of the "docile, dexterous, always-ready, and
cheap woman worker." These tropes can be seen in the racialized stereotypes of the physical dexterity of women, whose small hands and "nimble
fingers" are advantageous for completing certain tasks (Fernandez-Kelly
1983, 2001; Freeman 1993, 2000; Ong 1987; Pellow and Park 2002).
Sometimes these tropes are promoted through patriarchal and sexist ideologies that present women as secondary wage earners who are less likely
to demand higher wages or engage in union-organizing (Fernandez-
Kelly 1983, 2001; Hossfeld 1990). In effect, these tropes mark women's
desirability as workers at the same time that they serve to devalue and
legitimize their disposability as labor commodities.

As care workers, Third World women are ideal for a new economy that increasingly depends on "love" as a "new gold" (Hochschild 2002), a new resource to be extracted from less economically privileged nations. As nannies, maids, caregivers, and nurses who come from all corners of the world, these women perform labor that both provides much needed care work services and significantly supports the "lifestyles of the First World" (Ehrenreich and Hochschild 2002, 4).[12] They are often required to provide not only physical labor but also emotional labor, often undervalued (Hochschild 1983), which might include love given to children and families that are not their own. As race as well as gender matter in this process, employers also possess preconceived racialized notions about where this "love" comes from. For example, whereas in the early twentieth century Jamaican women were ideal nannies, reflecting the image of Aunt Jemima or the "Black Mammy," employers now perceive them as too "aggressive and difficult" (Stiell and England 1999) or as "uneducated island girls" prone to criminal activity (Bakan and Stasiulis 1995). In contrast, women from Asia and Latin and Central America are viewed as imbued with an ideal docility, which employers attribute to cultures with a strong work ethic and values related to family, loyalty, and authority.

The Philippines is a crucial resource of care workers who meet these ideal characteristics, in addition to being touted as highly educated, with a stellar competency in the English language (Constable 1997a; Lan 2003b; Parreñas 2001b; Pratt 1997). Similarly, countries facing a shortage of nurses turn to the Philippines because of a perception that it has a surplus of competent and "ready-to-go" nurses (Choy 2003; Guevarra 2003; Stasiulis and Bakan 2003). The Philippines' colonial history, especially as related to the United States, has set up a country that can produce this kind of a labor force, especially with the introduction of a U.S.-modeled educational curriculum and historical availability of educational opportunities and training in the U.S. schools that give meaning to the understanding of Filipinos as educated care workers. The country's labor export economy and the institutions (state and employment agencies) that sustain it shape how Filipino workers come to be understood as ideal, in the same way that other scholars have revealed about the role of labor mediators in reproducing racialized discourses about the productive femininities of various Third World women workers.[13]

However, our understanding of the mechanisms that labor mediators or brokers such as the state and employment agencies use to generate model workers is limited. Indeed, we know that the Third World is an ideal source of women's labor and that global capital operates on this trope of productive femininity. Nonetheless, how they vary across different occupations and the cultural logic that enable these ideological constructions are undertheorized. As Salzinger (2003, 10) argues in reference to how this trope influences production processes, "Docility, no matter who exhibits it, is produced on the shop floor, not acquired ready-made," and reflects "a potential worker whose productive femininity requires not creation but recognition, [and] is thus a transnationally produced fantasy."

While Salzinger underscored the transnational aspects of production, readers are left to discern the actors who enable this process. The ideal laboring subject is a product of specific labor processes and defined by what managers or employers perceive are necessary to a profitable production, but it is also a trope that must be understood in terms of a specific locale and particular histories. Here, I find Laura Kang's (2002) theorization of how Third World Asian female bodies matter for transnational capital instructive. Instead of assuming that global capital is somehow simply naturally predisposed to identify the Third World as a "natural source of lower wages or contingent workers," she underscored the need to examine the "transnational web of organization and individual actors" who enable this process. This level of coordination is the subject of this book.

In the chapters that follow, I tease out how this trope is "transnationally produced" by introducing the concept of *added export value*, a specifically racialized form of productive labor power that is pitched as the comparative advantage of Filipinos, as compared with other Third World subjects, in the global economy. By examining the brokering of two types of care workers—domestic workers and nurses—I highlight the ways that the state and employment agencies represent this added export value as a racialized form of productive femininity and unique Filipina labor power. I examine how they produce an essentialized Filipina labor power and market a racialized form of "docility." While I highlight the mechanisms that enable these discursive representations, I also underscore how workers themselves embody, accommodate, and challenge this power. I give voice to a group of workers—Filipino nurses—who are "products" and "implicated actors" (Clarke and Montini 1993) of these brokering processes.

DOING TRANSNATIONAL ETHNOGRAPHY

I carried out the first part of my fieldwork in the Philippines from September 2001 through June 2002, when I examined the process of labor brokering in employment agencies, state offices, and the popular press. I conducted repeated in-depth interviews of labor brokers (agency owners and officers, recruitment specialists, and receptionists) from six employment agencies (four nursing and two domestic work agencies). I chose agencies that were currently licensed by the state, had existed for at least ten years (long enough to have some history and reputation), and had an active recruitment activity focusing primarily on nursing or domestic work at the time of my fieldwork. I selected nursing agencies whose primary labor markets represented the United States, the United Kingdom, and Saudi Arabia, because these locations were the three top nurse recruiters at the time of my fieldwork. Finding domestic work agencies willing to participate in this project was made significantly more difficult by ongoing news reports of the labor exploitation of domestic workers abroad. Many agencies minimized their public exposure by not entertaining requests from researchers, like me, whom they perceived to be potential spies.

The participation of these six agencies demanded using several strategies, ranging from sending recruitment letters, placing numerous phone calls, and making repeated personal visits to follow up on the letters of request. The most critical strategy for soliciting participation came from the assistance of various liaisons and gatekeepers in the field. Among the critical gatekeepers were the agencies' receptionists, whom I got to know as I became a frequent visitor of their workplaces. At one point, one of them referred to me as a *bayani* (hero) for my persistence. These receptionists pointed me toward appropriate staff members who could respond to my queries; gave me tips about their schedules; and in many cases, personally followed up on my letters of inquiry and phone calls. The interviews with the brokers typically lasted between one to four hours and were often in English and, occasionally, Taglish.[14] These agencies allowed me to do participant observations in their premises, which included sitting in the waiting rooms, observing some of the interviews with prospective workers, and attending meetings that the agencies deemed relevant to my study.

I also interviewed state officials from the Philippine Overseas Employment Administration (POEA), the Overseas Workers Welfare Administration (OWWA), and the Commission on Filipinos Overseas (CFO), as well as representatives from the Women in Development Foundation (WIDF) and Kaibigan, two nongovernmental organizations appointed by the state to provide pre-departure orientation seminars to Filipino workers, especially those leaving to do domestic work. To learn about the implications of the increasing out-migration of Filipino nurses, I interviewed a dean and professor of one of the top nursing schools in the Philippines, staff nurses from two nursing units in a large private hospital in Manila that were facing a critical shortage of nurses, and the representatives of the Philippines Nursing Association. My access to former overseas workers or prospective applicants of the agencies I studied was limited to informal conversations in waiting rooms or to those who were not necessarily affiliated with these agencies (Guevarra 2006a).

At this time, the relationship between the state-appointed regulatory body (POEA) and the private sector (employment agencies) was worsening, and this made it difficult to find participants. As I relate in chapter 4, this was caused by agencies' claims that the dual role of POEA as a regulatory body and a labor recruiter results in an uneven playing field. Thus, many agencies were skeptical of outsiders who might hurt their image, a challenge I address in the next sections and elaborate elsewhere (Guevarra 2006a). Additionally, through the assistance and recommendation of labor brokers, state officials, and NGOs, as well as public advertisements, I conducted participant observations of pre-departure orientations for Filipino workers that were provided by agencies and the state, labor recruitment seminars, and national labor conferences in the Philippines. To gain a view of suitable depth and breadth of the labor-brokering process, I incorporated a focused textual analysis of labor-marketing tools related to overseas employment (print ads, Web sites, marketing brochures, and government documents).

During this fieldwork, I lived in metropolitan Manila, having carefully selected a place that put me close to areas with large concentrations of employment agencies. I was often within walking distance or a "jeepney" ride away from these agencies.[15] In fact, it wasn't until a few months later that I realized that I was much closer to an agency than I had thought. One night, my usual walk home down what was typically a relatively quiet alley was interrupted by a crowd of people who had assembled with curiosity around a jeepney that blocked the entire alley. I, too, was curious, and as I got closer to the crowd, I saw a striking image. A man opened the back door of the jeepney to unload ten or fifteen women, hurriedly leading them to a gated house that was situated next to my building. The women must have been in their midtwenties; their faces were overly made up and they were wearing tight-fitting cocktail dresses and two-inch heels that brought whistles, stares, and obnoxious comments from the alley men. I learned that this house was actually an employment agency catering to "entertainers," and what I witnessed was one of their "audition" nights during which prospective overseas employers saw the "commodities" that they were about to purchase. It now explained why this house had a security guard posted outside its gate, a sign that said *Bawal ang sumisilip* (No one is allowed to peek), and foreigners coming in and out of the place, and, further, why loud music often emanated from the house throughout the day and sometimes long into the night.

I lived on the twenty-third floor of a twenty-six-floor condominium building with one of those names that aim to evoke a sense of grandeur, one of the many buildings that are sprouting up throughout Manila, owned by upper-middle-class families who rent them out to those who can afford what is considered an exorbitant amount of money for the average Filipino. While a few families lived in the building, most of the residents seemed to be foreign exchange students studying at the nearby university or individuals on short- or long-term business trips. The only window in my unit offered a panoramic view of the surrounding squatter area, and smoke emanating from this neighborhood as trash burned was a common phenomenon. The walks through the alleys that took me to this building involved passing jarring scenes of children playing in dirty water, families living in dilapidated homes unlikely to make it through another storm, and individuals trying to make whatever money they could from selling every kind of street food possible. Yet it was also quite a lively and entertaining place, especially on weekend nights when the economic miseries faded in to the background temporarily as karaoke machines played full blast, inspiring a range of talent as well as valiant attempts thereto. Meanwhile managers in my building were dedicated to trying to create a high-class aura by providing a twenty-four-hour security guard, an on-site laundry service, an Internet café, a small convenience store, and building maintenance service for residents. I chose this building in part because it was close to De La Salle University, which hosted my stay and provided me with office space and access to the university's resources under the mentorship of Dr. Exaltacion Lamberte, fondly known as "Dr. Tata."

From 2004 to 2007, I conducted in-depth interviews of two groups of nurses in Texas and Arizona to capture the actual material implications of labor-brokering activities at the other end of the migration process and provide a more complete picture of how workers are transnationally produced. The nurses represent U.S. hospitals' current strategies for alleviating a national registered nurse shortage in the United States, and they were recruited through one of the agencies that participated in my project. Our interviews took place in their apartments or in restaurants after they came home from their night shifts or, more frequently, during their days off. To understand their presence as foreign nurses and the controversy behind the nurse labor shortage, I interviewed individuals who were actively involved in dealing with the labor shortage problems, such as the members of Arizona's Governor's Nursing Shortage Task Force, who represent nursing schools, hospitals, professional nursing associations, and other entities. I also worked with the Philippine Nursing Association of Arizona (PNAAZ), a key liaison to newly arrived Filipino nurses.

My access to nurses in both sites involved a number of strategies. In Texas, my key liaison was a Web site manager of a local Filipino organization who responded to one of my e-mail queries to the group. His wife was a nurse who was part of the first group of nurses recruited to Gray Meadows and she also became one of the participants in my project.[16] Both were crucial in referring my study to nurses they knew fit my criteria as well as pointing me to the only Filipino restaurant in town, which turned out to be another significant gatekeeper. Given that this was a small town, the owners of the restaurants were quite knowledgeable about newcomers to the area and willingly advertised my project to their customers, many of whom were nurses looking for the comfort of home-cooked Filipino food. The restaurant was strategically located, in that it was only a block away from the hospitals' "corporate housing"—the apartment complex that recruiting hospitals contracted to provide the first three months of free housing to the newly arrived nurses. After a couple of interviews, I was able to gather subsequent participants through referrals. In Arizona, PNAAZ introduced me to newly arrived nurses. The organization provides an active outreach and mentorship program to nurses coming from the Philippines, and I was able to gather participants through their referrals and invitations to meetings. Similar to the situation in Texas, one of the recruiting hospitals in Arizona also provides corporate housing to their "recruits," an arrangement that made it easier for me to find other nurses.

BEING "FILIPINA ENOUGH"

Many ethnographers, particularly feminist "ethnic insiders," have highlighted the unique politics and limitations of returning to and studying one's community.[17] My relationship with labor brokers and nurses whose activities I had come back to the Philippines to study was no exception. As a *balikbayan* (expatriate) returning to the Philippines after sixteen years and a *kababayan* (compatriot) of the brokers and nurses yet carrying U.S. citizenship, I was not (and could not expect to be) an insider to their communities. For both groups, I occupied a particular privileged position based on the "status identities" (Beoku-Betts 1994) that I carried in the field and that automatically positioned me as an outsider and contributed to my sense of estrangement in relation to these communities. Even though I was born in the Philippines and could speak Tagalog and Taglish, they evaluated me on the basis of my U.S. citizenship, educational attainment, and migration history.

For Filipino labor brokers in the Philippines, I was a Fulbright scholar, which they regarded as a marker of my class privilege. Although I was born in the Philippines, I was not "one of them" but instead a *balikbayan* who was fortunate enough to possess the economic resources to have the opportunities that many of them could only dream about. I also benefited from the local institutional support provided by a private university, De La Salle University, and from the Philippine-American Educational Foundation (PAEF), which heightened this privileged status.[18] I also could afford to rent an apartment and live alone in the heart of Manila, where the average Filipino is outpriced by the housing market and the cost of everyday living. Interestingly, these very same status identities helped negotiate my entry into the labor brokers' premises, for they made me seem "important enough" to entertain. Nevertheless, this did not mean that I did not have to mitigate their suspicion that I was an industrial spy, a journalist, or a state worker whose presence could potentially lead to the demise of their companies. As I describe in chapter 4, this is particularly important because of the contentious relationship between POEA and the employment agencies at the time of my fieldwork.[19]

As a Filipina American and daughter of a former overseas worker, whose sacrifices were at the core of the work that I sought to understand and critique, the process of immersing myself in this field was tenuous from the very beginning. My ability to do research in the premises of labor brokers entailed developing an acceptable identity based on the brokers' perception of me as a potential ally, a sympathetic outsider, and a culturally competent Filipina American whom they could trust and welcome in their communities (Guevarra 2006a). These very identities contributed to my vulnerability in the field and forced me to make particular ethical compromises to do this work. For example, when I was on their premises, especially in interacting with overseas worker applicants, labor brokers introduced me unhesitatingly as a researcher who was "on their side" and who was helping them challenge their public image as hustlers. As one labor broker explained to me, I needed to realize that contrary to POEA's portrayal of employment agencies as "leeches," they are, in fact, the "makers of new heroes." He claimed that without them, the heroes that the country proclaims as saviors of the Philippine economy would not exist and thrive.

While I saw labor brokers express their concern for the harm that workers may face overseas and exhibit excitement about their ability to assist Filipinos in realizing their dreams and attaining a new economic status, I was not blind to the industry's competitiveness and its profit goals. I also knew that despite the brokers' claims of my becoming their ally, they did not trust me. After all, I would eventually leave the field and publish my findings, putting them at the mercy of my representation of their work. In order to minimize my vulnerability and the possibility that this project could not be carried out, I did not disclose my family history and my knowledge of workers like my father who dealt with unscrupulous agencies. I did not introduce my critiques of their work or the labor export process in general. These measures were necessary to prevent any conflicts and pacify my fears that labor brokers would reflexively disallow my presence in their agencies and refuse to associate with me. I also feared that they would dwell on trying to prove themselves different from those unscrupulous agencies that I knew about, instead of providing a thorough description of their work. While my decision provided no guarantees, I did not want to take the risk that they would not see past my family history or experiences.

Similarly, Filipina nurses, especially those I interviewed in the United States, viewed my status identities as a U.S. citizen, a PhD holder, and a professor with great importance and pride, regarding me as a "success story" and, much to my discomfort, as one who had attained something much greater than what they had. Some kept referring to me as "Doc," despite my insistence that they call me by my first name; they emphasized the fact that I held a PhD at my age and they attached great intellectual merit to my research project. I knew that they entertained me partly because of the meaning that my status posed for them. For labor brokers, I was the successful *balikbayan* who, to some extent, represented the dream of "greener pastures" that they usually market to Filipinos. For Filipina nurses, I served as living proof and reassurance of the limitless educational and employment opportunities embedded in the American dream that they were chasing. But just as I needed to exhibit sufficient cultural capital and Filipino social disposition to be part of the labor brokers' communities, I also recognized the importance of correcting an assumption on the part of many of the nurses I interviewed initially of the impossibility of moving beyond a professional relationship. This assumption arose from their preconception of my Americanized disposition and from the enormous weight they placed on my PhD, both factors representing for them insurmountable barriers between us at the same time that they likely signified a ray of hope.

I made a conscious effort to conduct our interviews in Tagalog. While my interviewees appreciated my efforts, in some instances, and much to my gratitude, they permitted me to speak in English and forgave the times I misspoke and lost things in translation. That I could speak Tagalog minimized our social distance, especially for those who had just arrived in the United States at the time of our interview and felt very discouraged about their ability to speak English fluently and understand all its colloquial meanings. While language facilitated our interactions, I appreciated the times when I felt that the nurses could relate to me as they would to any Filipina acquaintance, friend, or family member. I also needed to be Filipina enough to relate to them and answer a barrage of questions that may have been exceedingly personal for someone who was not accustomed to this level of questioning: *Where is your family from? How long have you been in the United States? Are you married? Is your husband Filipino? Do you have any children?* The last question was especially important to them, and, as nurses, a number shared the medical consequences of delaying childbirth to a later age. Interestingly, a year after my first set of interviews in Texas, I contacted one of the nurses and the first question she asked was "Do you have a baby yet?" Although the question was mildly jarring, it signified this nurse's level of comfort and familiarity with me. This is important because although many regarded me as a class-privileged Filipina and saw a separation between us, they were, in fact, professionals themselves—highly educated and skilled individuals.

OVERVIEW OF CHAPTERS

This book is organized to underscore the multilevel aspect of the labor-brokering process. The first two chapters focus on the brokering process from the perspective of the state. In chapters 2 and 3, I illustrate the neoliberal ethos of the Philippine state in carrying out its overseas employment program in partnership with employment agencies and nongovernmental organizations. In chapter 2, I challenge the notion that the country is a natural source for or has a surplus of labor by highlighting the political economic and historical underpinnings of the Philippines' overseas employment framework and the development of an ethos of labor migration. I show the sociohistorical forces that created the conditions through which labor migration can be sustained and those that give meaning to its national identity as a labor exporter. In chapter 3, I specifically explore how the state aims to "manage labor migration" and its image as a responsible and responsive state by governing the conduct of Filipinos in ways that push them to model a neoliberal market rationality of economic competitiveness, entrepreneurship, and social accountability while projecting an image of social respectability for their families and their nation.

In chapters 4 and 5, I highlight the brokering process from the perspective of the private sector—the state-licensed employment agencies. I describe in chapter 4 the agencies' assertion of their role as "makers of new heroes" in the midst of a contentious relationship with the state.

I show not only how they operate as key gatekeepers to Filipinos' economic livelihood and perceptions of working abroad but also how they sustain the country's ethos of labor migration. I then examine, in chapter 5, exactly how agencies enact their role as the "makers" of these "heroes," as I illustrate how they sell the unique labor power—the added export value—of Filipina care workers as their comparative advantage over others. As social institutions, they draw from racialized and gendered ideologies to construct this added export value but also devise strategies that ensure they groom the workers to fulfill it.

The next level of the brokering process is represented in chapters 6 and 7, which capture the other end of the labor-brokering and migration process as I profile the voices of newly recruited nurses in the United States. In chapter 6, I describe the professional consciousness of Filipino nurses and the moral economy that supports their aspirations, desires, and determination to work overseas. I describe the simultaneous empowerment and estrangement they gain, as "American-dreaming" Filipinos, from these pursuits and the tensions that seem to redefine their perceptions of "the good life" and propel them back home. In chapter 7, I specifically focus on how Filipino nurses internalize and problematize their added export value as workers and how they distinguish themselves as offering a type of care work that is different from and "better" than others. I show the power of agency they exhibit as they manage their fears and vulnerabilities as foreigners and contract workers and how their promotion of their added export value is a fundamental dynamic of their moral economy and a crucial way of securing their future. In chapter 8, the concluding chapter, I summarize the implications of this project as I situate it in the larger context of transnational labor.

CHAPTER 2

Cultivating a Filipino Ethos
of Labor Migration

19% of Pinoys want to leave, say RP hopeless.
—Front-page headline, the *Philippine Daily
Inquirer*, June 26, 2002

EVERY SATURDAY MORNING, a television show called
May Gloria Ang Bukas Mo (There's Gloria/Glory in Your Future), features the current Philippine president, Gloria Macapagal Arroyo.[1]
In these shows, she often began with an inspiring message about the
place the Philippines occupies in the global economy and the economic
promise that foreign investments and overseas employment bring to
Filipinos. Viewers heard of potential business ventures such as the establishment of foreign-owned call centers or the presence of global labor
shortages in knowledge-based sectors such as health care, in which
Filipinos can participate. Alongside reports of a bright economic outlook, delivered with a sense of urgency, were strategic references to the
country's success stories—the overseas Filipino workers who not only
contributed to nation-building through their monetary remittances but
who had also transformed themselves economically and socially. In one
episode, President Arroyo excitedly hailed Filipino nurses in London as
the "new aristocracy," individuals whose wages afforded them material
luxuries and upward mobility, unavailable in the Philippines. She spoke
of them as class-empowered Filipinos who benefited from and represented the promise of wealth and limitless opportunities overseas. Every
week, she delivered a deafening message that the country's competitive
advantage was its human resources and repeatedly proclaimed Filipinos as
the Dakilang Manggagawa (Great Filipino Worker) and the Philippines as
the home of the Great Filipino Worker. Interestingly, this second phrase

TABLE 2.1

Overseas Labor Deployment from the Philippines

Type	1975	1985	1995	2000	2005	2006	2007
Land based	12,501	320,494	488,621	643,304	740,632	788,070	811,070
Sea based[a]	23,534	52,290	165,401	198,324	247,983	274,497	266,553
Total		36,035	372,784	654,022	841,628	988,615	1,062,567	1,077,623

SOURCE: Philippine Overseas Employment Administration.
[a]This is work that takes place on board maritime shipping vessels (for example, work done by Seafarers) or cruise ships.

appeared on an advertisement sponsored by the Philippines Department of Tourism that ran on the CNN's international network. It featured Filipino workers displaying their skillful and seemingly acrobatic abilities in handling a wide variety of tasks, leaving their customers in awe.[2] The commercial ended with the caption "Invest in the Philippines. Home of the Great Filipino Worker."

Beneath these glorious representations is a reality of hopelessness to which President Arroyo reacted and attempted to mitigate. The Philippines labor export policy was supposed to be a stopgap response to escalating unemployment, which began in the 1970s, during the regime of Ferdinand Marcos. Three decades later, unemployment persists, with an outflow of hundreds of thousands of Filipino workers (Table 2.1). In the most comprehensive figure available, the CFO reported that as of December 2007 approximately 8.73 million Filipinos were living overseas, with 4.1 million of these carrying employment contracts.[3] These expatriates represented 9.8 percent of the country's population and 4.6 percent of the Filipino workforce; in August 2007, the estimated population of the Philippines in was 88.57 million (Philippine National Statistics Office, http://www.census.gov.ph, 2008). So successful has the country been in exporting its population, the International Labor Organization has designated the Philippine Overseas Employment Administration (POEA), the country's overseas employment regulatory body, as a model for other labor-exporting countries (Tyner 1996).

The widespread desire to migrate from the Philippines is closely related to a growing sense of national hopelessness in a country in which the April 2008 unemployment rate was 8.0 percent and the rate of underemployment 19.8 percent (Philippine Census Bureau, http://www.census.gov.ph). According to the most recent official estimates, twenty-seven out of one hundred families (totaling 4.7 million families) were poor in 2006 (National Statistical Coordination Board 2008).[4] A survey conducted by Pulse Asia revealed that 19 percent of Filipinos agreed with the statement, "This country is hopeless, and if it were only possible I would migrate to another country and live there" (*Philippine Daily Inquirer*, June 26, 2002). While the survey pointed to unemployment and the Philippine state as a motivating force for encouraging labor migration, state officials are quick to denounce these claims. Beginning with the Migrant Workers and Overseas Filipinos Act of 1995, the state proclaimed that it no longer *promotes* overseas employment. Instead, it simply *manages* labor migration by supporting the desires, choices, and freedom of Filipinos to work overseas. The ubiquitous intimation of labor migration on Philippine streets, in the media, and in the public consciousness are supposed to reflect this shift in perspective.

Labor brokers and state officials often attribute the driving force behind Filipinos' presence in the global workforce and their desire to migrate to the fact that Filipinos are naturally adventurous and the Philippines has evolved a culture of migration. They further assert that the innate cultural traits of flexibility and adaptability and an English-speaking facility make Filipino workers marketable in the global economy. They promulgate the idea that the demand for Filipino workers stems from a global familiarity with Filipino workers who have the cultural capital to provide a desirable work ethic. But these claims beg the question of the conditions that brought about such seemingly global knowledge of Filipinos as workers. What enables state officials, labor brokers, and even workers themselves to make such culturally essentialist claims? Choy (2003), who studied the history of Filipino nursing migration to the United States, has argued that it has much to do with the development of a "culture of migration," facilitated by the educational and social infrastructure that resulted from the country's colonial relations with the United States.

Similarly, it is the development of an ethos of labor migration that characterizes the Philippines and defines the aspirations of Filipinos. I expand on Choy's conceptualization by examining not only the country's colonial history but also the state-led initiatives and transformations in state power that contributed to this ethos of labor migration—an unintended consequence of these forces. From the perspective of the Philippine state, overseas Filipinos are not merely migrants, they are laborers whose value is measured by the remittances they can potentially funnel into the country. The national identity of the Philippine state as a labor exporter and a manager of labor migration are informed, I argue, by its ability to cultivate and sustain the country's role as a global labor provider.

FROM A COLLECTION OF TRIBES TO EDUCATED CITIZENS

The Spanish colonization of the Philippines from 1565 to 1898 transformed the social and political landscape and the remnants of those changes are reflected in the current overseas employment framework. While the emphasis was on creating an agricultural export economy that set up a hierarchical social system stratified along race, class, and gender lines and concentrated wealth on the hands of a few elite landowners, the nation's conversion to Christianity was an equally important Spanish legacy that contributed to the social reorganization of the Philippines. Philippine scholars Reynaldo Ileto (1979) and Vicente Rafael (1988) note that this religious conversion served as an important ideological frame for the colonization of the Philippines and the submission of Filipinos to Spanish authority. It became the basis through which this colonial power governed Filipinos culturally. The narratives of suffering, sacrifice, and martyrdom became prominent themes with the introduction of Jesus Christ and his symbolic representation of redemption. Within Philippine society to this day, his suffering and sacrifice are popularized, retold, and collectively celebrated as narratives of Pasyon; his crucifixion is reenacted during the Lent season.[5]

The introduction of Catholicism was coupled with exhortations to ideal femininity, represented by the Virgin Mary, whom the church used as a vehicle for teaching Filipinos the values of purity and motherhood. So not only did the conversion of Filipinos to Catholicism carry the message of submission to Spanish authority, it also involved the promotion and adoption of religious ideals that still govern Philippine culture and shape Filipinos' outlook and way of life. In a fundamental way, it conditioned Filipinos' eventual submission to the Philippine state. These ideals have become especially evident in the ideological framework of the country's overseas employment program and pivotal in the way the state manages labor migration and characterizes Filipino workers' choices to work overseas as "sacrifices" or acts that serve the interests of both their families and the country and that the state attempts to reward symbolically and materially. As I explain later, the state's construction of Filipino migrant workers as God-fearing, self-sacrificing, highly productive workers and citizens echoes these ideals and is represented by the iconic figure of the *bagong bayani* (modern-day hero).

The subsequent colonization of the Philippines by the United States, in 1898–1945, contributed to the emergence of a vulnerable economy that became receptive to overseas employment as a program of development in various ways. First, a reorganization of the country's political and educational system under the directive of then U.S. president William McKinley's 1898 "benevolent assimilation proclamation" was aimed at converting the Philippines from a "collection of tribes" into an entity ready for self-government.[6] However, Filipinos resisted this effort, because it threatened the possibility of gaining independence and raised the risk of submission to yet another colonial power. This resistance materialized in the Philippine-American War, which lasted until 1903.

Americans met the mounting Filipino insurgence with an equal degree of suppression, which took the form of physical torture of Filipino prisoners; pacification campaigns that included the forced relocation of certain groups into containment areas; the 1901 Sedition Act No. 292, making it unlawful for Filipinos to participate in any form of resistance against the United States; prohibitions against nationalistic political parties; and press censorship (Cortes, Boncan, and Jose 2000). This is ironic, given that central to McKinley's benevolent assimilation proclamation was the deployment of the American ideals of peace, democracy, and freedom, all buttressed by the notion that the sole intention of the United States was to come to the Philippines as "friends, to protect the natives in their homes, in their employments, and in their personal and religious rights" (United States Adjutant General of the Army 1902, 858). However, as Rafael (1995, 128) aptly puts it, this discourse of benevolence established a racialized hierarchy that "infantilized [Filipinos] as racial others in need of nurturance and tutelage in the fundamentals of 'Anglo-Saxon democracy' not in order to turn them into Anglo-Saxons but rather into a 'self-governing people' separate from but equal to white civilization." Thus, the "benevolence" behind the U.S. colonization of the Philippines was ultimately a means of governing Filipinos, with the goal of raising their brown children as model imperial subjects who could be exhibited as *good enough* to be part of the U.S. empire but all the while ensuring their otherness.

This imperial project was starkly visible in the realm of education through the U.S. government-sponsored construction of public schools, equipped with American teachers, who came to be known as the Thomasites, after a group of volunteer American teachers who arrived on the U.S.S. *Thomas* in 1901 to operationalize McKinley's directive and replace American soldiers, who had previously provided American-style education to Filipinos. Just as the Spaniards sent missionaries to convert Filipinos to Catholicism as a covert means of having them submit to Spain's colonial authority, the Thomasites embodied America's attempt to transform Filipinos into a particular type of American citizen, one who was not only "educated" but also emulated the American way of life and embraced its ideals of law and democracy. As Racelis and Ick (2001, 4) note, "The Thomasites. . . . saw themselves as bringing more than just the basic literacy and numeracy skills. They were charged with inculcating democratic values and ideals into young Filipino minds, with a view to making the country a model of American-style democracy in the Far East." The Thomasites provided education that shifted from an emphasis in religion to that of American democratic principles of rules and laws while using the English language as a medium of instruction and "conversion."

The United States promoted higher education through the establishment of educational and training institutions and through the University of Santo Tomas and other universities established by the Spaniards. The Americans founded the University of the Philippines (1908), the first university to use English as the mode of instruction; the Philippine Public Library (1908); the Philippine nautical school (1914); and a midwifery school (1915) (Cortes, Boncan, and Jose 2000). Americans also established programs that trained Filipino municipal teachers and nurses, using curricula modeled on those in the United States.[7] As Choy (2003) describes, the institutionalization of U.S. nursing programs in the Philippines, beginning in 1907, was an essential "precondition" of the contemporary migration of Filipino nurses in the United States insofar as it provided them a U.S.-based nursing training and familiarity with a U.S. work culture. As will be evident in later chapters, the ability to market Filipinos as an ideal nursing workforce stems from a nursing education that closely mirrors that of the United States.

A COUNTRY IN DEBT(ED)

Filipino migrant labor streams were formed in the early part of the twentieth century, as colonial relations with the United States resulted in economic and trade policies that were detrimental to the long-term economic development of the Philippines. For example, the growth of the agricultural sector was hampered by U.S.-directed import-substitution industrialization strategies that favored capital intensive and urban-based industries and the production of selective export crops primarily for the American market such as sugar.[8]

This became evident when the United States began to use Filipino human resources in response to its labor shortages. With European and American expansion, beginning in the mid-eighteenth century, Hawaii's island economy of maritime commerce was displaced by an agricultural market economy based on the production of sugar.[9] In response to this shift and an insufficient local labor pool, plantation owners engaged in the recruitment of migrant labor, namely from China and Japan.[10] However, as a result of a 1909 strike led by Japanese laborers and plantation labor shortage, the Hawaiian Sugar Plantation Association (HSPA) saw the Philippines as a lucrative source of labor, especially given the U.S.-driven agricultural export economy in that country, which provided Filipinos with expertise in sugar cultivation. The first official group of laborers, the "manongs," left the Philippines for Hawaii as plantation laborers in the early twentieth century (1900s–1930s); in 1909 a rigorous program of recruitment for Filipino laborers began.[11] Thus, the legacy of an agricultural export economy inherited from the Spanish and preserved by the American colonial occupation through American trade relations may have sown the seeds of an environment that would later support the impetus of labor migration as a project of economic development.

As the number of applicants for overseas work increased, the Philippine government, through the Bureau of Labor, along with a small number of private recruitment agencies, took an interest in this business and participated in the placement of Filipino men for overseas farm labor. These "recruits" were primarily illiterate single men from the Ilocos region, in the northwestern part of the island of Luzon.[12] Between 1906 and 1926, about 100,000 Filipinos migrated to Hawaii (Villegas 1988) and by 1946, the Philippines witnessed the exodus of approximately 125,000 of its population (Sharma 1984). In addition to working on Hawaiian plantations, Filipino men found work in California, Washington, Idaho, and Montana as vegetable and fruit pickers; in Alaska and the Northwest as fish cannery workers; and in cities such as New York as domestic service workers.[13]

Even after independence, in 1946, postcolonial relations continued through military and trade agreements that influenced the Philippines' socioeconomic landscape. For example, these relations led to the devaluation of the local currency and contributed to large trade deficits as American businesses acquired special privileges and "parity rights" to exploit the country's natural and public resources, leaving local industries unable to compete.[14] Parity rights afforded foreign-owned corporations the same legal benefits as those enjoyed by Filipino corporations and were one of the conditionalities that the United States demanded from the Philippines under the 1946 Bell Trade Act in exchange for the "rehabilitation funds" that it promised as recompense for war damages. In addition, the Philippines agreed to continue "free trade" with the United States (until 1954), thus disallowing restrictions on import duties and fees coming from the United States, and to ensure that the Philippine peso continued to be tied to the dollar at a rate of two to one.

These conditionalities had severe repercussions for the Philippine economy as the country experienced an average annual trade deficit of $273 million in 1946–1949, culminating in a $161 million balance of payment in 1949 (Villegas 1988). As Villegas explains, the escalating balance of payment was not a favorable economic situation for the United States, because it needed the Philippines to maintain a stable export market for the raw materials (abaca, iron, sugar, and coconut) it exported to the United States.[15] In 1949, on the advice of the International Monetary Fund (IMF), the Philippines imposed temporary foreign exchange controls on U.S. imports. Finally, in 1954, when the Bell Trade Act expired, the Philippine government made its move to impose duty-free restrictions on U.S. imports, subsequently codified in the Laurel-Langley Agreement of 1955 (Cortes, Boncan, and Jose 2000; Villegas 1982). Under this legislation, Philippine goods entering the United States were subject to similar foreign exchange controls in place previously, but on condition that they would not be as high as those imposed for U.S. goods entering the Philippines (Cortes, Boncan, and Jose 2000). While this strategy allowed local industries to develop in the Philippines and contributed to a period many refer to as the "golden age of manufacturing" (Bello, Kinley, and Elinson 1982), this period was short-lived, ending in the 1960s. Given its comparable lack of expertise and technology, the Philippines was unable to compete with U.S.-made imports. The unavailability of well-crafted national protectionist measures to protect Filipino-owned industries against U.S. firms who set up assembly plants for goods primarily produced elsewhere only worsened the situation, because these American activities did not contribute a huge amount of money to the local economy.

While the Philippines was experimenting with this import substitution strategy and struggling to keep its manufacturing industry alive, its agricultural sector was in crisis. Much of the arable land was cultivated primarily for export/cash crops (sugar, pineapple, coconut) at the expense of food crops such as rice and there was a retrograde system of land tenure in place (Bello, Kinley, and Elinson 1982), factors that had caused degradation of the sector.[16] From these two parallel crises emerged a surplus labor force, which neither industry nor agriculture could accommodate. With a gradually declining economic landscape in the country and the availability of employment opportunities overseas, the migration of Filipinos regained momentum beginning with the exodus of World War II veterans and several groups of professionals (nurses, physicians, engineers, business entrepreneurs, and other workers related to technical fields) to the United States, Canada, and Western Europe (Gonzalez 1998; Sto. Tomas 1984). In the 1950s and 1960s, Filipinos also found employment as artists and musicians in East Asia and as contractors for American military bases in Guam, Okinawa, Vietnam, Thailand, and the Wake Island. Beginning in 1948, through the U.S. Exchange Visitors Program, Filipinos left the Philippines to receive advanced training in U.S. hospitals (Bergamini 1964; Ong and Azores 1994). Between 1957 and 1966, almost eight thousand Filipino nurses entered the United

States through this program (Ishi 1987). By 1968, among the nations participating in this program, the Philippines had the most representation, more than Canada, the United Kingdom, Ireland, Korea, and India. As I discuss in Chapter 6, the Exchange Visitors Program was instrumental in transforming the Philippines into a source of nursing labor for the United States.

When the 1965 U.S. Immigration Act was passed, migration of skilled professionals to the United States surged. This legislation was notably significant for facilitating the second wave of migration from Asia. It not only abolished the 1924 National Origins Act, which imposed the 2 percent quota per nationality, but also facilitated the entry of skilled professionals into the United States through "preference categories."[17] This legislation was important for the Philippines, whose highly skilled professionals (nurses, physicians, surgeons, scientists, lawyers, and teachers) represented the bulk of migrants coming into the country through the "third preference" category. Between 1966 and 1970, 65 percent of Filipino immigrants who entered through the professional third-preference category were highly skilled professionals (Keely 1973; Takaki 1998). For the United States, the legislation was strategic: in 1965 the country was facing its first national nursing shortage, prompting the U.S. labor secretary to waive the labor certification requirement for foreign nurses and to allow them to come to the United States even if they did not have prearranged employment (Ong and Azores 1994).

In the shadow of these migration processes was a country in economic crisis. With escalating trade deficits, coupled with the dictatorship of Ferdinand Marcos, the country, beginning in 1965, turned to the IMF and the World Bank for economic relief. These financial institutions imposed structural adjustment policies that favored an economic liberalization program of development that was detrimental to the Philippines' local industries, as they primarily supported the economic interests of foreign investors, wealthy Filipino elites, and Marcos's cronies. By 1969, the Philippines had a trade deficit of $257 million (Bello, Kinley, and Elinson 2000), resulting in part from Marcos's second term reelection and a huge expenditure of public funds, creating inflationary pressures that further devalued the Philippine peso and drove domestic prices sky high (Cortes, Boncan, and Jose 2000). Between 1970 and 1983, the nation's external debt climbed from approximately $2 billion to $24 billion

(Canlas, Miranda, and Putzel 1988). Meanwhile, rumors of Marcos's plan to remain in office beyond the constitutional limit of two terms pervaded the social milieu and prompted a number of public demonstrations across the nation. Responding to this crisis and to growing sociopolitical unrest and tensions between power-holding elites, landless peasants, foreign investors, economic nationalists, and presidential opponents, Marcos declared martial law in 1972.

Two years after declaring martial law, Marcos passed by executive order the Labor Code of 1974, an effort to reorganize the Philippines' labor policies with the intent of mitigating the country's escalating unemployment at the time. A critical aspect of the labor code was that it formally institutionalized the country's labor export policy (Asis 1992; Villegas 1988). The code minimized the role of private employment agencies in labor recruitment and, instead, firmly established government participation through the formation of the Overseas Employment Development Board (OEDB) (later renamed POEA) and National Seamen Board (NSB). OEDB and NSB handled all aspects of land-based and sea-based overseas employment, respectively.[18] The code also banned foreign employers from hiring Filipinos directly ("direct hiring") and mandated the former to go through the Government Placement Branch. Furthermore, it mandated overseas workers to remit a specified percentage of their earnings through official financial institutions.[19] Three years later, as concerns for the welfare of overseas workers mounted, the Welfare Fund for Overseas Workers was formed.

The 1974 labor code and the establishment of the country's overseas employment program were supposed to be stopgap measures to slow rapidly escalating unemployment and as a strategic response to the employment opportunities created by the 1970s Middle East oil boom (Asis 1992; Villegas 1988). Beginning in 1973, oil-rich countries, among them the United Arab Emirates, Kuwait, Saudi Arabia, Iran, Iraq, and Bahrain, sought workers for infrastructure and development projects related to the oil industry. From 1975 to 1977, Filipinos found employment in these countries as construction workers, doctors, nurses, engineers, and highly skilled mechanics, with Saudi Arabia a leading labor recruiter (Abella 1979).

Contrary to government claims, the presence of Filipinos as a global workforce is not the result of an innate Filipino cultural trait that has created a propensity for migration, but is a product of colonial and neo-colonial relations. These relations facilitated the country's dependence on overseas employment as a form of economic development and enabled labor migration to become embedded in the national consciousness of Filipinos.[20] The emergence and intensification of an ethos of labor migration in the Philippines were made possible by global market dynamics and colonial legacies that put the country into a trajectory of economic crisis. They created economic "opportunities" and directives that the Philippine state pursued and that contributed to the persistently high rate of poverty in the country. This, in turn, facilitated the formation of a society that can anchor and is responsive to the idea of labor migration as a nation-building strategy and a viable source of economic livelihood for its citizens.

PAYING TRIBUTE TO THE VALUE AND (HUMAN) COST OF LABOR MIGRATION

Following the introduction of the 1974 labor code, the institutionalization of labor migration continued with the consolidation of OEDB and NSB into one governing body, POEA, in 1982. POEA initially had the task of promoting, monitoring, and regulating overseas employment. In 1987, during the administration of Corazon Aquino (Marcos's successor), the organization's regulatory functions were expanded to include the licensing and monitoring of private recruitment agencies, market development, worker skill enhancement and testing, and accreditation of foreign employers (Asis 1992). In the same year, the Welfare Fund for Overseas Workers was renamed the Overseas Workers Welfare Administration (OWWA). This administrative body was in charge of welfare issues facing workers and of providing support to their families and dependents.

At this time, the primary deployment of Filipino workers was to the Middle East, which became a destination for workers in construction, health care (nurses and physicians), and service (hotel personnel and office clerks) until the mid-1980s. In 1985, of the almost twenty-six thousand medical workers who left the Philippines, approximately 82 percent were nurses; Saudi Arabia was their primary destination, followed by the United States, which faced a nurse shortage between 1986 and 1987 (Ball 1996). Although Hong Kong and other places had been importing domestic workers since the 1970s, it was during this period that a marked increase in the deployment of Filipina domestic workers occurred. In addition to the Middle East and Hong Kong, Malaysia and Singapore became open to Filipina domestic workers. With the growing number of domestic workers, entertainers, and nurses leaving the country, this period marked the beginning of a feminization of export labor. In 1987 alone, the POEA reported that of the 382,229 overseas workers who left, 47 percent were women (Department of Labor and Employment 1995). This number reflected a significant narrowing of the gender gap in workforce deployment from previous years. In 1975, Filipino men outnumbered women, the former accounting for 70 percent of total country deployment (Gonzalez 1998).

Thus, while the Philippines' official labor export policy began almost a decade before Corazon Aquino's administration, it was during her leadership that the Philippines first truly benefited from the dollar remittances Filipino workers funneled into the economy. In a 1988 speech to domestic workers in Hong Kong, she first officially referred to overseas Filipino workers as the *bagong bayani* (modern–day heroes) of the nation and named December as the Month of Overseas Filipino Workers in recognition of their economic contribution (Rafael 1997; Commission on Filipinos Overseas 1995). Labeling overseas Filipino workers as modern-day heroes was an attempt to downplay the absence of any governmental protective mechanisms for the country's overseas workers during this period. But it also calmed growing public discontent about the plight of migrant workers by summoning a kind of nationalist spirit rooted in the belief of one's role in nation building.

With an annual deployment of eight hundred thousand workers to more than two hundred nations, succeeding administrations maintained this program of development, understanding the importance of the contribution of overseas workers' dollar remittances to the country (Table 2.2).[21] A significant portion of the remittances entering the Philippines is sent by Filipino women, who, in 2006, constituted 60 percent of newly hired workers leaving for overseas employment. Most were employed as household workers, caregivers, and workers in the medical field (Philippines Overseas Employment Administration 2006b).[22] While earnings vary by occupation and employment destination, women abroad remit a significant portion of their earnings to their families in the

TABLE 2.2

Value of Overseas Workers' Dollar Remittances to the Philippines

Year	Amount (dollars)	% GNP
1988	857 million	2.0
1995	4.9 billion	7.2
2003	7.6 billion	8.9
2005	10.7 billion	10.0
2007	14.4 billion	unavailable

SOURCES: Bangko Sentral ng Pilipinas (BSP); Gonzalez 1998; Gonzaga 2006; Philippine Overseas Employment Administration (POEA).
NOTE: Figures are for cash remittances funneled through the banking system.

Philippines. In a nationwide survey of 1,150 overseas Filipino workers conducted by the Asian Development Bank (ADB) in 2003, the respondents who worked as domestic workers in Hong Kong remitted an average of $246 monthly, representing a little more than half their monthly salary (ADB 2004).[23] The state's interest in these remittances was certainly evident in a series of regulations imposed on workers, beginning with a 50 to 80 percent mandatory remittance of their earnings in 1974. In 1982, this was amended to require workers to remit through official banking channels, a requirement reinforced in 1991 through the formal accreditation of other agencies to become official remittance centers (Asis 1992).

While the state recognizes the value of workers' remittances, it faces the reality that their contributions can come at the cost of their lives. This is especially the case with women workers, the majority of the country's overseas employment workforce. In 1988, in response to escalating reports of the exploitative working conditions in which Filipino workers, especially domestic workers, were laboring, President Corazon Aquino instituted a worldwide ban on the overseas deployment of domestic workers. However, this was short-lived, because of the mounting protests and fears that the ban would only encourage illegal overseas recruitment circuits.[24] Similarly, the succeeding administration of Fidel Ramos faced mounting social unrest brought about by, among other things, the mysterious death of Maricris Sioson, an "entertainer" in Japan; the trial of Sara Balabagan, a domestic worker who stabbed her employer in the United Arab Emirates; and the execution of Flor Contemplacion, a domestic worker accused of murdering a child and her nanny in Singapore (Guevarra 2006b).

These cases were instrumental in revealing the lack of adequate social protection available for Filipino workers overseas, prompting the state to devise policy changes to redress these situations. These included setting minimum age requirements for entertainers and domestic workers, at eighteen and twenty-three years old, respectively; requiring that foreign employers be accredited by the Philippine Embassy and that entertainment "promoters" post a twenty-thousand-dollar bond to cover artists' claims against them; and, for all Japan-bound entertainers, setting up the Artist Record Book system, which imposed skills training and testing through the Technical Education and Skills Development Authority (TESDA) (Asis 1992; Guevarra 2006b).[25] Additionally, domestic workers were now required to speak and write English and receive basic housework training (Department of Labor and Employment 1995). All these measures were supposed to protect and minimize the "vulnerability" of women in the occupations covered by the mandates, while demonstrating that the state was attending to growing public unrest about its inability to protect its migrant workers, an issue that was at its height with the Flor Contemplacion case.

"IF NOBODY IS DYING, NOTHING HAPPENS"

Flor Contemplacion, a mother of four born into a poor family in Masbate, which, in 2000, was the second most impoverished province in the country (National Statistical Coordination Board 2004), left the Philippines in 1988 for domestic work in Singapore. In 1991, she was charged in the double murder of Delia Maga, a domestic worker, and the child of Maga's employer. Contemplacion confessed to the murders. However, evidence was brought forward that she had confessed under duress. The Singaporean government disallowed a reinvestigation of the crimes as well as the inclusion of new evidence, including autopsy reports from the victims, which may have benefited Contemplacion's case. The new evidence suggested that the cause of Maga's death was, not asphyxiation resulting from strangulation, as previously claimed, but bludgeoning, an act that the Philippine coroner suggested may have been committed by a man (May 1997). Despite then-president Fidel Ramos's appeals for clemency to the Singaporean government and the massive public outcry that radiated throughout the Philippines and Singapore, fuelled primarily by two nongovernmental organizations (NGOs), Migrante-Philippines and Gabriela, in 1995 Flor Contemplacion was hanged (Rodriguez 2002). Following her execution, Contemplacion became a powerful figure for many Filipinos, who viewed her as the national symbol of their economic plight, a martyr whose vulnerability mirrored that of the typical migrant worker. And because she represented the thousands of migrant workers whose remittances kept the economy afloat, she was also an important figure for the state, which, after the arrival of her body in the Philippines, proudly hailed her as a *bagong bayani*, another hero(ine) of the Philippines.

Most important, her death made visible the exploitative working conditions in which many migrant workers, especially Filipino women, labored and a state that was unprepared to alleviate these conditions, having no institutionalized protective measures in place. As Noel Josue, president of Kaibigan, a key NGO in the Philippines that provides social and legal assistance to migrant workers, explained, prior to the Flor Contemplacion case, the problems that overseas Filipino workers face had received scant attention from the state and were not widely known to the public. The case mobilized not only NGOs but also the public to unite and exert sufficient pressure for the state to respond quickly. After what Josue described as "marathon congressional sessions," the government passed the much awaited law RA 8042 (discussed in detail below) to protect overseas workers. As Josue put it, "Whenever there is a celebrated case, something good happens. . . . *If nobody is dying, nothing happens!* (interview by the author, April 25, 2002).

Thus, Flor Contemplacion's plight was a pivotal moment in Philippine labor history in humanizing the country's labor export policy and punctuating its ethos of labor migration and dependence on workers' remittances for national economic survival. It provided an important mobilization tool for NGOs and workers globally by putting the state in a precarious position to listen to what was becoming a deafening cry for protective measures against unscrupulous recruiters and abusive employers and for implementing social support services for migrant workers. Not only did the state need to defend its program of development, it also needed to save face. "The government had to act fast," Josue remarked, while underscoring the fact that this knee-jerk response was also influenced by current senatorial and local elections. Contemplacion's plight and the resulting call for protecting migrant workers became a promising political platform.

Popularly dubbed the Magna Carta of overseas Filipino workers (OFWs), Republic Act 8042: The Migrant Workers Act and Overseas Filipinos Act of 1995 put forth a rigorous program of welfare protection for OFWs. The provisions outlined in RA 8042 included clarifying the role of government agencies involved in overseas employment, the provision of legal assistance to migrant workers, and the grounds and penalties for illegal recruitment. While the law was supposed to encapsulate the notion that the state does not promote overseas employment but simply facilitates the "choice" of Filipinos to work overseas, it was also supposed to express the state's commitment to send Filipinos only to countries that upheld and guaranteed their individual rights and protection. It also spelled out the terms of deployment that are contingent on the state of Philippines' foreign relations with a particular host country while also setting forth a five-year comprehensive deregulation plan on the recruitment activities of the Department of Labor and Employment (DOLE) and POEA. RA 8042 also reflected the state-led transnationalism that the Philippine state was modeling, seeking to benefit not only from the remittances of its workers but also from their skills. This would happen through the provision of special incentives to professionals and other highly skilled Filipinos abroad in the field of science and technology to share their skills with the Philippines in the interest of national development. Most of all, it finally recognized the feminization of the Philippines' labor migration and the contribution of women to the Philippine economy, embodied in the promise to use what the state refers to as "gender-sensitive criteria" in its policies and programs.

At the height of the Flor Contemplacion case, President Ramos formed the multisectoral Gancayco Commission, or the Presidential Fact-Finding and Policy Advisory Commission on the Protection of Overseas Filipinos, in 1995. The commission was responsible for assessing current policies and programs aimed at protecting migrant workers and offering recommendations for improving them (Guevarra 2006b). Following its findings of the range of abusive situations in which domestic workers and entertainers found themselves, the commission introduced the notion of "vulnerable occupations," such as domestic work and entertainment, as a special category of state protection. The commission boldly recommended the gradual phaseout of these occupations and the creation of economically lucrative local employment for women. This would serve not only as a permanent measure to end these "vulnerabilities" but also as a way to correct the perception of the Philippines as a country of domestic workers and entertainers, which contributes to the marred image of the country and in particular, of the Filipino woman.

According to the Gancayco Commission Report (Gancayco 1996, 73), "Our nation has gained the embarrassing reputation that we are a country of DHs [domestic helpers], entertainers, and even prostitutes . . . that even in a certain dictionary, the latest definition of the word 'Filipina' is a 'housemaid.'" The importance placed on the country's image conveniently overshadows the fact that because of their sheer volume, these are the same workers hailed as modern-day heroes for the remittances they contribute to the country's economy. The uneasiness that this commission conveyed about the kind of vulnerability that the country's national image was experiencing is striking and captures the spirit behind the incorporation of the so-called gender-sensitive component in RA 8042. According to Section 2d, while the state recognized the significant role that men and women play in nation building, it also recognized the contributions of migrant women workers and "their particular vulnerabilities." In response, it claimed that "the state shall apply gender sensitive criteria in the formulation and implementation of policies and programs affecting migrant workers and the composition of bodies tasked for the welfare of migrant workers."

Following this policy inclusion, the state assumed the posture of a governing body that was responsive to and could appease its public at the same time as it continued to profit from the participation of women in "vulnerable" occupations. Thus, one way in which this gender sensitivity materialized was in the assurance that a "representative from the women's sector" was appointed to the governing boards of POEA and OWWA, the two key institutions facilitating the country' overseas employment program. Another way was to include discussions of the unique experiences that women face as overseas workers within the pre-departure orientation session (PDOS) provided by state-accredited providers.[26]

The inclusion of this policy has some interesting aspects, among them the types of tensions and contradictions that it presents. This "gender-sensitive criteria" can be read as the state's final recognition of the important contributions of women workers to the Philippine economy, the dangers they face abroad, and the commitment to protecting their well-being overseas (Guevarra 2006b). However, it can also be read as the Gancayco Commission's concern about the image of the Philippines that it believes is tainted by Filipino women who are seemingly perceived to be not only of low "quality" but also of questionable sexual mores. Ultimately, what resulted was a set of "gender sensitive" programs that sought to "empower" women workers in ways that addressed the vulnerabilities of both the women and the state, an issue that I discuss in the following chapter.

"We Have Naturally Evolved a Migrant Worker Culture"

A central tenet of RA 8042 is that the state does not promote overseas employment but simply aims to manage the process and, specifically, the choices of its citizens to pursue this opportunity. Reflecting this shift in perspective—from the state as promoter to the state as manager of overseas employment—was a white paper produced by DOLE in 1995, before passage of the law. This document explicitly defended the country's overseas employment program, arguing that labor migration may be the best tool for addressing some of the labor market gaps in the global economy. In this spirit, the paper prompted Philippine policy makers to engage in a shift of perspective from seeing their task not as "exporting the country's labor surplus" but as "*managing* effectively the *natural* processes of labor migration—which will continue even if we ban the outflow of our workers" (Department of Labor and Employment 1995, 1; emphases added).

This framework proposes that opportunities abroad are natural processes of globalization and that the desires and aspirations of Filipinos to work overseas are natural responses. As Ricardo Casco, former director of POEA's Welfare and Employment Services explained, the framework of managing labor migration is a response to the opportunities provided by global markets, which is ideal for the Philippines because "we [have] naturally evolved a migrant worker culture" (interview by the author, October 25, 2001). By assisting this so-called natural process of overseas employment, the state can claim that it is merely supporting the constitutional right and freedom of Filipinos to choose their employment. As the former Administrator of OWWA, attorney Wilhelm Soriano, also emphasized, "If Filipinos are given a choice, they would rather work here [the Philippines]. This is why working abroad is an option" (interview by the author, November 25, 2001).

But is it truly an option? While state officials and labor brokers overemphasize the concept of "option" or Filipinos' sense of adventure they obscure the economic realities that undergird the desire to pursue migration. The average salary of nurses in the Philippines ranges from 2,500 to 14,000 pesos (about $48–269) a month, with the higher end relegated to those working in the cities or possessing highly specialized skills.[27] As I discuss in the chapters that follow, Filipina nurses further explain that the inability to find employment after graduation is a strong incentive for pursuing overseas employment. Hospitals hire only those with significant experience; therefore, many recent graduates are forced to volunteer first unless they have a family connection to a particular hospital.[28] Of course the volunteer nurses also become a boon for hospitals insofar as the latter can benefit from the nurses' much needed yet unpaid labor at the same time that the hospitals further support the impetus of Filipinos to pursue overseas migration by providing the clinical training they need.[29]

The official minimum wage for domestic workers based on the 1974 Philippine Labor Code ranges from 500 to 800 pesos ($12–19) a month, depending on the regions in which they work, a wage far below that which they can earn overseas.[30] For example, a Filipina working as a domestic worker in Hong Kong earns a monthly salary of $3,670 (about $471).[31] But these factors all recede into the background to make way for constructing overseas migration as an action not born of coercion but allowing workers to realize their individual power to make choices and to fulfill their sense of adventure.

By "managing" labor migration, the state seeks to evoke the image of a governing body that responds to the demands and choices of its citizens, producing policies that can reflect at some times an all-controlling and dominating power and at other times, one that seemingly withdraws control and becomes a facilitator of its citizenry's demands. Exemplary of an "art of government" (Foucault 1979), managing labor migration is about how best to do so in ways that will be lucrative to the country. Meanwhile, underlying this framework is the reality that Filipinos are leaving because the country is unable to provide them viable jobs.

Nevertheless, Casco succinctly noted, "[labor migration] need not to be treated as temporary and that it can be stopped anytime. You have to accept and manage it to your advantage" (interview by the author, October 25, 2001). Viewing labor migration as a phenomenon to be managed instead of a program to be promoted or implemented, he argued, provides a greater degree of flexibility and responsiveness to global markets and challenges that may plague the Philippine economy. This involves reconceptualizing one's role in this process as a "public manager" instead of a bureaucrat. Unlike a traditional bureaucrat, as a public manager, he does not "operate the program by the letter" but instead "take[s] risks by passing a law and exercising discretion and judicious judgment for the essence of public interest and public service." he characterized the role of POEA as that of public managers who have "developed creativity to respond to the dynamic behavior of the migrant." This creativity can perhaps be seen in two key elements of this framework: marketing and labor diplomacy, which I discuss in the next section.

The state discusses its support of the country's overseas employment in terms of merely responding to Filipinos' choices and innate tendency to work overseas (dubbed the "dynamic behavior of the migrant"). As Casco explained, one of the "push factors" for Filipinos' desire to work overseas is the "natural aspiration for greener pastures which is pre-conceived as not here [but] somewhere else—in a developed country, in a high-tech country, in an environmentally sensitive country, in a less populated country, in a country where there is a World Trade Center" (interview by the author, October 25, 2001).[32] Thus, the framework of managing labor migration rests on a fundamental assumption that the state merely supports these "natural aspirations" without giving itself due credit for helping to cultivate them and contributing to the country's ethos of labor migration. As Casco further described, the recruitment activities promoted by the private sector and state bodies like the

POEA—many of which materialize in the classified ads, of which 90 percent are for overseas employment—bring a certain kind of hyper-awareness of opportunities outside the Philippines. "How could you not be aware? The labor market that you aspire to when you are a student and when you graduate is not the Philippines but the globe," Casco argued (interview by the author, October 25, 2001).

Casco captured the very tension and contradiction that underlie how the state envisions itself as a manager of labor migration. On the one hand, it paints itself as an actor aiming to secure a strategic position in the global economy and one that is accommodating the natural desires of Filipinos to go abroad. On the other hand, it undermines its own power in creating the very conditions it purports to manage. That is, the very process of managing labor migration through myriad state-driven initiatives, perhaps emblematic of the creativity that Casco described, only reveals the illusion behind the so-called claim that the country has naturally evolved a migrant worker culture.

FILIPINOS FOR SALE OR ON SALE?

Imagine entering an unremarkable government office building where you are greeted by hordes of people carrying passports and brown envelopes, waiting in endless lines to get their paperwork processed, negotiating with uniformed attendants—a scene you might expect of any bureaucracy. Indeed, once one is inside a POEA office, the layout and ambiance seem to confirm this. There is one big room filled with tables, mostly scattered about and without dividers for privacy. Only a handful of computers and phones occupy the tables. Yet filling this room is the cacophonic hum and clacking of printers, fax machines, and type-writers, coupled with the enormous din of simultaneous conversations in Tagalog and English. Hidden in a corner, managing this mayhem, is the private office reserved for the director of this division.

But upon closer inspection, this is not just a paper-pushing arm of the POEA bureaucracy. Beyond these seemingly mundane bureaucratic walls sits a social think tank, a laboratory, called the Marketing Division, a key organizational unit within POEA's Preemployment Services Office. The Marketing Division produces the ubiquitous "labor market updates" that one finds posted on this office's walls or on the POEA's Web site. From information regarding country-specific labor shortages and job opportunities, cautionary messages about illegal recruitment activities, or changes in overseas employment regulations or policies, prospective migrants can keep up with the ever-changing global market.

The updates are provided by the unit's Market Research Branch, which obtains its information from a number of sources. First and foremost are the officers of the Philippine Overseas Labor Offices (POLOs), who deliver on-site assistance to workers, attempt to promote "healthy" employment relationships, and supply POEA with information about any labor market development.[33] Currently, thirty-four POLOs are stationed in places where Filipino migrant workers are found in great numbers.[34] Second, the Market Research Branch obtains market information from the Internet, official and unofficial publications, conference proceedings, and migrant workers. Third, it incorporates relevant scholarly research as a source of information to the extent of encouraging employees who are pursuing master's or doctoral degrees to write papers pertaining to labor and employment.

Alongside the labor market updates are brochures and pamphlets featuring the human resources that the country offers, produced by the Market Promotions Branch within this marketing division unit. Even POEA annual reports proudly boast the number of "promotional materials" that this office produces and disseminates to prospective foreign employers. From producing "5700 marketing flyers," to developing brochures for such efforts as the "special hiring program for Taiwan workers," to providing a "PowerPoint presentation on the recruitment of Filipino nurses for U.S. principals," POEA attempts to display its "aggressive marketing strategies" (POEA 2004, 2005). Showcasing the varied skills, experience, and expertise of Filipino workers in such brochures as *Hiring Filipino Workers through POEA* and *Filipino Workers: Moving the World Today*, the Market Promotions Branch is in the business of selling the country's most prized commodities and their competitive advantage as global workers.

Prospective foreign employers perusing the brochures can learn about workers who have college degrees, who are adept at using varied technologies, who possess a range of expertise and experience, and who even uniquely provide service with "charm and cheerful efficiency." They may also receive a false impression that men make up the majority of the country's workforce deployment, given that women are largely invisible in these brochures and only appear once, assisting a male nurse. Highlighting Filipino managers, bankers, and accountants, the photographs place women in the periphery and direct the reader's gaze to male figures. While these representations obscure the gendering of Philippine migration, they make visible how the state's much touted gender-sensitive criteria is actually realized. As I show in the following chapter, they also reflect the anxieties behind the overwhelming number of Filipino women employed as domestic workers overseas and the resulting state initiative to professionalize the image of its labor export economy.

The Market Promotions Branch is also the brains behind the POEA's ballyhooed global marketing missions, another key component of its "aggressive marketing strategies." Government officials explain that different kinds of marketing missions exist, of which most are geared toward promoting the welfare and protection of overseas workers. However, these marketing missions often refer to activities that promote the Filipino workforce for newly opened labor markets. For example, in 1989, the POEA organized two marketing missions to Hong Kong on news of that territory's national labor shortage (Tyner 2000). In the fall of 2002, in an effort to take advantage of markets that opened for skilled professionals in the United Kingdom, the Netherlands, and other parts of Europe, the POEA partnered with the private sector in a project designed primarily to market Filipino workers (POEA 2003). In 2003, it sent marketing missions to Croatia and Slovenia, informed of shortages of health care workers there (POEA 2004). In 2004, the POEA ventured to Taiwan, whose information technology and electronic sectors reopened (POEA 2005). In 2005, the POEA conducted a successful Middle East marketing mission that it claimed resulted in "10 recruitment agreements and an estimated 2,300 job orders to be realized" (POEA 2006b, 16). Meanwhile, it held itself primarily responsible for securing the 126 job orders that a local Philippine employment agency received for Filipino entertainers (dubbed "overseas performing artists") for a newly opened Hong Kong Disney resort (POEA 2006b, 17).

Promoting Filipino workers became yet more evident in the first "in bound marketing activity" spearheaded by the POEA in 2005, an event that purportedly generated 15,462 foreign job orders (POEA 2006b). Not only was this three-day activity supposed to assist in identifying overseas employment opportunities, it was also meant to "promote the services of OFWs and showcase their skills and talents" as it served as a forum within which foreign employers and prospective workers could interact (POEA 2006b, 15). The focus on professionalizing the country's workforce deployment, an issue I discuss in the next chapter, was also reflected in the fact that the workers who are showcased here were "Filipino professional[s] and skilled workers and seafarers."

While prospective foreign employers have an opportunity to sample the country's offerings, prospective workers and their families can participate in a "local jobs fair and business forum," where they receive tips for managing their overseas earnings and savings by exploring investment, agribusiness, and franchising opportunities. The apparent message is that the state manages both the employment opportunities of Filipinos and the ways they can spend their hard-earned money. As I illustrate in the next chapter, the state's interest in their earnings is part of a larger project of conditioning overseas Filipino workers to see themselves as entrepreneurs and investors who can make more responsible decisions about how they spend their money, on the basis of the guidelines that the state puts forth.

Sharing Filipino Resources through "Labor Diplomacy"

In one of her *May Gloria Ang Bukas Mo* (There Is Gloria/Glory in Your Future) television episodes, President Arroyo called on the nation's educational institutions to keep up with globalization. She proclaimed, "If there is a big demand for nurses, [they] need to produce more nurses. If there is a big demand for I.T. [information technology] workers, [they] need to produce more I.T. workers" (field notes, January 12, 2002). In 2002, in a speech delivered on Migrant Workers Day, she clearly articulated that the country would be dependent on overseas workers' remittances and credited OFWs for their contributions, asserting: "The successful businesses put up because of your remittances are important economic pillars of the country." POEA's framework of "managing" labor migration was a central framework of President Arroyo's national economic development plan—the Medium-Term Philippine Development Plan (MTPDP) of 2001–2004 and 2004–2010. While these blueprints for the country's economic success focused on improving such areas as trade, tourism, the environment, housing, crime prevention, and political governance, a key issue was how to generate labor and employment opportunities for Filipinos. This is especially the case in terms of globalization processes. As outlined in the 2001–2004 MTPDP Plan, Filipino workers need to be competitive in order to "access larger markets" and that "skills-training and provisions of safety nets" are the key tools for doing so (National Economic Development Authority 2002, 3).

Arroyo's administration notably placed the need to develop, enhance, and update Filipino workers' skills as a strategic response to the demands of globalization. In the 2004–2010 plan, now current, the focus on skill building becomes more apparent and seemingly directed to meeting the demands of global labor markets. While both plans emphasize the importance of generating local employment, the impetus behind the call for enhancing Filipinos' skills is to make workers competitive for overseas employment. After all, in the 2004–2010 plan, the state clearly states that Filipino workers are "the country's comparative advantage" and thus the state needs to transform the country's educational and training programs in ways that fulfill the demands of "skills needed in a globalizing economy." In the state's doing so, the "standards for skills certification and assessment of competencies *shall be developed based on international standards* (National Economic Development Authority 13; emphases added).

The notion of workers serving as the country's "comparative advantage" is important for several reasons. First, it signifies the value of Filipinos to the state and suggests that its workers are bargaining chips by means of which the Philippine state attempts to gain a viable position in the global economy. Second, it reflects the commodification of Filipinos, whose global marketability depends on their acquiring particular features (skills, competencies, and so on) that would contribute to what I describe in Chapter 5 as their *added export value* and satisfy so called international standards. The Filipino workers that the state produces need to be *good enough* for international markets.

This language of exchange whereby Filipino workers become the state's resources to be harnessed and commodities to be traded supports the ways the state attempts to manage labor migration through the principles of "labor diplomacy." Philippine state officials often echo the notion that sustaining an ethos of labor migration is fundamentally about managing foreign relations. This is similar to what Pei-Chia Lan (2006) argued is the guiding principle behind Taiwan's legalization of migrant labor, as that state opened its borders to four countries of the Association of Southeast Asian Nations as a means of establishing or rekindling bilateral relations and political ties with them.[35] More important, it is a means through which Taiwan aims to facilitate the investment of Taiwanese capital in these countries, which Lan aptly characterizes as a "checkbook diplomacy" (40). For the Philippine state, under the concept of labor diplomacy, economic foreign relations with other nations are often heavily influenced by the presence of Filipino workers in those countries. As former POEA director Casco recounted, the Philippines uses labor diplomacy to press foreign countries to consider Filipino workers as "internationally shared human resources" who significantly contribute to the countries' national development. He explained how he made an effort to inform Filipino workers that they were the Philippine state's "strategic contribution to global economic development" and outlined various economies' dependence on this: "If we withdraw all of the domestic helpers in Hong Kong, wives [in that territory] can no longer work. If we withdraw all of the Filipino seafarers [from] all of the oceangoing vessels of the world, there will be no more shipments and cruise vessels. If we withdraw all our petroleum workers [and] construction workers, [all of] the infrastructure development will be affected. If we withdraw all of our nurses in the Middle East, I don't know how [the hospitals] can survive (interview by the author, October 25, 2001).

Through labor diplomacy, Filipino workers serve as invaluable resources and commodities that the Philippines "share" with global markets, which are dependent on their expertise and skills. As a result, the state envisions this strategy as a bargaining point for negotiating mechanisms that ensure the protection of overseas Filipino workers through formal or informal bilateral agreements with labor-receiving countries. The state claims that participating in overseas marketing missions and international conferences dealing with information exchange on matters like worker protection, full disclosure of employment terms, and labor market development are examples of labor diplomacy. As I show in the next chapter, by managing labor migration through labor diplomacy, the state seeks to influence the conduct of Filipino workers by encouraging them to envision themselves as "ambassadors of good-will" for the Philippines, emissaries who must preserve diplomatic ties with their host country.

However, labor diplomacy has its limitations and is hampered by competition when other labor-exporting nations offer workers at cheaper rates. POEA officials such as Carmelita Dimzon, former head of the Preemployment Services Office, observed that meeting with other labor-exporting nations prove unsuccessful because they often cannot agree about formulating uniform employment standards. For example, as she explained, if the Philippines demanded wages of $150 its workers, Sri Lanka and Bangladesh would settle for $80, a situation that explains the difficulties of forming global cross-class solidarity among labor-exporting countries (Carmelita Dimzon, interview by the author, October 25, 2001). As a result, for the Philippine state, managing labor migration involves dealing with emerging competition and finding ways to increase Filipino workers' competitiveness without sacrificing their wages. The kind of labor diplomacy that the Philippine state attempts to summon is based on generating highly skilled Filipino workers. The success of labor diplomacy rests on the ability of the state to respond to global market demands by marketing a comparative advantage that would pitch the country as an ideal supplier of labor. For the Philippines, such a comparative advantage is in its highly skilled, trained, and educated Filipinos, who not only will be capable of doing the work but also whose skills can be used as bargaining chips for securing conditions that will contribute to fostering improved foreign bilateral relations.

CONCLUSION

In this chapter I challenge the culturally essentialist claims about the Filipino labor export economy and illustrate the (neo)colonial legacies and varied state-led initiatives and policies that put the Philippines into a trajectory of economic crisis at the same time that they introduced Filipinos as exploitable human resources. I described the state's role as a manager of labor migration and the resulting unintended consequence of creating an ethos of labor migration. This ethos of labor migration is a phenomenon of the political, economic, and social context that produces the state's much touted Great Filipino Worker. It is based on the country's commitment to using overseas employment as a source of income and explains its addiction to overseas Filipino workers' remittances. This ethos of labor migration is also fundamentally grounded in creating a *culture of sacrifice* in which Filipinos become *implicated actors* (Clarke and Montini 1993) as both objects and subjects of the state.[36] On the one hand, as the country's resources, they are commodified as objects of the state that are offered to the globe as its comparative advantage in exchange for national economic survival. On the other hand, as the country's modern-day heroes, they are integral subjects of the state, as they are symbolically and ideologically touted and molded to save not only their families but also their nation through their remittances. Most important, this ethos of labor migration characterizes the extent to which the aspirations of success that Filipinos imagine and pursue reside outside the Philippines—an issue I take up in later chapters.

Thus, the national identity of the Philippine state as a manager of labor migration is maintained by its ability to manage both aspirations and its image as a responsive state. In the next chapter, I describe how the state carries out this task and specifically maintains this ethos of labor migration and sacrifice through the mechanism of "empowerment," attempting to affect the conduct of Filipino citizens so that they project a favorable image of the home of the Great Filipino Worker.

CHAPTER 3

Governing and (Dis)Empowering Filipino Migrants

We are proud of our overseas Filipino workers as our new heroes. They bravely chart international paths many of us have not dared venture in. They forge new courses of friendship and amity for the Philippines. They strengthen our economy and in many ways allow us to enjoy the fruits of their collective behavior.

—Former senator Leticia Ramos Shahani, RA 8042:
Migrant Workers and Overseas Filipinos Act of 1995

IN A ROOM filled with about thirty-five women, an impassioned woman stands proud, shouting, "You are not yet heroes. You are just soldiers right now!" This woman is Mildred Yamzon, cofounder of the Women in Development Foundation (WIDF), an NGO authorized by the Philippine state to provide pre-departure orientation seminars (PDOSs) to prospective domestic workers headed overseas. Alternating between the personas of a preacher delivering a sermon to her congregation and an army commander explaining survival tactics to her battalion, Yamzon powerfully transforms these sessions into something more than simply a place where prospective workers can receive guidance on travel to their destination. Rather, it becomes a space where women workers, whom some view as an endangered species, are made clearly and bluntly aware of the potential dangers they face overseas.[1] In partnership with the state, NGOs such as WIDF supply information to the women that is supposed to prepare and empower them, this information all narrated within the framework of giving meaning and tribute to their sacrifice in the name of their families and nation. Yamzon and her colleagues define their work as meeting the state's so-called gender-sensitive criteria by empowering the women to see their "comparative advantage" as Filipino workers and to view themselves as more than workers, to see themselves as professionals, heroes, ambassadors of goodwill, and investors.[2]

Promoting empowerment to support the vulnerabilities of all Filipino workers and elevate their social value in fact leads to their commodification. The state's framework for "managing labor migration" is built on this ideology of empowerment, which accords with the state's neoliberal ethos of governing Filipino workers by fusing together Filipino "moral" values of family and nationalism with Westernized notions of economic competitiveness.[3] The Philippine state's management of labor migration through the art of government is a means of ruling a population by influencing its conduct (Foucault 1991; Rose 1999; Rose and Miller 1992). It is a strategy that reflects a state that derives power and legitimacy from appearing less concerned about dominating its population than about empowering its citizens to self-govern. While claiming not to promote labor migration but instead supporting the choices of its citizens, it governs from a distance by defining and enabling the very choices it purports to support.

This form of empowerment derives from Western values of freedom, individualism, rationality, and self-accountability, combined with the neoliberal market rationality of economic competitiveness and entrepreneurship. All these values contribute to the production of a market-oriented citizenship and the formation of a gendered and racialized moral economy of the Filipino migrant based on what the state and its labor-brokering partners determine *should* be the obligations of migrants to their families and nation (Guevarra 2003). Ong (2006, 199) similarly discusses the "moral economy of the female migrant" to describe the system of "unequal relationships of exchange based on a morality of reciprocity, mutual obligation, and protection" and foregrounds the role of NGOs in this process.

My conceptualization of the moral economy of the Filipino migrant not only highlights its gendered dynamic but also identifies its racialized aspects whereby its formation is influenced by norms both of femininity and masculinity and of particular Filipino cultural and social values. While this moral economy is about the actual value systems that inform Filipino migrants' actions and the web of exploitative situations in which they are entangled, it is also about the disciplinary power of the state and its partners, which seek to define their social conduct and sense of belonging to the nation. The gendered and racialized moral economy of the Filipino migrant underscores the cultural logic that governs how overseas Filipino workers are supposed to behave, as model Filipinos who can embody an ethic of responsibility toward their families, nation, and the representation of the Great Filipino Worker, while maintaining their commodification and submission to a neoliberal state.

However, I do not suggest that workers do not respond to this power strategically. Following James Scott's (1976) conceptualization of "moral economy" as the standards or values upon which peasants respond to their exploitation and acts of resistance, I argue that Filipino migrants also respond to the disciplinary power that governs their commodification in ways that mirror *their* moral economy, whether this may entail embodying or challenging this power. I address this thoroughly in chapters 6 and 7, through my interviews with nurses. In this chapter, I focus primarily on the Philippine state's disciplinary power and highlight empowerment as the mechanism that enables this power in order to point out how the very moral economy that attempts to govern Filipino migrants by remaking them into being more than just workers may, in actuality, only contribute to their disempowerment and disenfranchisement.

(Dis)Honoring Heroes and Ambassadors of Goodwill

More than two decades after Corazon Aquino's official designation of overseas Filipino workers as the country's modern-day heroes, the label *bagong bayani* thrives. In December 2005, it was highlighted at Malacañang Palace's Rizal Hall, in a celebration of Filipino women and men working overseas who had earned the coveted Bagong Bayani Award (BBA).[4] Since 1989, POEA has annually celebrated the BBA, a state-sponsored tribute to overseas Filipino workers. "The Bagong Bayani Awards," went the announcement, "is a national search for the country's outstanding and exemplary Overseas Filipino Workers (OFWs), as our 'modern-day heroes.' The award seeks to recognize and pay tribute to our OFWs for their significant efforts in fostering goodwill among peoples of the world, enhancing and promoting the image of the Filipino as a competent, responsible and dignified worker, and for greatly contributing to the socioeconomic development of their communities and our country as a whole" (POEA, http://www.poea.gov.ph). This description demonstrates how the state defines the role of its migrant workers and rewards their contribution within Philippine society. They are the new "heroes" not only because of their remittances but also because they promote amicable relations with foreign nations and enhance the image of the Philippines as a reputable source of labor.

However, their heroism must also fall within the state's predefined criteria (POEA, http://www.poea.gov.ph).[5] For one, a BBA recipient can be a worker who demonstrates a unique work ethic and sense of loyalty to the job by having "manifested love, concern for the company and his or her coworkers" or "performed a heroic act or deed, or saved life or property, the performance of which is beyond the normal call of duty." A BBA recipient can also be a worker who displays a sense of community spirit, who has, perhaps, "selflessly offered his or her time, skills and/or resources, in collective or personal capacity to engage in such community services or activities that are beneficial to the people." Or a BBA recipient may be a worker who exudes a sense of nationalism and love for the Philippines by having "worked or been involved in the promotion, preservation, and development of Filipino culture and arts overseas" or has "excelled in his or her work as an artist abroad thereby earning recognition, adulation or honor for Filipino artistry and talent."[6]

While the state is quick to label its migrant workers as heroes, those who are worthy of the BBA must do more than just sustain their family and nation with remittances. The 2005 BBA winners, for example, included Leonor Mohammad Gile, who "worked with the Philippine consulate in Jeddah in solving the numerous problems of OFWs against their employers without expecting anything in return"; Zenaida Batillano, who was credited with "being the only Asian woman in her company's top management level who influenced the hiring of Filipinos for supervisory and management positions" and who "led the Filipino community in managing the Iraqi crisis in 2004 and became its pillar of strength and courage"; or the Filipino crew of the *MV Merino Express* who kept "alive their cargo of 56,000 livestock while battling extreme heat and thirst during a stretched voyage of 86 days" (press release, December 2, 2005, http://www.gov.ph).[7] The heroism that BBA showcased here was that of individuals who encapsulated the "greatness" that the Philippine state advertises about Filipino workers. Meanwhile, the

BBA deflects attention from and appeases public criticism of the state's inability to create an environment in which labor migration is no longer a necessity for economic survival. As former POEA director Ricardo Casco clarified, the BBA is supposed to recognize the "heroic deeds" of OFWs who "shine, giving [a good] name to the Philippines." The BBA, he explained, is one way that the state recognizes how they are "suffering away from their families" while "*unknowingly* contributing to their country's economic recovery and in the process, encountering tragedies" (interview by the author, October 25, 2001; emphasis added).

The BBA attempts to honor the social heroism of OFWs, their ability to endure these hardships and "tragedies" without realizing that they are key contributors to keeping the economy afloat. The idea of social heroism is not new to the Philippines, but is a remnant of Spanish colonialism. It is deeply rooted in Catholic ideals of suffering, sacrifice, and martyrdom, the predominant cultural norms that structure the ways Filipinos interpret their everyday lives in times of social despair and that imbue individuals who possess these ideals with a status of social respectability. Equally important, they are the same ideals that continue to play a part in defining Filipino nationalism and citizenship.

Referring to OFWs as modern-day heroes is a practice that began with an important historical and cultural figure, the first national hero of the Philippines, José Rizal.[8] As demonstrated by Filipino historians Reynaldo Ileto (1979) and Vicente Rafael (1997) Filipino nationalism has been historically articulated as beginning with Rizal, his life of suffering and sacrifice identified as its defining moment. Following Rizal's tradition, other Filipino (primarily male) heroes (Andres Bonifacio, Apolinario Mabini, and others) emerged and became symbols of sacrifice and courage after dying in the name of their country. Now, OFWs, who are disproportionately women, have become the Philippines' modern-day heroes, enduring the exploitative conditions in which their dollar remittances are produced and funneled into the country and the rising social costs, such as family separation and isolation, of migration. As Rafael explains, "By encoding OCWs [overseas contract workers] as national heroes, Aquino and her successor, Fidel Ramos, have sought to contain the anxieties attendant upon the flow of migrant labor, including the emotional distress over the separation of families and the everyday exploitation of migrants by labor contractors, travel agents, and foreign

employers" (276).[9] I add that by invoking Catholic ideals of sacrifice, suffering, and martyrdom through the *bagong bayani*, the state can make use
of these cultural particularities by seemingly empowering workers and
subsequently promoting its neoliberal mandate of generating responsible
economic citizens in ways that make cultural sense to Filipinos. For Filipinos, sacrifice and suffering are familiar and important values, so when
the state invokes them, Filipinos understand and respond accordingly.

While the notion of the *bagong bayani* has been popularly adopted for
commercial use and is starkly visible in institutions—banks, travel agencies, real estate firms, and megamalls—throughout the Philippines government officials insist on reformulating this cultural inscription. For
instance, Casco argued that referring to OFWs as modern-day heroes
does not empower workers but only commodifies them. He was adamant
that this "exaggerated" and "overused" term only signifies that the workers' only importance to the country lies in their earnings. He uttered disdain for the focus on their consumption power: "In reality, what should
be done is to explain to the OFWs that instead of wasting [their] money
with [buying] fake goods in Hong Kong or doing duty-free shopping,
[they] should buy this educational plan, memorial [cemetery] plan"
(interview by the author, October 25, 2001). Following his logic, if
OFWs are going to be *real* heroes, they need to be ones who are
endowed with certain responsibilities and obligations (buying an educational plan instead of "unnecessary" material goods). As responsible citizens, they must go beyond considering their role only as workers and
contribution only in economic terms.

Casco claimed that the state currently promotes a program of worker
empowerment based on the idea that OFWs are not only heroes but also
ambassadors of goodwill. In PDOSs, he described the message the state
imparts to them. His statement is worth quoting at length:

> Ladies and gentlemen, you must remember that you are a Filipino
> citizen and *you should help the country's image.* You are ambassadors of
> goodwill. How? If a domestic helper misbehaves and doesn't follow
> instruction, she will be the measuring cup of the image of the Fil-
> ipino worker. You are an ambassador of goodwill because you are
> going to work in an international environment. If you think that you
> smell better than [foreign employers] or that your religious practices

are superior, you better not surface that. You should understand each other. There should be cultural exchange, understanding. You should showcase your skills. You should take care of your employer. Be concerned about their interests. . . . We don't want [you] to be thrown into a situation where [you] stab [your] employers to death, do drug trafficking, steal or [commit] other crimes and ask the president to work for clemency. It is just so embarrassing. When [you] commit a crime, [you] are subject to the laws of the host country. You have to be jailed in the same manner that a foreigner in the Philippines would be if he [*sic*] commits a crime [here]. We should not have a situation where our president always works for clemency of criminals. [You] have to behave in proper decorum, [in] the way [you] dress, carry [yourselves]. . . . [As] Filipino citizens, [you] should help in government programs—promoting tourism and investments, especially those who are in the highest echelon. (Interview by the author, October 25, 2001; emphasis added).

"Empowering" workers to see themselves as ambassadors of goodwill is about creating a specific type of worker and citizen. First, Casco argued that if OFWs are going to avoid becoming "commodified" and overvalued in their economic worth, then they need to assume greater responsibilities. As Filipino cultural ambassadors, OFWs become partners in the Philippine state's project of managing labor migration through labor diplomacy by sharing in the responsibility of promoting good relations with host nations and being "concerned about their interests" and promoting "cultural exchange and understanding" in ways that contribute to a positive image of the country. A "misbehaving" worker mars the global perception that foreign employers develop to "generalize" about Filipino workers.

Second, he asserted that the status of ambassador does not afford overseas workers special privileges but instead should remind them of their need to be accountable for their actions. "That is why we try to exaggerate the awareness," added Casco, as he justified this practice of referring to Filipino migrants as cultural ambassadors. In saying this, he admits that the state knowingly recognizes the "exaggeration" of this construct. Yet it persists in promoting it as a measure of protecting itself from its own presumption of Filipinos' unruly tendencies or criminality.

In effect, the state shifts the burden of responsibility and protection from itself to the workers by implying that their best protection is empowerment—which they can achieve by becoming responsible and self-regulating. While these are fine virtues, this social labeling is disconcerting in that it is solely geared toward affecting the conduct of Filipino workers and not that of foreign employers or labor brokers.

Another official from POEA's Government Placement Branch discussed the importance of this kind of empowerment and complained about the emergence of "overcoddled" workers who had grown dependent on the state for protection. Workers, she observed, were no longer told be self-reliant or self-sufficient. As a result, "when things happen to the worker, it is the fault of the government. When a particular worker gets raped, it is the fault of the government." Although this official insisted that she is "pro-worker," she called for the need to create a different type of empowered worker. "When you empower the worker, you believe that when they get out into the field, they have the adequate bullets and when they [finish the battle], the first thing that [they] do is *behave. And when you behave, you can't go wrong.* So I am looking at the empowerment of the worker as a true and responsible worker" (interview by the author, February 18, 2002; emphasis added).

While I do not contest that this official genuinely cared for the livelihood of workers, the discourse of empowerment that she advocated is, nevertheless, disconcerting. First of all, she recognized the risks that workers, especially women, experience overseas at the same time that she minimized and normalized them by characterizing violence as a natural part of the overseas employment package and maintaining that empowerment is the instrument of protection and prevention. However, her very use of the word *empowerment*, while it intimates a minimizing of workers' vulnerabilities, also places the blame on them by attributing the violence they experience to their lack of discipline. This official's dismay at the blame put on the government for the sexual violence that women experience and her subsequent mention of their misbehaving tendencies implies that women (or perhaps, any worker) provoke this violence and become victims of their inability to control and manage their behavior—that, in fact, a worker who gets raped has no one else to blame but herself.

Second, and equally disturbing, is the continued reference to Filipino workers as soldiers, who, if given "adequate bullets" can survive any potential danger of working overseas because, as this official indicated, "when you behave, you can't go wrong." She assumed that the problems that overseas workers experience stem from their ignorance and ill preparedness for their eventual fate; she summoned workers to embrace the idea that their only source of protection is themselves. In this discourse of empowerment, the state casually retreats to the background and skirts around its very responsibility to the workers it reveres under the guise of promoting their individual autonomy and freedom.

As Rose (1999) explains, however, promoting individual autonomy and freedom is often geared toward disciplining individuals to conduct themselves in ways that support the state's nation-building projects. It is aimed at producing citizens who do not need to be governed by others but who can instead engage in "techniques of the self" and self-govern through personal accountability and responsibility (Foucault 1979; Burchell 1996). In this case, it is to serve the state's market interests. Thus, paying tribute to Filipino migrants as heroes or ambassadors of goodwill is fundamentally a means of disciplining their conduct at the same time that they are supposed to empower them. They are supposed to become more than just workers, to be almost mythical superheroes, who can act as autonomous subjects, able to embrace their responsibility to and sacrifice their lives for their families and nation.

(RE)PRODUCING WELL-INFORMED WORKERS

Empowering overseas Filipino workers to embody an ethic of personal responsibility and accountability as a means of their protection stems from the state's insistence on creating what they would call well-informed workers. This is at the heart of the dismay that the government official quoted above expressed about "overcoddled" workers. It reflects the state's general sentiments about the need to recognize that overseas employment is the choice that workers make and is, therefore, their responsibility. State officials affirm this by constantly referring to their simply *managing*, not *promoting*, labor migration. In the case of contract negotiations, for example, Carmelita Dimzon, POEA deputy administrator of general administrative and support services, asserted that the Migrant Workers Act (RA 8042) very clearly asserted that overseas employment is a matter between workers and employers. The government has no say in this process. She stipulated, however, that "it is the role of government to teach the worker and inform him [*sic*] of his rights and the consequences [of their agreement] if/when he signs the contract" (interview by the author, October 25, 2001).

Her statement is a compelling indication of a neoliberal state that governs on the basis of an overvaluation of individual "freedom" and liberty (Rose 1999). If freedom can be regarded as a formula of power realized through its exercise over others, then Dimzon's statement can be understood as one that reflects the state's aim to manage its migrants' conduct. Constructing neoliberal worker-citizens rests on recognizing and promoting individuals' autonomy and their capacity to make educated decisions. In her remarks, Dimzon presented a state that honors and respects the freedom of workers to make the final decision regarding their employment. Meanwhile, individual freedom allows the state to absolve itself from accountability to potential "welfare cases."[10]

For example, in the case of contract negotiation, by limiting its responsibility to dispensing workers with information that the state deems is necessary for their preparedness and protection, the state can argue that any problems arising between employer and worker must be resolved between the two of them. However, their contracts are based solely on a minimum set of provisions (such as work hours, wages, and employment benefits) that foreign employers follow and that are set out in POEA's master employment contract. Therefore, while the provisions of any final work contract may differ from those in the master employment contract, they have in essence been defined largely by the Philippine state. Further, the labor recruiters who serve as the official agents of foreign employers and workers fine-tune and negotiate the final contracts. The workers' role in this process is minimal, if there is any, and workers rely on the mercy of recruiters and employers to construct a reasonable employment package.

Nevertheless, the state insists on taking the approach that education is the best strategy of protection in order to generate these so-called well-informed workers. This outlook is evident in POEA's preemployment orientation seminars (PEOSs), which were integral to President Arroyo's human resource development projects. The seminars are part of POEA's migrant worker education program, which provides practical information for prospective Filipino workers about overseas employment. The seminars cover the application process, the educational and psychological preparation workers need to consider, and tips on how to avoid becoming victims of illegal recruitment. As Dimzon remarked, the thrust behind PEOS is the belief that "education is the best strategy for welfare" and that workers' protection derives from their making "well-thought-out" decisions. It is also in these sessions that state officials respond to public discontent about the impact of migration on families, especially on the children whom migrants leave behind and who are viewed as casualties of overseas employment; migrants hear about the difficulties of family separation and the possible resulting strain on family relations.

While the intention in constructing overseas employment as a family affair can be interpreted as a way to project an image of a state that responds to this discontent, I interpret it in terms of a state that seeks to ensure the productivity of its workers overseas. A former administrator of OWWA, attorney Wilhelm Soriano, would agree. As he himself remarked, "If migrant worker[s are] fully aware that the government and other sectors are looking after the welfare of their families back home, the more that [they are] able to concentrate on their respective jobs" (OWWA, press release, January 31, 2002). He echoed the state's underlying concern about the need to manage transnational families in ways that would ease migrants' preoccupation with their situation back home and their homesickness while ensuring that their performance met their employers' standards. It also underscored how the state attempts to discipline migrants' conduct as "responsible" individuals. Workers are expected to take care not only of the country's image but also of their family's welfare, even if they do so from a distance. They, not the state, are responsible for ensuring that they are not only productive workers but also good spouses or parents who will make sure that their relationships with those back home are not strained by and do not suffer from their decision to pursue overseas employment.[11] The focus on the family is specifically gendered, and as I explain below, women become specific targets of the state's disciplinary gaze (Foucault 1979), with the state's power judging, dictating, and modifying acceptable behavior and actions.[12]

Dimzon added that the government seminars empower workers by raising their self-esteem about the meaning and importance of their work and getting them to change their "paradigm." She explained the ways that the PEOSs inculcate in workers' minds the idea that their employers need them as much as they need their jobs. She asked domestic workers to consider the following: "You are domestic helpers in Hong Kong. Do you think that your employer can work without you?" Without such concepts, she feared, "they become very subservient . . . they just say yes, yes, yes" (interview by the author, October 25, 2001). While this may seem like sound advice, it does not account for the fact that there are limits and costs to this kind of empowerment, especially in light of how employers perceive the disposability of workers. For example, some labor brokers observed that Filipino workers were losing their "monopoly" on the market as ideal workers because with their education and English-language competency, employers perceived them to be more combative, more likely to "talk back," than workers of other nationalities. This is on top of the fact that foreign employers can demand a free replacement from their agencies when they become dissatisfied with a worker's performance. Therefore, the inability of the state to facilitate better working conditions for its workers guides the ways it wants workers to behave. Given the futility of lobbying for increased wages, the state redirects the responsibility to the workers by proposing that their self-assertiveness is a source of bargaining power; in reality, this strategy may be highly ineffective, placing workers at risk of losing their jobs.

Although prospective applicants can obtain educational information by attending a PEOS, available nationwide, they can also tune in to their local radio and television programming for what one POEA official proudly referred to as "PEOS on air."[13] Through guest appearances on television and radio shows, POEA officials advocate for the safety of migrant workers while they disseminate information about overseas employment. With PEOS on air, the task is the same—to "explain that people should have consciousness in preparing for jobs, livelihood, and lifelong learning" (Casco, interview by the author, October 25, 2001). In doing so, they develop a certain hyperawareness about the promise of overseas employment. Through a ubiquitous media presence, overseas employment becomes even more ingrained in the everyday consciousness of Filipinos and further cultivates the country's ethos of labor migration. The state runs a series called the Migrant Worker Education Program, whose goals are similar to those of PEOS; to introduce the notion of migration, specifically labor migration, in selected sites throughout the country.

One program even targets elementary and high school institutions as strategic points to insert information about overseas employment.

This program began in response to mounting criticism about the short duration (six hours) of POEA's PEOSs, which do not allow comprehensive coverage of essential matters that workers pursue in considering overseas employment. As a result, POEA and the Commission on Filipinos Overseas (CFO) developed a set of lessons called Education Modules on International Migration and Development. CFO officials and Casco claimed that these modules recognize the inevitability of migration and seek to further assist potential migrants, not to mention school-aged youths, in making "informed" decisions about migration. However, the uniqueness of this program derives from the fact that the modules are geared toward elementary and high-school students whose teachers are given training to incorporate information about overseas employment into their curriculum. For example, Casco explained that instead of creating one course on migration, the program selectively incorporates elements of migration as they appear relevant within the existing curriculum (within social studies, geography, economics, and so on). He reasoned that this is how "PEOS in school" operates. Although these modules do not state that they target labor migration per se, CFO and POEA officials admitted that they emphasize information about overseas employment. As Casco remarked, PEOS in school seeks to provide "that kind of education so that you are aware that eventually, [when] you become desperate and you cannot find a job [in the Philippines], you will go abroad" (interview by the author, October 25, 2001). Furthermore, he explained that prior to developing these modules, POEA already served as consultants to a significant number of elementary and high school teachers who incorporated aspects of overseas employment in textbooks. As a result, this same official observed some notable changes in some elementary school textbooks where they mention overseas workers such as Flor Contemplacion[14] and depict them, rather than the usual Apolinario Mabini or José Rizal, as heroes of their generation.[15]

Although these modules and educational programs function as an information clearinghouse for potential migrants, they gloss over questions about the grim future they inculcate in the minds of Filipino youths. Although the state claims to simply support the inevitability of labor migration as an outlet for people's economic despair, in fact, they are manufacturing its inevitability through this type of early learning indoctrination. The state makes labor migration inevitable by strategically failing to provide the infrastructure for young people and the citizenry at large that would allow them to see the Philippines as an economically viable country and local employment as a workable source of livelihood.[16] Moreover, these modules were created with no direct contribution from OFWs, thereby raising the question of the kinds of political and economic interests driving them. CFO officials have claimed that OFWs were not directly involved with the design of the modules but that their experiences, through existing research materials, were incorporated or guided the content and structure. Since the state depends on cash remittances from overseas employment and therefore is interested in generating citizens who understand the importance of this employment for national development and who will continue this tradition. Perhaps having the input of OFWs who might recount their frightening real-life experiences could discourage children and work against the state's intention of promoting overseas employment.

In addition to the PEOS and the Migrant Worker Education Program, PDOS is a mechanism for ensuring the deployment of "well-informed" workers. The institutions that provide these sessions vary according to the type of employment. Domestic workers who are recruited through private employment agencies must attend a mandatory one-day PDOS given by a state-designated NGOs in order to receive clearance for obtaining their overseas employment certificates.[17] Any worker, whether a highly skilled professional or a service worker, processed by POEA must go through a POEA-sponsored PDOS or, if that is unavailable, to an NGO. For all workers (nurses, teachers, seafarers, and so on) who go through private employment agencies, these agencies usually provide their own PDOS because many have received the requisite training from POEA.[18] Therefore, any PDOS given by agencies and NGOs follows the basic format outlined by POEA, whose framework revolves around "empowering" workers through instructive and morale-boosting education. They are intended to prepare workers about the country in which they will work and live, to describe the elements of the particular culture that they need to honor, and to offer them survival strategies that they can use when they encounter problems overseas. These sessions also give them practical information about airport travel tips and the documents they need to bring to make the immigration process go as smoothly as possible.

The sessions remind workers of the image they must uphold. As I highlighted at the beginning of this chapter, the statement of the Women in Development Foundation (WIDF) session leader, "You are not yet heroes. You are just soldiers right now," is a good example. The metaphoric use of war to describe the position of overseas workers as soldiers of the state seems especially poignant in supporting the notion that overseas workers are ambassadors of goodwill. As cultural ambassadors, they must act as good citizens by providing high-quality service to their employers because that will determine whether they deserve the respectable status afforded to national heroes. The session leader advised participants that even if they could not perform a certain task initially, they needed to endure and embody patience: "Kayanin ang trabaho" (Push yourself to do the work), she exhorted them. They were not simply contract workers, she added, but *Filipino* workers, who are known for the three M's: *masipag* (hardworking), *matalino* (intelligent), and *may abilidad* (highly skilled). She reiterated that foreign employers seek out Filipino workers because of the quality of their work and service, and this is the name and reputation they need to protect and uphold. With this approach, she empowered Filipino workers to view themselves as valuable workers by naturalizing and racializing certain traits, making it appear as if Filipinos were *naturally* inclined to exhibit this behavior. Thus, their task was to realize this and draw from their natural abilities.

Racializing these traits provided a space for socially repositioning Filipino workers as a superior to others performing the same job. It is a strategy of empowerment that this particular speaker presented skillfully, to the extent that she generated a positive response to her statements even when they could have been offensive. For example, she scorned Filipino workers who compromised their professional image by behaving inappropriately in public. Referring to domestic workers in Hong Kong, she stated that although domestic work is a respectable job, Filipinas threaten this respectability when they congregate in public and behave in a manner that she deemed inappropriate (talking too loud, selling food and various commodities, and consuming food in public) because of the public criticisms mounted by Chinese employers. Another speaker emphasized that "professionalism is an attitude," and workers should reenvision themselves as "professional caregivers," not as *chimays* (servants). She encouraged them to see themselves as "managers" and as "export quality" as a way of modeling this professional attitude.

Filipino workers must also know how to manage their finances effectively; this is a critical component of the PEOS. NGO instructors teach overseas workers how to prioritize their finances and spend according to their means. One of the session leaders encouraged participants to list the "dreams" they wanted to fulfill and those that inspired them to work overseas. These dreams included paying for the education of their children or siblings, owning a home, obtaining financial capital for starting a business, purchasing certain material goods (food, clothing, appliances), and establishing savings. Then, the speaker presented the stark reality of the actual take-home pay after personal expenses were deducted and showed that this amount was not necessarily sufficient to fulfill all of these dreams. For example, a domestic worker earning a total of 352,320 pesos for a two-year contract will take home only 188,920 pesos after deducting certain expenses (agency fees and other personal expenditures). The instructor pushed the idea of prioritizing finances and realistically budgeting the money that participants could spend on each of their dreams. She listed options such as having children attend public instead of private schools, providing smaller start-up capital for business ventures, spending less on food and clothing, and aiming for lower personal savings over the two-year span. These sessions deliver a clear message that overseas employment can offer only minor economic relief and presents significant limitations on what workers can accomplish.

Nevertheless, by modeling Filipinos as members of a workforce who possess all this knowledge about the kind of economic actors they are supposed to emulate for the benefit of a state that sees itself only as a facilitator of their choice to work overseas, the state can accomplish a couple of things. First, it can parade them as model economic actors for the country and their families when they can conduct themselves as well-informed workers who behave as professionals, act as effective financial managers, and be capable of asserting their rights independently. Second, and more important, the state is relieved of any responsibility for their overall well-being, since these well-informed workers are already equipped with the knowledge needed for their protection.

Upgrading and Professionalizing Overseas Filipino Workers

As stated in the text of RA 8042, that overseas employment Magna Carta, the "ultimate protection to all migrant workers is the possession of skills." This is a tenet that drives the state's ongoing efforts to professionalize the image of the Philippines' export workforce by encouraging workers to upgrade their skills, another mechanism of empowerment. The state's rationale is that the abuse and maltreatment that workers receive from foreign employers result from the former's lack of adequate preparation and competencies. The possession of specialized skills by Filipino workers should allow foreign employers to the workers as invaluable commodities for purchase. This was echoed in the PDOSs I attended and is also strikingly apparent in the content of promotional materials, such as the splashy marketing brochure titled *Filipino Workers: Moving the World Today*, that are made available to prospective foreign employers. This particular brochure showcases four categories of workers encompassing business and management personnel, health care providers, operations and maintenance workers, hotel workers, and seafarers.

Not only does the brochure specifically market a highly skilled and professional workforce, it does so in ways that respond to neoliberal demands of global markets by describing Filipino workers in the way they do. Workers, says the brochure, are *highly educated*, having received "extensive educational training," with some having attained master's and doctoral degrees in the Philippines. They are *English proficient*, making them "ideally suited in any multi-racial working environment." They are *malleable* in that they have the "natural ability to adapt to different work cultures." They are certainly *highly skilled*, given their engagement in "constant training and retraining." They also have *top work credentials*, evident, for example, in "years of hotel training apprenticeship and actual work experience." They also offer *added bonus qualities* such as "hospitality," "charm and cheerful efficiency," an "innovative spirit," and a "strong desire to heal."

These descriptions are intended to create a professionalized image of Filipino workers and at the same time to direct their conduct in ways that fulfill what the state advertises as their natural traits. For example, empowering workers by motivating them to upgrade their work skills may be one way of boosting their global marketability but it is also a way of ensuring that what appears in these ads put out by the state are sufficiently fulfilled in reality. Although state officials and labor brokers argue that these are true, common, or even natural traits of Filipino workers, they have manufactured and socially constructed the traits to fit the neoliberal demands of global markets for "high quality" labor commodities.

The state has accomplished this by essentializing and racializing the traits as a way to fit Filipino workers into an international mold of flexible workers.

The situation is slightly different for those, such as domestic workers, who fall outside the so-called professional category. The state, in response to the demand of foreign employers for "technically" trained domestic workers, allows private employment agencies to require the workers to undergo basic housework training through one of the state-accredited training centers. State officials affirm that upgrading work skills may also be employed as a means of lessening the vulnerability of workers to workplace violence and maltreatment. At the time of my fieldwork in 2001–2002, discussions about how to upgrade the "vulnerable" skills category, which encompasses domestic work, pervaded POEA. Proposals about categorizing it as "professional caregiving" include implementing changes that entailed improving workers' technical skills such as providing them expertise in first aid or proficiency in the host country's language; reconceptualizing their work by eliminating live-in arrangements and replacing it with the hiring of workers on a daily basis and for a specific amount of time; changing workers' image by altering their social demeanor and the way they dress to summon a degree of respectability and reflect professionalism.[19]

Beginning in December 2006, part of this vision to professionalize domestic work was fulfilled through a series of policy reforms that POEA instituted (www.poea.gov.ph).[20] Three of these policy changes were supposed to be beneficial to workers. For one, the minimum salary that workers can earn overseas was increased from two hundred to four hundred dollars, a change that must be stipulated in the standard employment contracts that foreign employers follow. In addition, agencies can no longer collect placement fees from workers via any means, whether prior to their departure or on site through salary deduction. Instead, the cost of hiring domestic workers must be shouldered by foreign employers. Finally, foreign employment agencies, which serve as the counterpart agencies to Philippine-based agencies must now undergo a rigorous pre-qualification certification from the Philippine Overseas Labor Office (POLO) before they can officially partner with the Philippine-based agencies. With this certification, employers agree to assume a vital role in upholding the humane treatment of Filipino domestic workers, providing any type of needed assistance to them, and mediating between them and their employers.

Of these policy changes, two reflect the state's perception of how to upgrade and minimize the vulnerability of domestic workers through the ideology of empowerment. First, the state perceives that the vulnerability of domestic workers stems from their age, which they believe reflects one's level of maturity, thereby increasing the minimum age for working as a domestic worker from eighteen to twenty-three years. Of course, this again essentializes the vulnerability of domestic workers by suggesting that the maltreatment and abuse that they face result from their age rather than the work situation or the perception of foreign employers of the nature of domestic work. This policy change also disturbingly shifts the burden of responsibility from the employers to the workers, whom the state mandates should be old enough to understand how to protect themselves. Second, the state perceives that proper skill training and competency are integral components of workers' empowerment and their ability to withstand the demands of their work and participation in a new culture.

As a result, all domestic workers must obtain an NC2 certificate from the Technical Education and Skills Development Authority (TESDA), which proves their "core skills competencies" in the area of household maintenance, handling of laundry, and food preparation (www.tesda. gov.ph). One can obtain this certificate by passing a three- to four-hour skill assessment administered by one of TESDA's accredited assessment centers or attend 216 hours of training through a TESDA-accredited training center.[21] It is probably to the advantage of most workers to bypass the training program, since it can cost anywhere between from 10,000 and 15,0000 pesos ($218–$327), an exorbitant amount, given that with the minimum wage, the typical average monthly earning of a domestic worker in the Philippines is 2,000–2,500 pesos ($44–$54) (Visayan Forum Foundation 2006).[22]

The NC2 certificate proves that a worker knows how to clean a home, operate various household appliances, and safely handle food; further, it attests that the worker knows how to model a prescribed professional demeanor. The TESDA training module for NC2 certification titled Competency-Based Curriculum Exemplar outlines "learning outcomes" that include knowing how to "participate in workplace communication" with employers and household members, "work in a team environment," "practice career professionalism" by skillfully managing work priorities and maintaining interest in professional development, and "practice occupational health and safety procedures" (www.tesda.gov.ph). Thus, the professionalized domestic worker that the state attempts to manufacture through this process is one who has the proper attitude and perception about her work, which is supposed to contribute to amicable relations with her employers.

However, this process ignores the reality that most employers of domestic work view themselves as consumers of a kind of service that is tailored to their individual needs (not one that is a produced through a generalized labor process) and is backed by an actual guarantee of satisfaction. As I discuss in the next chapter, domestic placement agencies offer a ninety-day guarantee to employers in case their worker does not meet their needs. The problem may not necessarily be in the inability of domestic workers to see themselves as professionals but in the refusal of employers to see the workers as such and as anything more than their servants.

Another new requirement for domestic workers is that they attend a three-day country-specific language and culture orientation seminar as part of meeting a higher competency standard for working overseas. The impetus behind this program, which is paid for by OWWA, is to minimize the "cultural crimes" committed by Filipino workers. In 2006, the Philippine Department of Foreign Affairs (DFA) reported on hundreds of overseas Filipino workers who were detained in Saudi Arabia for engaging in activities construed to be cultural crimes, among them gambling; alcohol consumption; and being seen in public eating or shopping with the opposite sex, especially one who is unmarried. As highlighted on POEA's question and answer component of these policy reforms, posted on their Web site, the changes are meant to "equip [workers] with a basic knowledge on the culture and language of their employer." POEA further states that this is important because "most of the crimes committed by our workers abroad are called 'cultural crimes' or those that are not, by general standards in our country, illegal but are being prohibited in certain countries/states since they offend the culture, practice or traditions of the people" (www.poea.gov.ph).

In line with the notion that overseas workers are supposed to be the country's cultural ambassadors, this requirement seems to work especially well to enhance the image of Filipino domestic workers as culturally competent foreign workers at the same time that the state absolves itself from responsibility of any cultural crimes that Filipinos may be accused of committing. It is also a response to complaints launched by foreign employers in recent years about the perceived unruliness of Filipina domestic workers who congregate visibly in public places to meet with friends or enjoy meals together—acts that are deemed unprofessional and likely to sully their employers' reputation (Chang and Groves 2000; Constable 1997b). In one of the PDOS training videos for Taiwan-bound domestic workers that OWWA makes available as a component of this orientation program, two major sections cover topics such as "Coping with Chinese Culture," and "Code of Discipline," both of which provide a laundry list of do's and don'ts that emphasize the appropriate decorum that Filipinos must embody and display in order to maintain good working relations with their employers and the host country. These include obtaining an employer's approval for every activity outside the home and avoiding those like prostitution, gambling, theft, or establishing sideline businesses (namely, outside employment). Thus, this orientation program may be not only about empowering workers but also about disciplining them to be model migrant workers who must act within the prescribed boundaries of acceptable conduct based on their status as foreigners and servants who will know their place in their host countries.

More recently, the focus on upgrading domestic workers was pushed further with the creation of the Supermaid training program, which was a response to some thirty thousand repatriated Filipino workers (a majority of whom were domestic workers) from the war in Lebanon in the summer of 2006. Introduced by President Arroyo, the Supermaid training program is supposed to further enhance the technical capabilities of Filipino domestic workers and their capacity to land higher-paying jobs as they offer employers expertise that goes beyond household maintenance. A Filipina supermaid is ready to respond to medical emergencies and accidents by implementing the proper first aid treatment and preventive measures. She is able to execute the appropriate procedures for responding to physical threats and dangers such as evacuating from highrise buildings. While already carrying an NC2 certificate, a supermaid will also need to undergo an additional 116 hours of instructional training. As Augusto Syjuco, the head of TESDA, succinctly put it, domestic workers "will become upgraded domestic helpers with a higher price" (Mediavilla 2006, A1). It is as if these skills are supposed to give them extraordinary powers to help them deal with their vulnerability and endow them with the knowledge and preparation to do their work and elevate their social and professional status.

By upgrading work skills, the state also hopes that Filipino workers will maintain their global competitiveness. POEA officials described the different programs that address the mounting competition with other labor-exporting countries (for example, Bangladesh, Indonesia, Sri Lanka, and India) that tend to settle for lower wages. They believe that that the competitive advantage of Filipino workers is skill development and that this training would also promote self-improvement and the betterment of the country. For example, OWWA provides a series of worker reintegration programs that are supposed to assist returning workers by giving them skill development training programs and financial loan assistance for establishing businesses. These programs include providing scholarships for workers or their families so they may receive vocational or technical training or take courses in science and technology; the programs also provide career development grants that allow workers (such as seafarers) to upgrade their skills for global employability.

According to Carmelita Dimzon, head of POEA's Pre-Employment Services Office, the Philippine state, through the assistance of private foundations, also established overseas resource centers that provide on-site vocational training programs in computer, sewing, and other technical skills. The impetus behind this is to promote continuous education and skill building in ways that may eventually lead to the pursuit of higher-wage jobs or other income-generating activities. As Dimzon noted, workers "should not just be [overseas] thinking of their families at home. During their *spare time*, they should be able to do something *more productive*." "They can earn their master's degrees while away," she proudly asserted, in relation to domestic workers who make use of the availability of distance learning education programs whereby some domestic workers are able to take online courses offered by universities in the Philippines, among them Polytechnic University Philippines and the University of the Philippines (interview by the author, October 25, 2001; emphases added).

Thus, the neoliberal state aims to create autonomous, self-motivated workers who will strive for self-betterment in the spirit of economic entrepreneurship and competitiveness. In doing so, it will invest in creating the conditions that will support these "technologies of the self" (Foucault 1979; Burchell 1996), or self-improvement mechanisms, that, in this case, enable workers to strive for labor productivity and competitiveness. While learning how to establish small businesses in the Philippines or obtaining a master's degree can be beneficial for the workers, both strategically fulfill the state's neoliberal economic mandates. Within these mandates, work, in itself, is not productive unless it does something to give workers the skills that they can use to sustain themselves economically at the end of their overseas contract. The state has now found a solution to its unemployment problem—treat workers as entrepreneurs and investors and let them create *their* employment and infrastructure for generating their income. Thus, the state's impetus to professionalize its workforce through various skill development and training programs allows it to not only address any vulnerability that its workers face overseas but also upgrade its own image as a labor provider *only* of professional and high-quality workers.

TURNING WORKERS INTO ENTREPRENEURS

In a segment of her television program, *May Gloria Ang Bukas Mo* (There Is Gloria/Glory in Your Future), President Gloria Macapagal Arroyo described the growing number of overseas Filipino nurses in London as a "new aristocracy," because of the economic value of their earnings and consumerism. She described their ability to purchase luxury goods while representing overseas employment as a lucrative and exciting endeavor. Although the country was not dissuading workers from coming home, she admitted that the kinds of employment available in the Philippines could not compare to those available overseas. She encouraged Filipinos to perceive themselves not simply as workers but as investors—overseas Filipino investors (OFIs). She urged workers, as OFIs, to view the Philippines as a place of retirement and investment, not necessarily as a "suitable" place of settlement to return to at this time.[23] Those who successfully fulfilled such a calling could expect to be recognized at the presidential level and hailed as one of the "OFW Entrepreneurs of the Year." Among the 2006 winners were a medical doctor whose earnings in Saudi Arabia helped finance a cattle ranch in the Philippines; a civil engineer who contributed his earnings to build homes for the homeless in his hometown; and former domestic workers turned venture capitalists who invested in establishing such businesses as a remittance/freight/travel service, a garden resort, and a banana plantation or engaged in enterprising activities such as selling Filipino food and products abroad (OWWA, http://www.owwa.gov.ph).

OWWA's former director Wilhelm Soriano explained that referring to overseas Filipino workers as OFIs signifies a new state strategy for replacing a "culture of employment" with a "culture of entrepreneurship." It is meant to invite overseas Filipinos to imagine themselves as entrepreneurs and the Philippines as a worthy place of investment. Upon returning to the Philippines, Soriano proclaimed, "we will prove to them [OFWs] that the land of milk and honey is in their motherland," while also explicitly stating that while the Philippine state may not generate jobs, it can "help them find ways of earning a living." It does this by encouraging Filipino workers to invest in the country by engaging in business ventures or to send greater dollar remittances to their families in ways that boost their consumer spending. He remarked, "What is happening now is that when they come here, they are scared of spending money and starting up businesses for fear of losing money. But if they have a formal training that would boost their confidence, [they would feel safer]" (interview by the author, October 25, 2001).

"Empowering" workers to envision themselves as entrepreneurs mirrors the idea that overseas workers are significant insofar as they are economically viable to the country. The state seemingly crafts such economic viability by culturally invoking what the workers should feel is their sense of duty and indebtedness, an *utang na loob* (indebtedness) to their country that can be honored by making financial investments in their motherland. This indebtedness comes from benefiting from the opportunities that the state's overseas employment program provides workers, and the different reintegration programs the state expects will be repaid in the form of social and economic investments that bring national economic stability.

The First National Conference on OFW Integration, held in Manila on April 12, 2002, opened with a dramatic performance of a song delivered by OWWA's in-house choir that narrated individuals' determination to ease the pain of a suffering nation through love, dedication, and a willingness to die for it. As the lyrics *Hindi ka maaapi, pag-ibig ko sa iyo, ina ng bayan* (Because of my love for you, you will not be oppressed, my motherland), were repeated several times, the song revealed how the state manufactures this indebtedness—*utang na loob*—by summoning workers' sense of patriotism. As OFIs, workers are well positioned to economically uplift their country. This neoliberal notion of entrepreneurship again allows the Philippine state to manage labor migration by developing citizens who can proactively generate their livelihood. By promoting the Philippines as a land of milk and honey, state officials such as Soriano indirectly inculcated the idea that the country is fertile with wealth and opportunity and that the task of overseas workers is to explore, nurture, and benefit from them. After all, they owe it to their nation. Meanwhile, it is through the notion of entrepreneurship that the state is able to govern Filipinos by tokenizing their intellectual capacity and labor power and promoting an illusion of freedom. As Rose (1999, 4) explains, *governing* differs from *dominating* insofar as "to govern is to recognize the capacity for action and adjust oneself to it. . . . To govern is to presuppose the freedom of the governed. To govern humans is not to crush their capacity to act, but to acknowledge it and to utilize it for one's own objectives." The Philippine state and its efforts to turn workers into entrepreneurs exemplify this.

In support of these endeavors, the state will impart to migrant workers formal training, education, and even the financial assistance necessary to realize their capacity for entrepreneurship. This is evident in such programs as OWWA's Livelihood Development Program, which grants monetary loan assistance for "income-generating projects" and is available to OFWs or any of their beneficiaries and to community-based organizations that OFWs may have formed. Although the program's goal is to provide monetary assistance to workers, its underlying objective is to affect the conduct of Filipinos by creating self-reliant and independent individuals who can produce their own means of livelihood. Under the leadership of another former OWWA administrator, Virgilio Angelo, in conjunction with the Philippine stock exchange, OFWs and their families were offered an orientation seminar on stock investment. An orientation was conducted on December 12, 2002, as part of OWWA's Pamaskong Handog sa OFWs 2002 (Christmas Tribute to OFWs 2002), a program for welcoming migrant workers who came home for the holidays. The orientation sought to educate workers on the benefits of stock market investments for themselves and their country, which Angelo perceived would ultimately generate local employment opportunities for the workers, their families, and their communities.

The state rewards these kinds of activities through the introduction of a new tribute, the Model OFW Family of the Year Award (MOFYA), introduced in 2005. The award commemorates "OFWs and their families who have used the gains of working abroad to the best advantage . . . [and] recognizes the results of [their] successes in terms of enterprise development and generation of employment opportunities as they optimize the gains of migration" (OWWA, http://www.owwa.gov.ph). Like the Bagong Bayani Award (BBA), the MOFYA is supposed to showcase migrants whose earnings have contributed to creating an entrepreneurial spirit that sustains not only themselves but also their families. Unlike the BBA, the MOFYA comes with specific monetary rewards, including a house, electronics (mobile phone and personal computer), ten thousand pesos worth of Philam Bond, Philamlife personal accident insurance of one hundred thousand pesos for two family members, and a five-thousand-peso livelihood package.

According to OWWA's current administrator, Marianito Roque, this recognition is "a testament to their achievement. We know how much they had to sacrifice and how hard they had to work. It's [only right] to acknowledge them" (OWWA, http://www.owwa.gov.ph). The award, however, does not merely pay tribute to these sacrifices; it also allows the state to respond to the growing public anxieties about the consequences of migration on families. The existence of transnational families is perceived to contribute to a host of problems, among them marital dissolution and juvenile delinquency. Most pressing is the care crisis (Asis 1992; Cruz 1987; Parreñas 2001a, 2001b, 2002, 2005) pervading the Philippines as a result of children who are left without the care of parents, who are working overseas. As suggested in OWWA's award description, posted on their Web site, "While migration brings about the solutions to a lot of financial constraints, migration also [takes a toll] on the family's unit day-to-day existence given the lack of proper guidance afforded to the children. Children normally are subjected to the abnormal situation of coping with one or both of their parents sadly absent to attend to their needs." With this award, OWWA hopes that OFWs can learn from and be "inspired" by others about how to manage their earnings so they may create alternative income-generating activities, which would minimize the need for migration (OWWA, http://www.owwa.gov.ph). Thus, the state pitches MOFYA as a celebratory token for OFWs who dedicate their lives to the upward mobility and survival of their families, while acknowledging the strain that migration puts on the family—so much so that it makes it appear as if this strain can be minimized by ensuring that OFWs manage their earnings effectively and become the "enterprising OFW families" that make the state proud.[24] The entrepreneurial spirit that emerges here is one that is also supposed to serve as a model to inspire other so-called self-sacrificing heroes.

In 2006, the country's model OFW families were a nurse in Riyadh who invested in establishing a residential building, a construction store, a farm, and a house rental; an electrician on a luxury liner whose overseas earnings produced a nurse in the family and financed the establishment of a taxi business, a convenience store, a boardinghouse, and a buy-and-sell business; and an engineer working on highways in Saudi Arabia who was able to send his children to school abroad and his family on trips to Europe. These awardees are not only exemplary entrepreneurs but also model family members, as OWWA highlighted. The nurse, OWWA announces, supports a paraplegic father by providing him with "life's comforts." The electrician is honored for diligently maintaining "constant communication" with his family despite the distance and the cost. The engineer is heralded for his attempts to mitigate family separation by devising overseas excursions, which "provide the family an opportunity to spend time together to bond" (OWWA, http://www.owwa.gov.ph).

Upon the return of its overseas workers to the Philippines, the state is committed to cultivating this entrepreneurship permanently. This was most evident in the formation of the National Reintegration Center for OFWs (NRCO) in March 2007. Through NRCO, the state seeks to facilitate "brain gain" and maintain the competitiveness of the Philippines as a labor source by not only generating productive workers but also enlisting entrepreneurial returnees. As current Philippine labor secretary Arturo Brion asserted, while other migrant-sending countries may attempt to compete with and imitate the Philippines' overseas employment program, "the National Reintegration Center will keep us at number one position [as labor providers], giving the Philippines a total edge from deployment to the productive social and economic reintegration of OFWs on their return (DOLE, http://www.nrco.dole.gov.ph).

In creating this center, the state demonstrated that it is diligent in maintaining its competitive edge in the global economy in ways that go beyond simply promoting an "ideal" workforce. It also promotes itself as a creative force that manipulates its labor export economy to allow the country to benefit from the fruits of migrants' labor, namely, their finances, skills, and overseas experience. The center's goal is to develop reintegration programs that allow the state to harness the workers' "new attitude," "investable assets," skills, and "goodwill for communities" for income-generating ventures that advance brain gain (http://www.nrco. dole.gov.ph).

As Secretary Brion further stated, "Brain Gain is the logical sequel to a conscious and managed overseas employment program. We have demonstrated the world-class quality of our human resources and employers worldwide acknowledge this." Thus, the state, through NRCO, will develop the means for using the resources of returning modern-day heroes for the benefit of the local economy. Brion added, "We will ensure that the rich talents of our Filipinos worldwide will be put to good use by our industries and to enrich research in science and technology. We will make sure that any OFW who has saved enough and wishes to invest in the country has a safe and profitable investment package that is tailored-fit for his [*sic*] needs and his resources. We will put out opportunities for OFWs to invest into their communities to address the latter's social infrastructure needs. We will network with other government agencies and NGOs to make sure that each OFW who intends to go into business is prepared to be an entrepreneur" (DOLE, "The Secretary's Page," http://www.nrco.dole.gov.ph).

Secretary Brion's statement accords with Rose's (1999, 139–142) elaboration on the tenets of neoliberalism; Rose sees neoliberalism as constructing an "enabling state" that must consider individuals as partners who, once acclimated, "would govern themselves within a state-secured framework of law and order." As Rose notes, "The powers of the state thus [have] to be directed to empowering the entrepreneurial subjects of choice in their quest for self realization" (142). In this vein, he asserts that the state not only governs through freedom but also cultivates enterprising, entrepreneurial, and self-regulating individuals who can engage the market productively. The Philippine state exemplifies these principles by providing the institutional and ideological mechanisms that are supposed to empower individuals to envision themselves as possessing the intellectual capacity to become investors and the "freedom" to engage in profit-making ventures.

However, the state is the primary empowered actor here. It benefits not only from the billions of dollars of remittances that enhance its GNP but also from the investments that workers commit to the country upon their return. Secretary Brion's statement above reflects a state that entitles itself to use the resources of its modern-day heroes to address the "needs of [the] local economy," while acting as some sort of guarantor that will ensure that their talents "are put to good use." This is at the heart of what it means for the Philippine state to be a manager of labor migration—to assume the position of *directing* how workers should spend their overseas earnings while cloaking its ineptness to sustain a local economy that can provide a living wage to its citizens. So much does it behave in this manner that it has to rely on the workers, the very individuals who are responding to this ineptness, for the capital to jump-start a struggling economy.

MAKING PRODUCTIVE WOMEN WORKERS

In 2002, the country's First National Reintegration Conference, organized by OWWA and several migrant-specific NGOs, was held.[25] The impetus of this two-day conference, beginning on April 12, was the state's recognition that the reintegration of Filipino migrants into the country was the weakest link of all state programs pertaining to overseas employment. The aim of the conference was to devise strategies to better reincorporate returning migrants into the country as productive citizens and community members and to restore family ties weakened by extended separation. Throughout the conference, State officials reiterated that while "overseas employment is temporary," it had become an enduring phenomenon of Philippine society whose social costs must be addressed. These social costs included estranged relationships between workers and their families, family ties and relations being defined by an economic dependency on migrants' earnings and remittances, and erosion of "educational values" among children who see themselves working in the same low-wage jobs as their parents (for example, as domestic workers).

In their discussions, session leaders attributed the vulnerability of families to a combination of two factors. First, they explained, family ties were weakened in the absence of a "mother who provides the emotional support and essentially holds the family together."[26] No particular focus was given to fathers. They argued that family members who lived for an extended period without the presence of a wife or mother become susceptible to various social problems, among them alcoholism, drug abuse, juvenile delinquency, and marital breakup. Second, transnational families become vulnerable to a "culture of dependency," which contributes to growing unemployment among the migrants' family members. NGOs repeatedly urged workers, especially women, not to use material goods, such as cell phones, or to promote unnecessary and lavish consumerism, as in building "palatial homes" equipped with modern appliances, as ways of managing and strengthening family relations. Instead, they motivated workers to invest their earnings into productive microenterprise ventures that they envisioned would stop their families' overdependence on their earnings and the vicious cycle of labor migration.

The state's concern about the ability of women workers to manage their families financially is echoed in the state-mandated pre-departure orientation seminars (PDOSs) provided to women leaving the country to work as domestic workers. In these seminars, a representative from a Philippine bank relays extensive information on how women can remit their overseas earnings to their families through official channels to make it easier for the state to tap into their remittances. Since workers often send money through informal networks, such as friends, in order to avoid fees, these representatives discuss the benefits of remitting their salaries through banks and the ease, efficiency, and security they can provide to them and their families.

But being a "good" mother, albeit from a distance, is not just about managing financial matters; it is also about providing emotional support to the families the women leave behind. While some studies of Filipino migrant workers and their children revealed the social costs of migration (Asis 2002; Constable 1999; Cruz 1987; Parreñas 2001a, 2002, 2005), the claim that overseas employment has led directly to the escalation of social problems is debatable. Other studies presenting the effects of maternal migration on children are contradictory (Asis 2004; Go and Postrado 1986; Parreñas 2002). As Parreñas (2002, 2005) argues, the pain and problems resulting from the absence of a mother in a household can be mitigated by more active participation from their spouses or families left behind.

Nevertheless, when state officials, scholars, NGOs, and labor brokers discuss the implication of overseas employment on the family unit, women migrant workers (particularly mothers and wives) are held especially responsible. Male spouses, families, and even employers typically escape such scrutiny. By blaming women and placing the primary responsibility of caregiving, marriage, and household maintenance on them, the Philippine state escapes responsibility and accountability, supporting the notion that they are not promoting labor migration but merely managing the choices of Filipinos to work overseas. The state can then argue that since these women *chose* to work overseas, they, not the state, are accountable for the consequences of their choices.

This discourse of responsibility is also evident in POEA's PEOSs. For example, Carmelita Dimzon elaborated on the questions asked of applicants that seek to "empower" their decision-making process regarding overseas employment: "Do you know what the real social costs are and the problems that may arise? Would you really want to leave the country leaving your husband behind? Aren't you afraid that your husband will find another woman? Aren't you afraid your children will finally forget all about you and whoever lives with them will be far more acceptable to them?" (interview by the author, October 25, 2001). These questions demonstrate the state's attempt to raise workers' consciousness about the possible real social costs of their decision to migrate. Further, and more important, they reflect another way of governing the conduct of the workers. Dimzon's narrative reflects the anxieties about this "care crisis" and projects a gendered moral mandate for women's responsibilities in the family. Becoming a good worker entails being good wives and mothers whose empowerment stems from the ability to manage families from a distance. The state's interest in the family can be viewed as an attempt to ensure the deployment of productive and psychologically prepared workers. But in the case of women workers, it must deal with two demands simultaneously. It must strike a balance in satisfying global demands for "flexible" workers *and* in maintaining cultural mores about Filipino women's obligations in the family.[27]

These gendered cultural mores are also reinforced in the PDOSs provided by the Women in Development Foundation (WIDF).

According to Helen Chavez, WIDF program director, the extended absence of women and separation from their families make their reintegration into their children's lives especially challenging. This is because during the women's absence their children have not only changed, but also acquired new sets of values and attitudes that affect the way they relate to their families—both of which result in mutual estrangement. During one of the sessions provided to domestic workers, WIDF session leaders used the rhetoric of sacrifice to remind women that although they were working overseas to help ensure the financial stability of their families, they must also make the effort to guard their families' emotional stability. This could be done by their providing emotional support to their children through phone calls and to their spouses through "love letters" that reaffirmed their commitment to their husbands, instead of "business letters" instructing husbands how to manage the remittances the women sent home (field notes, November 17, 2001).

What was strikingly apparent in these discussions and in the general discourse on the care crisis is the focus on a traditional construction of the family and married women in particular. The fact that single women are seemingly invisible from the state's disciplinary gaze and its care crisis discourse does not necessarily mean that only married women are leaving the country. Rather, it simply highlights a heterosexist state that does not account for the multiple social locations that women occupy in society. On the basis of the 2000 Philippine Census of Population on Housing, the National Statistics Office revealed that the numbers of single and of married women overseas workers were almost equal and that the rest were either widowed, divorced or separated, or involved in common-law or cohabitation arrangements. (Ericta et al. 2003). The only time that this complexity is addressed is during discussions of a persistent concern about Filipinas' sexual promiscuity.

For example, the public discourses circulating around the social costs of migration also include concerns about the sexual exploitation of Filipina overseas workers and about the stereotype of them as "morally suspect" (Constable 1997a, 1997b) or as "sexual providers" (Chang and Groves 2000). These elements have created a state that is interested in making sure that Filipina workers are responsible wives and mothers and that they are also sexually responsible Catholic women.[28] The content of a PDOS training video produced by OWWA for Taiwan-bound domestic workers is a good example of one medium of discipline that the state uses to address this concern. On this video is a long list of reminders aimed at regulating their work tasks, social conduct, and physical appearance. For one, domestic workers must make every attempt to work more closely with their female employer and maintain a good distance from their male employers. They must avoid wearing perfume. And finally, they must not wear "tight-fitting jeans" and "transparent clothes" in the presence of their employers. They are reminded that they must always inform their employers of their whereabouts—making sure not to "sleep in other people's homes without getting the permission of their employer."[29] The video heightens workers' awareness that they have an image to uphold—not only of their employers but also of themselves. And doing so requires modeling the appropriate gender identity and sexuality.

As women workers manage their transnational families as good mothers and wives, married women must also ensure that they are sexually responsible while overseas. The seminar provided by WIDF contained a section on sexual health education that addressed the issue of "homesexness" as a problem caused by migrant women's separation from their male partners.[30] The same seminar provided the following tips to help women cope: prayer and faith, reminding themselves of their ultimate goal—which is "not $ex but $"—and the need to pay their debts and communicating frequently with their husband and children.

Empowering women workers by instructing them to manage their sexuality is not simply about uplifting Filipino women's image overseas; more important, it is about protecting these women from sexual violence. In the same WIDF seminar described here a group leader highlighted several alarming statistics: four overseas Filipino workers die every day by suicide, murder, or sickness; seven rapes occur each day; and overseas Filipino workers are "damaged goods" (physically and emotionally) as a result of exploitive working situations (field notes, November 27, 2001). In response to these statistics, the leader informed a room filled with women bound for domestic work in Hong Kong, Saudi Arabia, and Malaysia that self-presentation was key to their survival. Women heard a resounding message that they could minimize their vulnerability by engaging in behavior and demeanor that established clear boundaries between them and their employers. As this session leader repeatedly stated, "Be friendly, not familiar," emphasizing a notion that the women should not construct themselves as sexually available to their male employers and that they must be assertive and confrontational with men who exhibit inappropriate behavior toward them. She provided examples of what to say and how to display this assertiveness and offered additional methods of self-defense protection against sexual violence.[31]

Meanwhile, nowhere in these presentations is there mention of the official procedures for reporting cases of sexual abuse or identifying any organizations that can help workers. Despite the fact that cases of sexual harassment may not necessarily be recognized as a civil rights violation in certain countries, they are, nevertheless, an infringement of an individual's human rights—an issue that is invisible in these presentations. Instead, workers are simply turned into their employers' private properties. Although the objective is to educate and prepare workers, the overwhelming message that comes across is that women become vulnerable as workers and that they are accountable for how this vulnerability plays out.

While the state and its NGO partners claim that the seminars are designed to prepare women workers for the challenges of overseas employment and mitigate the complications of family separation, their strategies contribute to Filipino women's disempowerment. They are disempowering insofar as they perpetuate gender inequalities in Philippine society, which render women solely responsible for the social reproduction of families. They also designate Filipina migrants, not the state or the foreign employers, as socially responsible for the creation, elimination, or prevention of social problems that are regarded as social costs of migration.

The concern with transforming women into responsible economic actors by encouraging them to invest their earnings in business ventures deflects attention from structural constraints created and maintained by a state that is incapable of producing viable sources of local livelihood. As a result, when women renew their labor contracts to continue working overseas, the oft-cited reason highlighted by NGOs or state officials is their misuse of earnings rather than the scarcity of living-wage jobs in the Philippines. Similarly, while the efforts made by these NGOs reflect a genuine concern for the escalating abuse faced by women workers overseas, the type of "gender sensitive" education they provide is also disempowering because it reproduces dangerous stereotypes that foreign employers attribute to Filipinas. They also reify the reality that the Philippine state cannot protect its workers sufficiently and thus shifts the burden of responsibility of worker protection onto the women.

Thus, what these programs ultimately reveal are the ways in which women workers are implicated much differently from how men are within the state's framework of managing labor migration. Unlike men, who are often recognized as the primary breadwinners of their families and whose overseas migration is understood as meeting the need to fulfill this role and obligation, women are prescribed with a different and more complex set of expectations. They are directed to present an economically competitive and entrepreneurial attitude at the same time as they are summoned to model an image of femininity and motherhood. The state may view them as modern-day heroines for their role in lifting the nation up from poverty but it also recognizes their positions of diverse responsibility within society in the Philippines. "Empowering" them entails holding them responsible for sustaining gendered cultural mores by focusing on their responsibilities in managing their family and social/sexual lives.

The state, through its NGO partners, becomes gender sensitive only insofar as it recognizes women's role in the public discourses regarding the social costs of migration and the escalating vulnerabilities of Filipino families. In the end, the state has accomplished its underlying goals—to create an image of being a gender-sensitive institution, to appease criticisms from its own citizenry about their inability to protect workers, and most of all to benefit economically from the export of its citizens under the guise of "empowering" its most "vulnerable" workers.

CONCLUSION

In this chapter, I described the basis upon which a neoliberal Philippine state defines Filipino migrants' relation and obligation to the country through a market-oriented form of citizenship. The state's policy shift from *promoting* to *managing* labor migration reflects a disciplinary process through which the state governs its overseas Filipino workers by inventing strategies for affecting their economic conduct in ways that mirror and serve the state's capitalist interests. Its uniqueness rests on its ability to employ creative, albeit problematic, measures that aim to maintain its competitive advantage as a global labor provider. Its invisible hand rules

Filipinos from a distance by attempting to summon nationalism through overseas employment, while firmly clarifying that it is a matter of choice among Filipinos. Although the Philippine state does not directly proclaim that overseas employment is the only means through which workers can generate a stable economic livelihood, it is institutionally and ideologically conditioning Filipinos that their future resides outside the Philippines and that their goal should be to transform themselves into global economically competitive workers.

The ultimate goal of this Philippine capitalist state is to produce responsible economic citizens through empowerment, a mechanism that acts as a form of discipline and labor control that constructs Filipino citizens as particular objects (labor commodities and representatives) of the state. It reflects a neoliberal state that rules its population by relegating and deflecting responsibility for economic livelihood and progress onto its citizens, under the guise of upward mobility, self-betterment, and protection. It does this by "empowering" them through an ethic of responsibility to their families and nation. When officials empower Filipino workers to embody the identities of heroes, ambassadors of goodwill, and entrepreneurs, they commit symbolic acts that demonstrate the state's insistence on defining workers as more than just income generators for their families. Rather, the workers must act as model Filipino citizens who will protect the image of the state and the Philippines as the home of the Great Filipino Worker. Empowering Filipino workers by culturally inscribing them as modern-day heroes or upgrading their skills is not necessarily about protecting them. Rather, these strategies manufacture a workforce that can effectively compete in the global marketplace. Empowering women to manage families and their sexuality as part of their responsibility as overseas workers is not simply about a concern for the degradation of families. It also reflects the state's concern for its image and its need to discipline and control those whom it considers potentially unruly subjects who may taint the image of the "Filipino woman" and most important, that of the Philippines.

Underlying this neoliberal framework of managing labor migration is a gendered and racialized moral economy of the Filipino migrant that links family and nationalism with capitalist ideals of economic competitiveness and entrepreneurship. Through this moral economy, Filipino migrant workers become *economic* citizens of the Philippine state.

The state pays tribute to their sacrifices while it seeks to ensure that their earnings are funneled into the economy. Then, when they return, it devises mechanisms that strive to "productively" reintegrate them into Philippine society. It is a moral economy that is racialized insofar as it hinges on some notion of a culturally essentialist labor power that is supposed to make Filipinos ideal workers and it is also gendered, especially as women migrant workers' productivity is informed by the state's perception of their responsibilities as women, wives, or mothers. Ultimately, the gendered and racialized moral economy of the Filipino migrant that is produced through this mechanism of empowerment captures how the state directs Filipino migrants to become the model citizens of the Philippines and defines their sense of belonging to the country.

However, this moral economy depends on the ability of its citizens to take up a "capillary functioning of power" (Foucault 1979) and self-govern by crafting what Foucault refers to as "techniques of the self." That is, Filipinos themselves also construct their own mechanisms of discipline. After all, producing a marketable workforce also depends on Filipino workers' complicit actions and decisions. If governmentality reflects a set of social processes designed at affecting the conduct of individuals, then its success relies on the possibility of promoting discipline among them. As Rose (1999, 22) explains, "Disciplinary techniques may be embodied in an external regime of structured times, spaces, gazes, and hierarchies. But the goal of discipline is to reshape the ways in which each individual, at some future point, will conduct him- or herself in a space of regulated freedom." To what extent Filipino workers respond to, accommodate themselves to, or resist the disciplinary power and moral economy surrounding the state's mantra of managing labor migration is an issue that will be addressed in chapters 6 and 7.

CHAPTER 4

Delivering "Our Contribution
to the World"

Our government seems overly focused in happily
punishing the recruitment agencies. I can't blame them.
There are those who abuse [their privileges and the
law] and this has created a bad reputation for the
overseas employment providers. What happens is that
when we provide good employment opportunities for
a thousand, there will be one casualty—a sad story or
one unfortunate incident that happens. But as a result,
the benefit of the one thousand is overshadowed by
this one incident.

—Victor Fernandez Jr., president of the
Philippine Association of Service Exporters Inc.

ON JANUARY 17, 2002, the usual hustle and bustle of Malate, one
of Manila's busiest districts, was interrupted by a crowd of men and
women who marched through its streets. Beginning at Malate Church
and ending in the historic Intramuros, the marchers forged through
the unruliness of the everyday traffic, hopeful that their umbrellas and
bandanas would protect them from the oppressive sun of a typical
humid Manila afternoon.[1] They were certainly much braver than I,
whose participant observation of this event was interrupted by momentary escapes to a nearby air-conditioned coffee shop, where I waited
for the main event to unfold. Tightly huddled together, the marchers
advanced quietly but in solidarity, determined to reach their final
destination, the Philippine Department of Labor Employment (DOLE)
office. Mostly dressed in black, the marchers presented a mysterious
image to the increasingly curious public that they passed, who compared
their gathering to a funeral procession. Even some of the DOLE
guards jokingly asked among themselves, "Did anyone die?" The two

87

six-foot-long banners that preceded the demonstration read "War on Terrorism: Protect License Agencies, Prosecute Illegal Recruiters" and "Justice for Overseas Employment." They hustled to the front of the DOLE building, positioning themselves in front of the press, which was waiting to capture the perfect image for next morning paper and create a headline of whatever standoff might happen. A truck approached. On top sat a man dressed in red, conspicuous in this sea of blackness. Holding a microphone and flanked by two giant speakers, he screamed at the top of his lungs that it was a protest against an "injustice" that would affect the lives of overseas Filipino workers. Everything would lead one to believe that these were overseas Filipino workers protesting about an exploitative system, but a closer look at the picket signs revealed otherwise. Two signs captured my attention: "Employment Providers: Pag-Asa ng Bayan" (Hope of the Country) and "Employment Providers: Makers of New Heroes."

The rally had, in fact, been organized primarily by the Federated Association of Manpower Exporters (FAME), a professional association representing six hundred recruitment agencies in the Philippines, and the man in red was one of their members. The rally was composed mainly of labor brokers—various staff and recruiters of Philippine-based private employment agencies and their allies—whose mobilization effort was fueled by the impending release of stringent new overseas recruitment rules from the state. These policy revisions were aimed directly at eliminating illegal recruitment practices within the private sector by increasing the licensing fee requirements for employment agencies and outlining a more precise classification of recruitment violations and corresponding penalties.

For several months, prior to the rally, while the labor department moved forward with the revisions, the private sector clamored for public attention and sympathy to their plight as victims of misrepresentation. They proclaimed incessantly that they were not the "leeches" that the state made them out to be. After all, they produced and delivered overseas Filipino workers to the world, and were the "makers of [the state's much touted] modern day heroes." In fact, it was only a year before this policy change, on July 30, 2001, that President Arroyo issued Proclamation No. 76, declaring 2002 the Year of the Overseas

Employment Providers in "grateful recognition of the significant contribution of private licensed agencies and their associations in helping provide overseas employment and welfare protection to millions of Filipino contract workers since 1976" (Arroyo 2001) As "employment providers," agencies claimed that they were not enemies but partners of the state in its overseas employment program. Despite this outcry and as a result of the escalating increase of illegal recruiters and the state's goal of professionalizing the country's labor export program, the revised rules were implemented, beginning in May 2002.

How do these volatile relations shape the brokering work of employment agencies? How do they manage the contradictory position they occupy in relation to the Philippine state, which sees them both as partners and as enemies? The rally I described above represents the contradictions in this relationship and the ways that the private sector has increasingly defined their role as brokers in relation to what they view as the state's escalating crusade to mar their image and take over the recruitment industry. They want to address the state's apparent amnesia about the private sector's role in ensuring that the Philippines is, indeed, the home of the Great Filipino Worker. In this chapter, I consider agencies as social institutions that define the contours of the Philippines' transnational labor export arena. They are not simply "global circuits of labor" (Tyner 2000) that provide institutional mechanisms for enabling foreign employers to recruit from the Philippines, following a linear process of contract procurement, labor recruitment, and worker deployment.[2] Rather, they are social institutions insofar as they can creatively manage and shape Filipinos' comparative advantage as workers and the quality of overseas job opportunities that become available to them. In the context of these tensions and contradictory relations with the state, I show, through their brokering practices, the meaning behind the phrase "employment providers: the makers of new heroes." Constructed as partners and enemies simultaneously, employment agencies ultimately have the same mission as the state—to sustain the country's culture of labor migration. However, they insist that, unlike the state, they do not merely seek to *manage* labor migration; they *promote* it, by providing the actual mechanisms and carrying the burden for making it happen, which they claim deserves appropriate recognition.

KEY
DFA: Department of Foreign Affairs
DOLE: Philippine Department of Labor and Employment
OWWA: Overseas Workers Welfare Administration
POEA: Philippine Overseas Employment Administration
NGOs: Nongovernmental organizations
POLO: Philippine Overseas Labor Office

4.1. The Philippines' labor-brokering landscape.

MANAGING A COMPETITIVE EDGE

In 2006, approximately 1,442 private employment agencies were thriving in the Philippines, facilitating more than 95 percent of the country's overseas labor recruitment of Filipinos (POEA 2007). These agencies are situated within a global playing field that is shaped by the agencies' negotiations with stakeholders, who each play an instrumental role in defining their success in brokering Filipino labor.

It is through their interactions and negotiations that Filipino workers are circulated as global labor commodities and become "implicated actors" (Clarke and Montini 1993) whose value, much like that of the state, is primarily defined by the financial interests of employment agencies, their so-called "partner."[3]

As Figure 4.1 illustrates, the uniqueness of the Philippines' brokering landscape pertains to this highly institutionalized labor-brokering process, where the state, represented by DOLE's POEA and OWWA, is supposed to work with employment agencies in facilitating the ability of the Philippines to serve as a labor resource. The 1995 Migrant and Overseas Employment Act (RA 8042)—the Magna Carta of overseas Filipino workers—set up this conglomeration of administrative bodies (Department of Foreign Affairs [DFA], Department of Labor and

TABLE 4.1

Employment Agencies and Primary Labor Recruitment/Markets

Agency name[a]	Primary labor recruitment	Primary labor market(s)
Tricorder Enterprises	nursing	U.K., U.S.A.
Holodeck Placement	nursing	U.S.A.
Exocomp Staffing Services	nursing	Saudi Arabia
Riker Manpower Services	nursing	Saudi Arabia
Starfleet Inc.	domestic work	Hong Kong
Troy International Services	domestic work	Hong Kong, Lebanon, Singapore, Taiwan

[a]Names are pseudonyms.

Employment [DOLE], Philippine Overseas Employment Administration [POEA], and Overseas Workers Welfare Administration [OWWA]), each given a particular charge, to ensure the protection of overseas workers.[4] As I discuss below, managing the agencies' partnership with this conglomeration of state bodies underlies the tension within this arena. While agencies act as local agents of foreign employers, their business practice is ultimately governed by the regulations established by these state apparatuses.

More than 90 percent of the agencies are located in the city of Manila (Tyner 2000). Many, including the six I studied, are in areas with a heavy concentration of employment agencies with diverse labor markets (Table 4.1).

Most of the agencies are visibly and conveniently clustered around commercial entities, such as travel agencies, photocopying and fax centers, ID and passport photo services, medical clinics, Internet cafes, and financial loan centers, making them easily identifiable from a distance. Although some of the agencies are in stand-alone offices, a majority rent space within multiple-floor office buildings. Sometimes, they share these buildings with other agencies, making it convenient for applicants to go from one agency to the next, intensifying the competition between them.[5] It is often easy to discern the agencies that are currently active based on the visible presence of foreign job orders posted around their

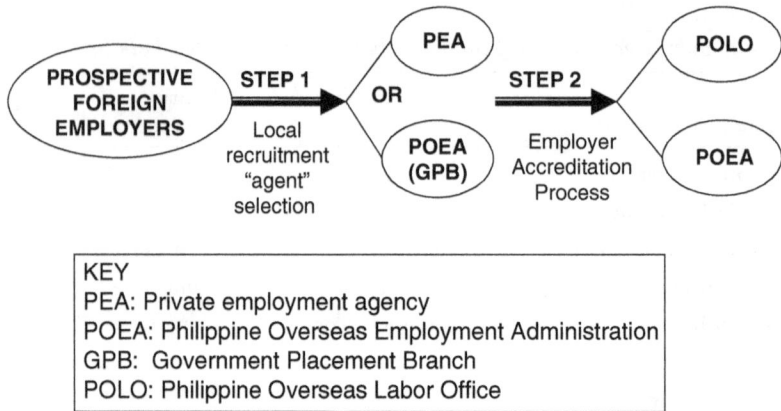

4.2. Hiring process of Filipino workers for land-based employment.
SOURCE: Philippine Overseas Employment

offices or advertised in newspapers and on the radio or by the number of prospective overseas workers waiting patiently in their offices.

The process of initiating the hiring of Filipino workers, particularly for land-based employment, proceeds in two principal stages (Figure 4.2). Prospective employers first select a local Philippine agent from the private sector or the government who will represent them and fulfill their labor needs. In most cases, employers solicit the service of private employment agencies unless the employer is a government facility or government-owned or -controlled company that may prefer to go through another government body, which, in this case, is represented by POEA's Government Placement Branch. The next step requires that employers submit recruitment documents to begin the process of accreditation as employers and to verify their need for Filipino workers. The accreditation process is typically initiated by employers through the help of the local Philippine Overseas Labor Office (POLO) in their country. Alternatively, if there is no POLO in the country, employers go through their chosen local Philippine agent, who facilitates the accreditation process through the POEA. This two-step process completes the employers' administrative responsibilities, leaving the rest of the recruitment process in the hands of the employment agencies, as employers wait eagerly for their workers. What this process, as diagrammed here, doesn't quite capture are the complexities of and tension in these exchanges, especially in terms of how agencies are selected and the actual work that goes into generating qualified workers.

Within this competitive labor export industry, certain agencies stand out, possessing particular characteristics that depends on the nature of their labor specialization (job orders, place of destination, and reputation of foreign employers) and their relationship with and official recognition from POEA. Agencies compete on the basis of work categories, skill specializations, and employment destinations—all of which influence the amount of profit they secure. An agency marketing employment to the United Kingdom would earn more for the workers it brokered and would have an easier time securing a labor pool, compared with one marketing to Middle Eastern countries. As I discuss in this chapter, because of the perceived differences in the sociocultural environment and religious practices of the Middle East, nursing and domestic work applicants do not consider these locations ideal. Moreover, employment agencies, beside being labor specific and country specific, compete based on the type of foreign clientele they represent. Being able to secure a contract with a so-called top-notch employer in a given industry contributes greatly to an agency's reputation.

Some agencies in the Philippines have become popular because of having received POEA awards. POEA administers competition for these annual awards and judges agencies on the basis of their volume of deployment, track record of recruitment violations, technical capabilities, foreign exchange earnings, and maintenance of welfare and allied services to workers.[6] Receiving the awards and official recognition from POEA afford them certain benefits. For example, under the Client Referral Assistance program, the marketing branch of POEA provides referrals to prospective foreign employers regarding agencies that can serve as their agents for fulfilling specific job orders. Thus, agencies that have received special recognition from POEA become the administration's primary referrals. Also, some awardees have the ability to obtain direct access local personnel registry divisions and to participate in recruitment and marketing job fairs sponsored by the state and the Public Employment Service Office.

As POEA notes on its Web site, prospective employers can benefit from these "top performing" agencies, which "have been conferred these awards in recognition of their outstanding and exemplary performance in

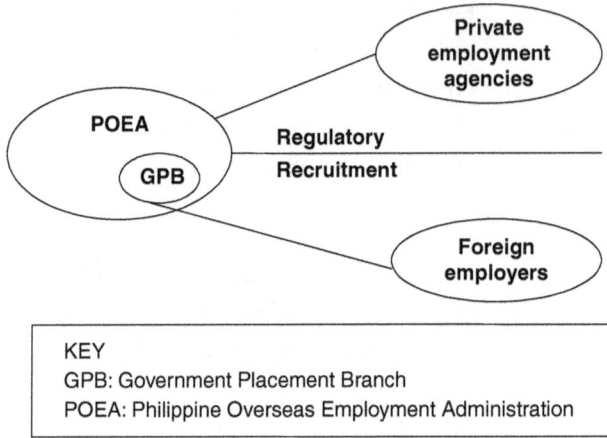

4.3. The Philippine state as a "regulatory" and "recruitment" body.

the field of overseas employment and for their vital role in uplifting quality of life of millions of Filipinos by providing them gainful overseas employment" (http://www.poea.gov.ph). Through a system that provides a government seal of approval, prospective employers are reassured of the quality and legitimacy of a particular agency. Meanwhile, as I discussed in the previous chapter, because the state, through POEA, is also a labor broker, primarily of highly skilled workers, agencies are also competing with it when it comes to this workforce deployment (Figure 4.3). Agencies, then, must manage these very tenuous relations because ultimately, their reputation and ability to obtain foreign labor contracts are at the mercy of POEA, which is simultaneously their regulator and their competitor. This dual position of the state is what agencies characterize as the unlevel playing field on which they conduct their business and to which I now turn.

AN UNLEVEL PLAYING FIELD

In May 2002, POEA implemented a policy change that severed its already tenuous relationship with the private sector through a revision of rules and regulations that govern the overseas recruitment and deployment of land-based workers. While the state interpreted these new rules as increased protection of Filipino workers through the elimination of "fly-by-night" agencies, the private sector saw them as insidious strategies for killing the recruitment industry. The revised policy was supposed to thematically reflect the current state mantra about the role of the private employment agencies in brokering labor: "Difficult to enter, easy to operate, and easy to go." The principles guiding this slogan were made visible through informational seminars provided to the private sector by POEA during February 21–27, 2002, to offer guidance on interpreting the implications of this new policy on businesses.[7] In a seminar I attended, POEA repeatedly attempted to convey the message that the rules were not meant to be punitive but rather a way to "clean up" and professionalize the industry's image (field notes, February 27, 2002).

POEA officials viewed these revised policies as containing amendments that ensure that only legitimate businesses—defined as financially capable and "professional"—will thrive. This is best captured by the fact that the new regulations made it significantly harder for new agencies to enter the recruitment business for two reasons. First, the financial requirements to start a recruitment agency significantly increased.[8] While the private sector sees these financial increases as a hindrance to doing business, POEA views them as helping the industry by minimizing competition within the private sector. Second, agencies must show proof that their sole proprietor, partner, or chief executive officer holds a bachelor's degree and has at least three years of business experience. According to POEA's director of the Licensing and Regulation Office, Viveca Catalig, "The labor market is changing and you are not exporting commodities but people; therefore, you are better capable to negotiate with foreigners if you have the proper educational background" (field notes, February 27, 2002). Revising the requirements for the financial and social capital needed for starting a recruitment agency is ultimately part of the state's attempt to professionalize the image of the private sector and, more important, a response to the continued presence of illegal recruiters.

During the seminar I attended, referred to above, a POEA official pointed out, "There is always this complaint that you have an image problem. How do we help you improve your image? I think that you have to work together with government" (field notes, February 27, 2002). In this context, the state presents itself as looking after the best interests of the private sector by helping businesses maintain a sense of integrity. But it became clear to me that the state is just as concerned with the private sector's image as it is with its own. Given that POEA's supposed primary function is that of a regulatory body that monitors the activities of the private sector in ways that ensure a reputable overseas employment program, it is ultimately implicated in any actions (positive or negative) committed by employment agencies. Further, given the persistent presence of illegal recruitment cases that plague the industry, the state is repeatedly called on to figure out how to mitigate them. Tightening the rules under the guise of professionalizing the private sector can be interpreted as one way of highlighting a responsive state that is committed to these efforts.

Complementing this "difficult to enter" aspect of the policy change is POEA's claim that it is committed to making it easier for agencies to operate their business. The "easy to operate" mantra indicates that licensed agencies no longer have to obtain prior approval from POEA in advertising overseas job vacancies as long as the jobs are included in the personnel requests submitted by registered and accredited foreign principals. Similarly, agencies can advertise for personnel pooling without obtaining prior approval from POEA.[9] Another provision that is supposed to assist agency's operations is in the area of accrediting foreign employers and principals. Whereas the POEA was previously responsible for this process, the new rules now shift the responsibility of verifying the recruitment documents of foreign employers and principals to the officers of POLO.[10] This shift is expected to speed up the recruitment process because these documents can now immediately be verified at the work site instead of being sent to the Philippines first, thereby minimizing any delays. However, some labor brokers remarked that giving the sole authority of verifying labor contracts to labor officials is unjust because they do not trust their abilities to make sound decisions, as they may not necessarily have sufficient background in the business of brokering labor. They also felt that this shift in responsibility was a limitation on their ability to go to another administrative unit for appeal.

Finally, POEA officials explained that while it may be difficult to enter this arena as a new agency, it will not be the case in terms of being expelled from it.[11] The "easy to go" component of this policy change outlined a rigorous set of recruitment violations and corresponding administrative penalties. The notable change comes with the kinds of "administrative offenses" that result in an automatic cancellation of an agency's license. Such offenses include the deployment of underage workers and the overcharging of placement fees beyond what is allowed by a host country's prevailing laws and by POEA. While POEA claimed that these changes were justified by the need to enforce policies that effectively eliminate unscrupulous brokers, the private sector argued that it does nothing to protect the industry from fraudulent workers. During the informational seminar with POEA, a few brokers brought up this issue, saying that they might engage in deploying underage workers unknowingly, because applicants can falsify the documents they submit to them. Their attempt to shift the responsibility to applicants was met with insistence by the POEA that they exercise "due diligence" in verifying the age eligibility of applicants. "You can commit any other forms of misrepresentation—just not the deployment of underage workers. If you do this, then this is a real defiance of the policy," an official firmly announced (field notes, February 27, 2002).

While the state believed that the "difficult to enter, easy to operate, and easy to go" policies would, indeed, uplift the private sector's image, the private sector was unconvinced. Labor brokers felt that the new amendments, along with the existing regulations, were not necessarily created in the spirit of "helping" them but would further hinder their business efforts. While the state viewed the new rules as a way of professionalizing and improving the image of the private sector, labor brokers perceived them as further "unleveling the playing field." As a labor broker and vice president of Troy International, an employment agency, remarked, the overseas recruitment rules had become so stringent that they actually created an environment that makes it easy to commit mistakes; the broker resented the fact that POEA, with whom the agencies competed, didn't face the same vulnerability.[12] He reasoned, "How can you compete in this arena? The playing field is not leveled. You are competing against your referee, who can change the rules at will. You probably know the golden rule—he who has the ball makes the rules" (interview by the author, January 15, 2002).

Part of the inherent conflict in the labor-brokering process results from the dual positions of power that POEA occupies, which the private sector claims subsequently compromises its ability to act as a fair regulatory body because it is also a labor broker. As the broker above noted, POEA has constructed a system that gives it an unfair advantage in recruitment because of the absence of another regulatory body to police it. Complicating this unlevel playing field is the hotly contested issue that POEA was supposed to undergo a comprehensive deregulation plan regarding its role in the overseas employment program. As outlined in Section 30 of Republic Act 8042: The Migrant Workers and Overseas Filipinos Act of 1995, "Within a period of five years from the effectivity of this Act, the DOLE shall phase out the regulatory functions of the POEA pursuant to the objectives of deregulation." This deregulation plan was originally intended to make labor migration "strictly a matter between the worker and his [*sic*] foreign employer" (POEA 1995).

However, Philippine state officials reasoned that the process of deregulation was also contingent on labor market conditions and the welfare of migrant workers. As Carmelita Dimzon, POEA deputy administrator of general administrative and support services, argued, "The spirit of the law is that we could be phased out only if the conditions set in that law are met [such as] if the economic conditions of the country shall have improved by 2000 or the workers shall have been empowered and have been able to make their decisions based on information provided by the government" (interview by the author, October 25, 2001). Since neither illegal recruitment activities (such as exacting placement fees from workers) nor the deployment of unprepared and therefore "unempowered" workers has necessarily decreased since the implementation of RA 8042, in 1995, the state believes that its regulatory functions are still needed. Director Dimzon further clarified that "deregulation," in principle, does not necessarily mean "absence of regulation" but "is just a reduction of regulatory functions."

Interestingly, this is precisely how the private sector perceives deregulation. It wants reforms resulting in increased facilitative procedures that allow its businesses to work more efficiently. Although both parties define deregulation similarly, they differ in terms of what they imagine will be its effects. For POEA, deregulation would create an unruly arena with labor brokers primarily deciding the fate of the workers. State officials envision that the state will always have the role of empowering workers. Therefore, it claims that even if the spirit of deregulation were embedded in the notion that employment should be a matter solely negotiated between workers and their employers, the state is ultimately responsible for intervening and educating them so that they can make well-informed decisions.

On the other hand, for the private sector, deregulation is a mechanism that would further enhance overseas employment insofar as it ensures the Philippines' monopoly in the labor market as a workforce supplier. Lessening the regulations and creating more "facilitative procedures" would allow the Philippines greater access to different markets because the recruitment rules would not be so restrictive. The private sector wants the state to refocus its efforts, moving away from excessively trying to regulate the private sector and toward actively promoting Filipino workers and opening new markets. But might this also be the impetus for the state's refusal to engage in deregulation?

For one thing, deregulation would minimize the ability of the state to participate in an endeavor that generates sizeable income for the country. Second, public pressures for governing the private sector would only increase, especially given the pervasive problems of illegal recruitment circuits. More important, it is a state committed to professionalizing the workforce deployment of the country and promoting a particular kind of highly skilled and "upgraded" workforce—a task that it believes can be accomplished only through active monitoring of the private sector, which is responsible for brokering the majority of so called nonprofessional workers (domestic workers and "entertainers").

Nonetheless, labor brokers criticized the revised policies as unrealistic and not market driven. This is especially the case when it comes to the issue of the placement fees that employment agencies collect from workers beyond what is allowed by the laws of host countries and by POEA.[13] Labor brokers constantly argue with the state over its failure to respond to foreign markets, which they claim necessitate working with brokers in other countries who serve as liaisons to finding employment for workers. Alfredo Palmiery, president of the Federated Association of Manpower Exporters (FAME), another professional association representing the private sector, explained that in 85 percent of the labor market, they are dealing directly not with the employers but with intermediaries—the local foreign brokers who are responsible for finding a suitable employer match for Philippine employment agencies' pool of candidates and for monitoring workers' needs as they complete their contracts. He reasoned that because of global competition, these intermediaries are forced to make their employer fees competitive by charging them less than what would be ideal. They try to make up for this loss by collecting sizeable fees from their overseas partners such as the Philippine employment agencies. While the state's response is to simply close these markets, Palmiery interpreted this as an unreasonable move because these intermediaries are gatekeepers of several markets, many of which are the top recruiters of Filipino workers and include Hong Kong, Taiwan, Saudi Arabia, and the United Arab Emirates (interview by the author, February 11, 2002). Workers again become implicated in this reasoning as he justified the displacement of the costs of paying their intermediaries' fees based on the dictates of the market. No consideration is given to the workers, who are already likely to be in dire financial straits, only to find themselves accumulating additional debt because of the market. It also seems a good strategy for absolving themselves of any accountability for the workers, since the intermediaries are technically in charge of how workers fare in their employment situations.

Ultimately, the primary goal of agencies is to protect their profit interests and safeguard the markets that enable them to realize this. Therefore, when the state pushes them to explore markets that do not have high-cost intermediaries, they see this as a threat to their livelihood. During the seminar noted above, state officials claimed that agencies can avoid overcharging placement fees if they cater to higher-paying employment (that is, highly skilled work). The officials encouraged agencies to "scout for higher-paying positions" that would increase their profit margins and allow them to collect greater one-month placement fees (field notes, February 27, 2002). The private sector responded by reiterating that the land-based workforce deployment of the Philippines was still disproportionately concentrated outside the "professional" category. Therefore, the state's program for professionalizing the country's workforce deployment and gradually phasing out the more "vulnerable sectors" (domestic work and entertainment work) does not make much business sense.

The sense of threat provoked by these suggestions stems from the ways that the private sector finds it difficult to conduct its business because it is always competing with POEA, which, it claims, has an undue advantage. A labor broker from Riker Manpower Services, an agency that has existed for more than twenty-five years and whose primary clients are in Saudi Arabia, claimed that just by virtue of being affiliated with the government, POEA "already creates a sense of safety for applicants." Applicants already assume that POEA works with better-paying employers than those of employment agencies, which are seen as focused on turning a profit. "I would assume that these agencies got a cut from their employers while POEA wouldn't do such a thing," the broker remarked (interview November 20, 2001).

Although the private sector is responsible for the bulk of the country's total foreign labor recruitment, it believes that because agencies are typified as already unscrupulous, they must work very hard at trying to build a reputation of being credible. In contrast, POEA, as a representative of the state that pitches itself as always on the side of workers, is likely to garner more trust from applicants. It is this perception of trust with which agencies like Riker must contend and that is compounded by the agencies' impression that the state perceives them as their adversary, an issue to which I now turn.

"We Are Not the Enemies"

The agencies believe that the unlevel playing field on which they conduct their business is worsened by the lack of true recognition of their contributions as employment providers. As a labor broker from Troy International stated in an impassioned tone, "To think that [the] year 2002 has been declared the year of the employment providers! They [the Philippine state] always hail workers as *bagong bayani* (modern-day heroes) and yet they look at the employment providers who are the manpower agencies as the enemy. They never look at the agencies as their partner" (interview by the author, January 15, 2002). Brokers believe that the state, given its administrative position, faces an inherent restriction in terms of its ability to fully promote labor migration. For one, its regulatory functions and its preoccupation with its own image derail it from pursuing the market aggressively. The private sector views the state as being more attentive to managing (and redressing) its image as an entity that cannot provide local employment to its citizens or protect overseas workers instead of strengthening Filipinos' monopoly in the global marketplace.

Labor brokers envision that the only way for the state to truly meet its so-called desire to optimize the benefits of labor migration is for it to work together with the private sector, fully embracing market realities and assuming a proactive stance in promoting Filipino workers.

However, it is noteworthy that although labor brokers see the state as insufficiently market driven because it does not directly promote overseas employment, they may simply be underestimating the "marketing" work of the state in promoting Filipino workers. As I discussed in chapter 3, maintaining a monopoly in the global marketplace is a pressing concern for the state. POEA officials recognize that the Philippines faces numerous competitors that are also producing marketable workers and are working on devising strategies for coping with emergent global competition (by upgrading workers' technical skills and other efforts).

Nevertheless, the private sector demands that the state undergo a shift in perspective so that instead of viewing its work as that of *managing* labor migration, it sees itself as *promoting* it. Refusing to actively promote labor migration only leads to stigmatizing overseas employment. According to Victor Fernandez Jr., president of the Philippine Association of Service Exporters Inc. (PASEI), "It is not shameful to be deploying Filipinos abroad. In fact we should be proud [of it]. There is that term 'OCW'—overseas contract worker—which should actually mean *our contribution to the world*. We are trying to repay what the other countries have done [for] us" (interview by the author, February 25, 2002; emphasis in original.[14] He characterized the state as viewing overseas employment as stigmatized because it represents the state's inability to generate viable jobs at home. "The only way you can remove that embarrassment is to create more jobs. You do not fight overseas employment by coming up with more rules," he reasoned. For labor brokers such as Fernandez, overseas employment can also be viewed as a form of resource exchange, whereby the Philippines "offers," or barters, Filipinos as prized commodities and "contributions" to the global marketplace, making it appear as if the country is indebted to the world. Although many brokers are aware of the long-term detrimental effects of overseas employment on families, the former believe that the families are precisely the primary motivation for workers' decisions to work abroad. Hence, they believe that they are simply assisting workers in fulfilling these pursuits and call on the state to arrive at the same realization.

This is particularly important as the private sector anticipates emerging competition for the Philippines. Labor brokers enumerated that other labor-exporting nations are brokering their workers for lower wages and have less bureaucratic red tape to impose on foreign employers, which gives them an advantage. According to FAME's president, Alfredo Palmiery, Indonesia is a viable source of domestic labor because its local agencies do not face any state-mandated placement fee ceiling that limits the amount of fees they can collect from placing applicants. This allows Indonesian agencies to partner with a greater number of foreign brokers from labor-receiving nations who are responsible for finding household employment and whose fees are often covered by the placement fees that applicants pay. Similarly, a labor broker from Tricorder Enterprises, an agency marketing primarily to the United Kingdom and the United States, explained that while Filipino nurses may currently be in demand, this will not always be the case as the Philippines. "Even the qualified nurses are starting to dwindle," he noted, while describing the deterioration of the "quality" of nurses who leave the Philippines (interview by the author, October 16, 2001). He attributed this deterioration to the scarcity of hospital training programs that prepare new graduates to make them globally competitive.

Labor brokers like him fear that the overemphasis of the state, through POEA, on regulating the private sector detracts from the key issue of maintaining the Philippines' position as a global labor provider. They contend that the Philippine state should not harbor a false sense of security about Filipino workers' comparative advantage and instead work with the private sector to form a better-coordinated partnership that will sustain it. They understand that their contentious relations with POEA comes from the fact that they are more firmly committed to facing the reality that labor migration is inevitable because of the scarcity of viable local employment. The issue is not so much about what can be done to minimize it but what can be done to prepare for its eventuality. They wish for a kind of partnership with the state that is based on this realization and at the same time they demand a degree of autonomy for doing their work.

But undergirding these wishes and the present adversarial relationship between POEA and the private sector is the fundamental question of who protects the workers in light of the much contested *joint and solidary liability clause*. This clause stipulates that agencies are primarily responsible for claims that arise from the labor contracts they facilitate, such as handling the employment relations between workers and their employers (POEA 2002b). Labor brokers view the clause as an unfair state tactic of displacing the sole responsibility of a worker and employer's performance onto the private sector. They argue that their only responsibility is to find employment for the workers; it is not to monitor workers' performance overseas. As Victor Fernandez explained, "There is nothing that a recruitment agency or whatever we call ourselves—the overseas employment providers—that we can actually do, or there is very little that we can do the moment that we deploy the worker. We can only say, we were responsible for deploying that particular worker, but how he [sic] fares abroad, in another country, in another environment, in another culture, would be very difficult for us to control or to manage." He believes that holding the agencies solely accountable for the workers' fate overseas is just one way that the state tries to cover up its inadequacies and incompetence in handling workers' problems overseas (interview by the author, February 25, 2002).

An example of the inadequacies to which Fernandez referred is the inability of the Philippine state to formulate strong bilateral agreements with foreign nations; the private sector views the joint and solidary liability clause as a means for the state to appease the public and reduce its concern about much needed on-site protection for workers by displacing the burden of responsibility onto another entity—the private sector—and, consequently, putting the private sector in the position of being an enemy of the state. Further, other labor brokers claim that the clause assumes that workers are the only victims in this process. A broker from Exocomp stated that the private sector also needs protection from "professional complainants"—applicants who he claimed make a career out of filing complaints or lawsuits against agencies in order to make money from them. There are individuals, this broker maintained, who apply to an agency just to file a complaint and others who are repatriated to the Philippines unexpectedly and blame the termination of their contracts on the agency (interview by the author, November 9, 2001). A list naming some of the most common professional complainants circulates within the private sector in an attempt to warn and protect agencies. As is evident, the private sector has recast itself as vulnerable, as a potential victim of unscrupulous applicants who, in reality, may actually know of their rights and how to exercise them.

Labor brokers argue that displacing the responsibility of worker protection solely on the shoulders of employment agencies will only encourage irresponsible behavior among workers. According to a labor broker and owner of Starfleet, a domestic work agency with more than twenty years' experience sending domestic workers to Hong Kong, the new rules and regulations, which reaffirm the joint and solidary clause will only "diminish the work ethic" of workers. This is because the new rules convey a message that if workers are unsatisfied with their jobs, they can simply complain to POEA and demand a refund from the agencies instead of first attempting to resolve the situation with their employers. So what labor brokers try to project is that they are not the state's enemies but are key partners of the state in attempting to promote the competitiveness of Filipino workers in terms of their skills and of their work ethic, so they will meet the standards of "greatness" that Filipino workers are supposed to embody. After all, labor brokers believe themselves to be not just employment providers but also "makers" of the country's heroes—a role they continually attempt to emulate in the midst of their contentious relations with the state and that which I describe in the following sections.

"We Even Deploy Those Who Are Underemployed"

Employment agencies are well attuned to the fact that they are responsible for more than 95 percent of the country's workforce deployment and pitch the idea that *they*, not the state, are the key facilitators of this process. They claim to have a solid understanding of Filipinos' economic needs and how labor migration has become a means to an end. They profit from what Choy (2003) refers to as Filipinos' "collective desires" to migrate that are shaped by how they imagine or are made to imagine what working overseas (or in particular, the United States) promises. As brokers, they understand that their job is to support these pursuits and help bring economically and professionally promising opportunities for work and leisure to their compatriots. PASEI president Victor Fernandez offers this apt description:

> We may be producing a lot of technical workers [and] highly skilled workers, but our economy cannot absorb all of this. A person who may be a good manager, a good financial analyst, even a good lawyer will find that the labor market is so constricted and the employment

opportunities so limited that they cannot expand their horizons so [they look] overseas. We have lawyers in America working as waiters. We have pharmacists who are actually working as service crew people. . . . We may have fully employed people here, like an EDT [emergency duty team] manager or a nurse but the type of equipment they are using becomes obsolete as time and technology catches up with them, so you can see that there is very big potential [in terms of labor power and talent], but you can't use them here in the Philippines (interview by the author, February 25, 2002).

The kind of political economy that Fernandez defined is one devoid of hope—the economy is unable to "absorb" and maximize the actual and even potential talents of its own human resources. As a result, those seeking work are pushed out into another employment landscape, one that is more ready to consume their labor and better equipped to accommodate their financial, professional, and personal aspirations. In discussing this with me, Fernandez wanted me to understand that "it is not only lack of opportunities here in terms of income but it is also about the development of one's own natural talent and resources." After all, he claimed, "we do not only deploy the unemployed. We even deploy those who are underemployed." It is in this context that labor brokers find their calling. For the private sector, brokering Filipino workers for overseas employment is, first and foremost, about mediating the ability of Filipinos to earn a decent living wage. Even if the employment or place of destination is less than ideal, the promise of a living wage wins out. Brokers do not worry, for example, about recurrent discussions regarding a proposed wage cut for domestic workers in Hong Kong, which may deter Filipinos from working there. From their perspective, even with a wage cut, an overseas job offers a better income than what workers can earn in the Philippines. A broker from Troy International confidently explained, "Overseas Filipino workers hold the view that it's better to die . . . in the Middle East in the event of a war than to die in the Philippines for not having anything to eat" (interview by the author, January 15, 2002).

His statement describes a dismal Philippine economy lacking any comparative advantage over its global counterparts. In this scenario, Filipinos ultimately have one "choice" to make, and it is this choice on which labor brokers depend. Interestingly, the Troy International broker's reasoning depicts Filipinos as always suffering, as victims, whether of war or of poverty; in doing so, the broker further reifies an ethos of labor migration based on a rhetoric of sacrifice, and ethos that the private sector, in partnership with the state, manages and maintains. While I acknowledge the labor exploitation of overseas workers and the emotional pain that comes from working overseas and being separated from one's social networks, I also point out that it is this kind of representation that labor brokers co-opt in the interests of their image. First, it allows them to sell undesirable labor markets as good-enough employment destinations despite abysmal labor regulations or political instabilities. Second, it permits them to assume the role of saviors who understand the sacrifices that Filipinos make and who will relieve their suffering by providing them a job.

Labor brokers promulgate this type of image in the job advertisements that the industry circulates.[15] One particular ad for a nursing position exemplified the promise proffered by brokers. Above the headshot of a white woman with inviting eyes and wearing nursing cap fashioned from the flag of the United Kingdom is a caption that reads, "Be a nurse in the UK! We guarantee over a million pesos a year in salary. We ensure fast deployment and absolutely no placement fees." The ad depicts an exciting offer, not only of becoming something different (perhaps as good as a white nurse) but also of being somewhere else. The crucial aspect of this offer, the one most likely to draw in readers, is the reassuring statement that the agency being advertised can broker an *identity transformation*, one that amounts to earnings of "over a million pesos a year." This identity transformation is an elevation in social status primarily based on material (economic) resources that reposition Filipino migrants as breadwinners and economic saviors. Not only can the agency make this happen quickly ("fast deployment"); it is a transformation that is at no cost to the applicant, since the agency can "guarantee" "absolutely no placement fees." Similarly, placement agencies for domestic workers make such economic opportunities visible through advertisements that boast the ability to "earn HK$3,670," a monthly salary that is approximately equivalent to 21,000 pesos ($472). This figure is significant because it represents earnings that are twenty times what domestic workers can obtain in the Philippines doing the same type of work.

The economic promise denoted in these ads is also proffered during recruitment seminars or job fairs that foreign employers and Filipino employment agencies jointly organize in the Philippines. In these gatherings, labor brokers remind Filipino workers of the global demand for the latter's skills and the viable jobs that await them. For example, one seminar provided by a Philippine nursing agency representing U.S. hospital clients in Florida, Chicago, and Missouri opened with an urgent call for Filipinos to help relieve the "chronic and critical shortage" of nurses in the United States (field notes, October 8, 2001). "There is a need for about two hundred thousand nurses in America," screamed an immigration lawyer who was working with the agency as she pleaded to an audience of about one hundred Filipinos, mostly women, to "pitch in to this current crisis in American health care." She offered a reassuring guarantee that there would be placement for all "qualified" nurses. In another recruitment seminar, a representative from a U.S. nursing registry providing nurses to California and Arizona facilities reiterated the exhortation and enumerated an extensive explanation for it. Presenting "U.S. hard facts," he listed factors contributing to the U.S. health care crisis: an aging nursing workforce, a growing disinterest among Americans to pursue nursing, and the large population of baby boomers who would soon need health care services (field notes, November 8, 2001). He explained that "the U.S. will need approximately two million medical personnel by 2007," an alarming overprojection (at the time) that he repeatedly voiced throughout his presentation.

We Make Undesirable
Markets Desirable

Employment agencies seek to remind the state of the everyday challenges inherent in finding viable jobs for applicants and of the agencies' agility in adapting to an ever-changing global labor market. This is evident in how they respond to labor market instabilities such as finding new employment destinations when certain places suddenly stop recruiting from the Philippines. For example, when the United States ended nursing recruitment from the Philippines around mid-1990s, agencies clamored for other markets into which to funnel their overflowing pool of nurses. Agencies such as Tricorder Enterprises, now known for marketing to the United Kingdom and the United States, then actively pursued Saudi

Arabia as an alternative market, until such time that other and "better" markets opened up. By labeling certain markets as better than others, brokers pointed to the challenges of selling undesirable employment locations such as the Middle East to Filipinos for a variety of reasons.[16]

One of Tricorder's labor brokers, commenting on this point, noted that it is difficult to recruit nurses for Saudi Arabia because of differences in religious and gender norms and practices (interview by the author, October 16, 2001). The problem is compounded by the reputation of workplaces in the Middle East as being particularly unsuitable for Filipino women. Because the region is predominantly Islamic, the cultural environment requires a degree of social adjustment for Filipino Catholic women.[17] Labor brokers and former Filipino nurses I met in the Philippines who previously had worked in Saudi Arabia repeatedly pointed to laws and cultural norms that imposed mandates on women's appearance and restrictions on their public conduct. Women mentioned their "lack of freedom," describing time limits on their leisure activities and restrictions on single women to "freely" associate with men in public. Further, having found themselves in a context in which only women are allowed to care for male patients in Saudi Arabia, coupled with facing cultural stereotypes of Filipino women as being sexually available, they shared stories about the resulting vulnerability of Filipino women to sexual advances and abuse.[18]

The existing wage rate classification system in Saudi Arabia contributes to the difficulty of selling this market. Under this system, migrant workers are paid according to the actual converted economic value to their countries of the workers' earnings (Woodward 1988). The rationale for this system is that it will create a wage scale that brings some parity to labor markets. But what has emerged is a seemingly race-based wage classification whereby workers from the Third World are classified as the lowest paid. Nursing labor brokers explained that Filipino workers occupy "level 4" of the wage scale.[19] The scale constitutes an unjust system because it does not compensate workers on the basis of the work they do. Instead, as a broker from Tricorder explained, even if Filipino nurses perform the same exact job as that of British nurses, Filipinos would still be paid less. But employers justify the differences in wages of migrant workers by stressing the value to their home countries of riyals, Saudi Arabia's local currency.

A labor broker at Riker Manpower Services, the agency mentioned above, who previously had worked in Saudi Arabia as a nurse for six years, verified this and blamed the practice for the tension among nurses in her unit. The tension was caused not only because nurses performing the same work were paid differently, but also because it created a perception that these differences were based on Filipino nurses having a much lower skill level. The unintended consequence of the wage classification system is that workers have come to believe that a salary level is a measure of a country's degree of economic desperation and social standing with respect to the global economy, thereby promoting the notion of some kind of a willingness on the part of workers to accept any wage.

As a result of these wage disparities, as well as the cultural norms and practices of the Middle East, Filipina nurses tend to scorn this region as an ideal place to work. Agency brokers must craft creative strategies in response, since the that part of the world remains a reliable destination of Filipino workers. In 2007 alone, POEA reported that for the past three decades, the Middle East region (Saudi Arabia, the United Arab Emirates, Kuwait, and Qatar) remained the top destination for Filipino workers and represented 45.3 percent of the total deployment for that year (POEA 2008). Despite its undesirability as place of employment, it is nevertheless the source of lucrative income-generating opportunities that are too hard for the private sector to pass up.

Much of the work of labor brokers thus entails devising ways of luring Filipinos to work in the Middle East, persuading workers of its benefits, so to fill the agencies' job orders for Saudi Arabia and other countries of the region. A broker from Riker claimed that her agency "never rejects candidates" and that every worker who comes through their door is qualified for a job. They rarely turn away prospective applicants and instead attempt to look through their existing job orders. "All nurses are qualified," she reasoned, while she described the agency's efforts in finding them a job that fits their training (interview by the author, November 20, 2001). At the time of my fieldwork in 2001, a central concern at Riker's office was not having a sufficient labor pool to fill the influx of job orders from its Saudi Arabian clients. Because Riker's primary and preferred recruitment strategy, headhunting in the predominantly Muslim southern Philippines, is a financial burden to the company, any time a "qualified" candidate seeks its services, that person delivers a welcome cost savings to Riker. Because labor brokers are fearful of traveling to the southern Philippines (Mindanao), where news of kidnapping and terrorist activities abound, they are happy when such provincial headhunting activities are curtailed. Thus, job candidates are not rejected, to the extent that they are of use when it comes to Riker's economic interest and the personal preferences of labor brokers.

In other cases, brokers must convince applicants who are already applying for a different job, in another area of the world, to reconsider Saudi Arabia as a viable alternative. This was the case during a meeting between a nurse recruiter from Riker and two nurses who planned to apply as live-in caregivers in Canada.[20] These female applicants expressed their preference to work in a Western country, despite knowing that they would essentially be deskilled, working as caregivers who would not be in a hospital setting but in a home and whose work would not allow them to practice their clinical training skills. The women preferred such work because of their fears about going to the Middle East, with its different religious and cultural practices and its unstable political climate. The recruiter explained to the women repeatedly that their fears were unwarranted and that working as caregivers was not just a disservice to their education and nursing training but represented significant downward occupational mobility. While she justified to me this practice of trying to persuade the women as being an example of her agency's efforts to provide applicants with jobs that fit their skills, I knew that she was anxious to supply her foreign clients with a pool of qualified nurses—an effort that comes with an economic payoff for Riker.

WE KEEP THEIR DREAMS ALIVE

A persistent challenge faced by the industry is that most Filipinos pursue overseas employment with the aim of going to the United States. The reality is, however, that this often entails an arduous process, since there is a long waiting period for U.S. immigrant visa approval and the completion of exam requirements. This is especially the case for nurses. Given this situation, agencies concoct schemes that transform certain countries into stepping-stones to the United States while also ensuring desirable profit margins for those agencies. One example can be seen in what I refer to as the "work while you wait" program offered by

Exocomp Staffing Services. Exocomp, a sixteen-year-old company in the Philippines, is known for having Saudi Arabia as its primary geographical niche and supplies various workers to its clients there, of which nurses constitute a large part.

Beginning in 2000, it has explored the possibilities of working with a U.S.-based nurse staffing agency, offering job placement of Filipino nurses under an immigrant-based visa. But because the waiting period for these visas (called EB3 visas) can be as long as two years, Exocomp offers its U.S.-based applicants an opportunity to work elsewhere, such as Saudi Arabia, first, while they wait for approval of their U.S. visas. As an Exocomp broker explained, "If they want immediate deployment and work overseas while waiting for their immigrant visa, we tell them we can deploy them in *three weeks* to the Middle East with a contract of one year. So while they are working in the Middle East and after they finish their contracts, they come back and their immigrant papers for the U.S. are ready (interview by the author, November 9, 2001; emphasis in original).

The broker further explained that this "option" can help mitigate the financial constraints that some of the agency's clients face in terms of being unable to pay for the cost of a U.S. application by using their savings in the Middle East.[21] This is a good plan for covering the cost of taking the U.S. nursing board exam, the National Council of Licensure Examination (NCLEX), which Exocomp's current U.S.-based client, a nurse registry, requires for all applicants.[22] During an orientation in which Exocomp first gave an overview of the employment opportunities being offered by the registry, the questions and concerns raised by applicants pertained to the exorbitant cost of taking the exam (see Table 4.2)[23] (field notes, November 18, 2001). Exocomp and a representative from the registry quickly attempted to appease the forty prospective job applicants in the room through this work-while-you-wait program by emphasizing how working in the Middle East was an efficient way for the applicants to realize their American dreams.

This broker stated that she worked in Saudi Arabia and thus could identify with the applicants' apprehension and fears about working there but encouraged them to think of it as temporary work and only as a "stepping-stone" to an eventual career in the United States. While this was certainly reassuring to applicants who longed to earn a living wage, it was

TABLE 4.2

Total Expenses for a Nursing Work Application to the United States

Requirement	Cost (dollars)
CGFNS testing	300
NCLEX application fee	80
NCLEX testing	120
NCLEX review	300
Airfare to Saipan	585
Hotel in Saipan	300
TOEFL testing	150
Total	1,835

NOTE: Figures are based on those presented by brokers to applicants between 2001–2002.

also a profitable venture for Exocomp. First, the agency was able to profit from using this pool of U.S.-bound workers to fill any already existing job orders to the Middle East. Second, if workers decided to go through with applying for a U.S. immigrant visa through this same agency, Exocomp was then able to secure future contracts with its U.S.-based client, amounting to a significant sum, of five hundred dollars, for each applicant (field notes, November 18, 2001).[24] If their system worked perfectly, Exocomp would make double the amount from the *same* applicant.

Moreover, this work-while-you-wait program is a good image builder for agencies like Exocomp, because it allows them to represent themselves as always able to provide some kind of employment to Filipinos, even if it may not be their "dream job." But in doing so, they strive to keep these dreams alive in the process. This is evident in ads that other agencies produce. In one agency's ad, nurses bound for the United Kingdom have not even left the Philippines but are already made an enticing offer for their next overseas job in the United States. "Headed to the UK but still want to work in the U.S.A.? Keep that dream alive with HCCA," advises the ad as it summons these Filipino nurses not to give up their (American) dream. Through a transnationally coordinated process carried out by brokers in the Philippines, England, and the United States, the agency promises to process the women's visas as they finish their U.K. contracts. It is in this process that an agency exhibits itself as a creative force that is able to maximize the offerings of various labor markets under the guise of providing Filipinos an opportunity to make their "American dream" come true, which this ad heightens by listing various monetary and relocation incentives. The exhortation to "keep that dream alive" is an attempt to signify not only the agency's role as employment provider but also its capacity to be a bastion of hope to Filipinos.

WE TRANSFORM LIFESTYLES AND IDENTITIES

Labor brokers perceive their role as providing a pathway for Filipinos to pursue not only work but also leisure. They claim to support Filipino migrants' so-called innate sense of adventure and desire to travel, both of which they envision can be realized by working abroad. This philosophy influences the way that Holodeck Placement, an agency that has been in business for more than thirty years and has a strong nurse recruitment arm, conducts its business. One of its labor brokers expressed the view that "Filipinos are naturally adventurous. So there is always a tendency to leave whenever you see a job opening that would suit your skill and experience even if you are not that interested. You just try it out until you end up working overseas" (interview by the author, October 27, 2001). Another broker, from Riker Manpower Services, claimed that this sense of adventure can also be motivated by a desire to "escape" family life. Referring to her experiences, she pointed to the desire to move away from one's family and comfort zones, even if it is just to "break the daily routine." She identifies with those who she claims may not have imagined working overseas but used this opportunity as a way to realize their desires for being in a new social setting. "At one point in my life, I went out of the country just to know how it is, how it feels to live alone away from your family," she exclaimed (interview by the author, November 20, 2001). Brokers capitalize on these observations to illustrate forces that shape Filipinos' desires for migration that go beyond the usual economic logic. However, it is this kind of representation of Filipinos that allows brokers to portray overseas employment as a kind of adventurous pursuit that promises not only travel but also a sense of personal and economic independence, all of which contribute to elevating the social status of Filipinos.

Recruitment seminars and classified ads are good sites for examining these dynamics. While some emphasize amusement parks such as Disneyworld in Orlando, Florida, or natural wonders such as California's beaches, others focus on the lifestyle changes that earnings bring. Included in the information packet distributed to prospective applicants in a recruitment seminar organized by an agency representing hospitals from Florida and New York is a flashy brochure advertising workers' "future home" (field notes, November 13, 2001). While showcasing Florida's "sunshine and beaches" and New York's "culture and sophistication," this agency assumed a level of consumerism and cosmopolitanism while doing well to elevate the social and class status of Filipino nurses who apply through it. No longer are they viewed simply as workers; they are consumers and purveyors of culture and entertainment as they enjoy the features of New York: "the world's best shopping," "the best and most varied cuisine in the world," museums and galleries, Broadway shows, and nightlife. And this relocation can be a form of R&R if they choose to go to Florida, which offers them a "recreation paradise" and even a "large indoor shopping mall."

But regardless of the destination, such representations blur the boundary between work and leisure by transforming overseas employment into a ticket to reconfiguring one's class and status identity through American-style consumerism. Portraying overseas employment as a form of adventure ultimately makes it possible for brokers to represent themselves as facilitating the ability of Filipinos to live (the American) dream. And it is specifically an American dream of consumption that underscores the kind of buying power that Filipinos will gain from overseas employment.[25] Thus, if the "American dream" is supposed to represent the "good life," what it seems to ultimately promise Filipinos is a life of materialism and conspicuous consumption. As I show in chapter 6, it is the pursuit of this type of American dream that some workers begin to question and problematize.

The emphasis on workers' class transformation is crucial because it gives meaning to what brokers believe is another key contribution that they deliver as employment providers. A broker from Troy International applauded the agency for helping enable a positive social transformation among workers it sent to Japan. "These people, when they applied here, you think they look like domestic workers. . . . Physically, they don't look good. . . . And when they come back [to the Philippines] after six months, their transformation is huge! Physically, they are now good looking, their skin is whiter, they are financially stable—even if it was only six months after. . . . We are very, very glad when we see that they have gone through those changes. *We helped them* (interview by the author, January 30, 2002; emphasis added).

The idea that overseas employment is a transformative process is a sentiment that is shared by other brokers in the industry. As employment providers, they believe that they give Filipinos an opportunity to obtain the material means to improve themselves, although this is a problematic characterization of this transformation. No longer do they look like maids—they are now seemingly high-class individuals who are to be envied, possessing financial stability and the social (and physical) capital of whiteness. Brokers claim that overseas workers become noticeably different in terms of appearance, demeanor, and sense of confidence upon their return to the Philippines. Professing themselves to be key actors in this process, they take credit for these changes as they view themselves as some sort of lifestyle coach facilitating this identity transformation.

"WE PROVIDE A SERVICE STRAIGHT FROM THE HEART"

Brokers carefully pitch themselves as allies of workers and as people who care about workers' well-being and understand not only their dreams but also the sacrifices they bear being away from families. Recruitment agencies typically hire brokers with overseas work experience as a way of connecting with prospective applicants and responding to myriad concerns that can be best addressed by those who share similar experiences. Agencies recruiting nurses typically ask their foreign employer clients to send current staff nurses, who are Filipino, to address prospective workers' concerns. The nurses serve as token "success stories," narrating alluring lines to Filipino applicants, promising that they, too, can be recipients of similar overseas fortune. They also demonstrate to prospective workers that the latter will not live in isolation but will be welcomed by a community of Filipinos.

One advertisement from an agency that caters to recruiting nurses to the Baylor Health Care System is a good example. "Nurses, remember when you imagined your dream job? It's waiting for you at Baylor—in the heart of Texas," this ad announces as it invites Filipino nurses to consider this employment destination as a way to fulfill their American dream. The ad contains a photograph of a tightly huddled, seemingly welcoming group of nurses, labeled the "Baylor Filipino Family." The text reads: "At Baylor, we are proud to provide a home away from home for our growing Filipino family. With our continued education, excellent salary and benefits package, and thriving Filipino community, we are looking forward to welcoming you as one of our newest members." Following this is a list that outlines a relocation bonus of forty-five hundred dollars and the different fees that the employer will cover, including airfare to the United States and immigration services, while it is professed that "no salary deductions whatsoever in the Philippines or the United States" will be taken from the applicants. In this ad, this agency has constructed a *dream* job for Filipinos, one in which they will benefit from both a robust financial package and a ready-made Filipino community reconstructed as a kind of "home away from home" that will alleviate Filipino workers' homesickness and fears.

Labor brokers emphasize their ethic of care by assuring applicants of an equitable working arrangement in which they will be properly compensated. The ad describe above indicates that nothing would be deducted from the salary, while another ad seeks to reassure applicants that they will "receive salaries in full, without deductions and commissions" or will be "be paid [the] same salaries as American nurses." These ads confront and respond to common instances whereby the actual wages that nurses receive are reduced because of the "cut" that agencies take from their paychecks. The agencies present themselves as allies of workers who look after their financial interest by consciously promising to treat them as equals, despite their foreign status. Whether it is actually true is another question, but for now, it is the promise that all workers want to hear to dispel any ambivalence about going abroad or seeking the service of this particular agency.

The notion that the agencies are caring providers extends to the way that they provide service to their applicants. Holodeck is one agency that puts a high premium on having received favorable recognition from POEA about its services, which are prominently displayed on its ads, on its Web site, and in its office. It touts these awards as evidence of its not engaging in unscrupulous activities. As one of Holodeck's recruitment specialists characterized it, the awards are indication that the agency is in the business of providing a service that is "straight from the heart" because it tries to minimize the hardships that Filipinos undergo during the application process (interview by the author, October 27, 2001). The specialist also claimed that Holodeck does not show any favoritism and ethically conducts business by avoiding the *palakasan* system; that is, it does not accept gifts or bribes from job candidates to expedite their applications or to guarantee their hire.[26] He made a point of noting that even relatives or friends do not receive any special treatment, in an effort to create an equitable system for all applicants. For Holodeck, the branded image that it projects is of an agency that not only provides all applicants an equal chance to pursue a particular opportunity but also sees itself as an ally of the workers primarily and proclaims to understand and tries to minimize their hardships through its service.

In contrast to not having the *palakasan* system, other agencies, such as Troy, noted their unmatched commitment to "full disclosure." Troy is one of the leading providers of domestic labor in Hong Kong and has more than thirty years' experiences as a recruitment agency in the Philippines. Troy explains that its applicants leave completely aware of where their money goes in terms of the payments they make to their agency. Troy's operations manager proudly detailed this process, which includes providing applicants copies of the "remittances" that outlines the fees that their foreign intermediaries (agencies) charge them in order to find their local employment overseas. This kind of complete financial disclosure is, according to this broker, their "most important policy" and one that sets it apart from other agencies. "We have to tell the workers where the money goes. We tell the workers that in accordance with POEA rules, this is the fee you have to pay us, but since we have this foreign intermediary, an additional payment is needed. But we emphasize to them that this additional payment doesn't go to us. We tell them that we could show the records of the remittances we send to [foreign] brokers." In this way, agencies like Troy are able to justify and downplay the fact that they are often overcharging their applicants, by projecting an appearance of complete transparency.[27] But this kind of disclosure serves a dual purpose. As this same broker emphasized to me, "We have to be honest with the workers . . . so they know our beliefs and stance so that if they have any problems, they will not be so quick to sue us because they will realize we've taken care of them" (interview by the author, January 30, 2002).

Troy evidently uses its full-disclosure policy as a manipulative means of garnering the trust of its applicants, who it hopes will not turn against it. By showing proof of its transactions with its foreign intermediaries, the agency believes that it is not cheating applicants with extra fees but simply addressing the economic reality of domestic labor recruitment and the need to work with foreign brokers. Under the guise of caring for them, its interactions with applicants are filled with reminders from Troy's brokers about the arduous process through which they have found them a job that will uplift them economically. However, this full-disclosure facade also mitigates the agency's vulnerability to applicants, who it knows ultimately have the power to report it to POEA but who it hopes can be duped enough into buying its rationale for this illegal activity. The rub is that while applicants may know about POEA rules, they are not necessarily quick to report illegal activities because having to pay a placement fee greater than a worker's one month salary is common practice within the industry. As a result, most choose an agency on the basis of which one offers the lowest fee. Troy may be violating the law but its fees of sixty-five thousand pesos are considered a bargain compared with those of others that may charge as much as one hundred thousand pesos. And from the perspective of the state, Troy believes that having to charge applicants additional fees is just the reality of the global marketplace and that instead of punishing it for this wrong-doing, the state should recognize that ultimately, agencies like Troy are able to secure this domestic labor niche and should instead relax the laws to make it easier for the industry to conduct its business.

For other agencies, caring for applicants is fundamentally about securing overseas jobs by modeling a certain kind of professionalism that makes the agency ideal as a source of labor for foreign employers. Starfleet, which prides itself on being one of the "pioneers" in the industry in sustaining a strong domestic labor market in Hong Kong, is owned by a Filipino national whose motto is "We are professional in an unprofessional industry." By this, he proudly claims that the agency does well to receive a steady stream of job orders because it offers its foreign clients workers who are *overqualified* for domestic work. This is based on the fact that 60 to 70 percent of its applicants are college graduates and that it is one of the few domestic labor providers that offer a live-in one-week training program to prospective domestic workers. This particular training provides an in-depth curriculum on housework and caregiving, tailored to the demands of employers in Hong Kong. He emphasized the fact that the workers the agency commonly send overseas are nurses and teachers who are thus able to incorporate this educational experience in their work.[28]

Because of the top-quality workforce it provides, Starfleet invests quite heavily in marketing workers through what its owner and staff members claim is the most professionally delivered videography of its applicants. These videos are sent to prospective employers to browse through and act as advertisements for Starfleet's applicants. The meticulous process through which Starfleet conducts its videography enables applicants to develop personal relations with the agency staff, who get to know and capitalize on the marketability of each candidate. For example, if they are teachers, they make sure that what they narrate on screen aptly highlights how their educational background will be an *added* asset to employers. If there are qualities or features about the applicants, such as their weight or facial appearance, that staff members believe may work to applicants' disadvantage, lessening their likelihood of getting selected, they help to concoct methods for addressing these issues on and off camera. Compared with the other domestic work agencies I studied, Starfleet exceeds by far the amount of time and effort that they spend on this process, which I illustrate in the next chapter. As with other agencies, Starfleet believes that the level of attentiveness it provides to securing overseas jobs for Filipinos proves the nature of the hard work that it performs and in ways that surpass anything that the state is able to do.

CONCLUSION

In the POEA seminar held for the private sector following the impending release of new recruitment rules and regulations, a state official ended what had been a contentious session with the following statement: "You are free to roam the paradise so long as you don't eat the forbidden fruits—overcharging applicants or deploying underage workers. So we are like Adam and Eve. We can roam the paradise so long as you don't eat these forbidden fruits or else you will die for sure" (field notes, February 27, 2002). He sought to reduce the outcry of injustice that the private sector had brought forward by characterizing the labor export arena as a paradise where the state and the private sector coexist and whose fruits (except the "forbidden" ones) they can both enjoy. But as I showed in this chapter, this paradise does not exist. This is because both actors, while they are both involved in sustaining the country's overseas employment program, marketing Filipino workers, and profiting from their remittances, have interests and positions that conflict. On the one hand, the state, as I described in the previous chapter, seeks to *manage* labor migration at the same time that it strives to uphold an image that it has workers' interests at heart. And one way it does this is by regulating the private sector, whose profit motives it deems influential in shaping its unscrupulous tendencies. The private sector, on the other hand, aims to *promote* labor migration and believes that it is its market-oriented perspective that is precisely what makes this labor export economy thrive and that the punitive and unlevel playing field in which it operates does not recognize its contribution.

In this chapter, I described how agencies carry out the brokering process through their conceptualization of their role in this process as the unrecognized "true" makers of the state's much hailed heroes. They see themselves as key partners of the state that enable Filipinos to partake in viable employment opportunities abroad. They believe that they not only are providing the means for Filipinos to elevate themselves economically and socially but also are imparting them with tools that can make them ideal representatives of their country—a goal that the Philippine state also upholds. It is in these kinds of actions that brokers establish themselves as actors who ably resuscitate Filipinos from a state of hopelessness.

As a social institution, these employment agencies do not only recruit labor but also play an instrumental role in how Filipinos come to imagine what it means to work abroad. They aggressively instill the notion that the promise of the *good life* is outside the Philippines while downplaying the various social costs of this pursuit. Their very survival depends on their ability to co-opt and shape the life aspirations and collective desires of Filipinos to migrate but also on their capacity to maintain Filipinos' competitiveness in the global economy. Unlike the state, they perceive themselves to be a creative force that is able to harness the human resources that the state is unable to support. Not only do they provide the pathways for Filipinos to earn a living wage but they do so by employing myriad techniques that respond efficiently to labor market realities.

Following the principles of neoliberal economic competitiveness, employment agencies see their role as cultivating a workforce whose members construct overseas employment as an obligation not only to their families and country but also to international relations, acting as the country's key global "contribution." In this "paradise," the private sector aims to prove that it is not made up of "leeches," as the state often seems to imply, but rather is a key force in maintaining an image of the Philippines as the home of the Great Filipino Worker and is also a creator of Filipino modern-day heroes.

CHAPTER 5

Selling Filipinas' Added Export Value

Filipinos are easy to [teach]. All they need is a little bit of training and they already know what to do. [Foreign employers] save on training costs. With very little time, they could easily adjust. There are not too many problems teaching Filipinos. Sometimes, even when the skills required for the job do not match the capability of the Filipinos hired for that job, they make it a point to deliver the kind of work and service that employers want.

—A labor broker from Holodeck, a nursing employment agency

A BRIGHT SPOTLIGHT illuminates a tiny room equipped with a television monitor and video camera. The videographer, Marco, directs a job applicant dressed in a maid's uniform to the back of the room to stand with her back against a white wall. Marco asks her to put her feet together and her heels against the wall. He gives her a cardboard sign that reads, "File #345: Maria Reyes," and tells her exactly how to hold the sign up against her chest, keeping it steady at all times. Marco views her on camera, and dissatisfied with how she looks, fixes the collar of her dress. Meanwhile, Maria observes herself on a television monitor that is connected Marco's camera, which directly faces her. "I am too fat," she says. Observing this, I find myself trying to console her, assuring her that she "looks great." Marco laughs and tells her to "get ready" and to give him that *ngiti ng mayaman* (wealthy person's smile). He encourages her to stand still as he attempts to capture her complete "body shot" while she holds her cardboard sign for about five seconds. Then, with his right hand, he motions her to come forward, to take two steps away from the wall, and then signals her to stop at the yellow line on the floor. He zooms the camera to focus on her face and, with fingers of one hand, silently counts to three; on the third count, he points to her. Maria begins reciting a scripted speech that Marco had given her the week before in which she tries to persuade her prospective employer why she would be their ideal maid (field notes, March 7, 2002).

This scene captures a typical session in the recruitment process of the agency Starfleet as it generates video representations of prospective domestic workers for Hong Kong–based employers. Employers will scrutinize these videos and from them they select a maid for their household. While this videography process is unique to domestic work recruitment, it fundamentally symbolizes the spirit of the labor export industry. Given the level of competition among labor brokers, the success of any agency in crafting a reputable and credible identity depends on its ability not only to promote a unique service, but also, and more important, to deliver workers who have the requisite skills and knowledge to perform a given job. The meticulous process through which domestic workers' videos are produced is emblematic of the process through which these *ideal* workers are manufactured for global industries that are determined to find a cost-effective workforce. Besides providing jobs to Filipinos, brokers also groom them to increase their marketability. Marco's calculated orchestration of applicants' appearance on screen mirrors a key element within the larger set of disciplinary techniques that brokers deploy to project Filipinos' comparative advantage. Labor brokers in nursing and domestic work industries endeavor to market this "advantage" through specific ideological constructions of their marked value as global labor commodities.

The construction of Filipinos as ideal nurses and domestic workers relies on the "trope of productive femininity" (Salzinger 2003, 2004) that shapes how Third World women come to be imagined as suitable laboring subjects. Although labor brokers are keenly aware of men's participation as nurses and domestic workers overseas, this trope of productive femininity guides how they inhere women with an assumed predisposition and suitability for performing nursing or domestic work. However, it is also a racialized and locally specific construct.

Alongside the popular political economic discourse that holds that the Philippines has a surplus of highly skilled labor is a naturalized view that Filipinos are cost-effective workers as a result of specific racialized and gendered behavioral attributes that determine their work ethic. As the quotation above illustrates, agencies that broker occupations such as nursing, which is disproportionately represented by women, do not market only women workers. They also sell *Filipinas*, by promoting a discourse of productive femininity rooted in a culturally essentialist logic in which the Philippines is a *natural* source of a cost-effective and desirable workforce that has innate caregiving abilities, is multiskilled, and is educated. But the invocation of and reliance on this trope come from a specific source: the trope that sustains Filipinas' *added export value* as nurses and domestic workers is created through the labor-brokering activities of employment agencies, in partnership with the state. These activities are emblematic of a "transnational web of organization and individual actors" that Kang (2002, 187) argues challenge the oft-cited economic essentialist claims that transnational capital is the only entity responsible for the identification of the Third World as a labor resource. The work of marketing Filipinas' competitive advantage, while driven by economic logic, is also deployed culturally and ideologically.

In this chapter, I illustrate another aspect of the brokering process that employment agencies perform in order to establish the Philippines as an ideal source of labor by describing their perceptions of Filipino workers' "worth" as workers and how they attempt to uphold and defend these perceptions and constructions. I compare the work of brokers in two different industries because this provides a lens for seeing how their understanding of the value of the workers who work in these occupations shape how they market Filipinos differently. I extend the concept of *productive femininity* and develop the concept of *added export value*, which highlights a racialized form of labor power that is used to construct Filipinas as ideal care workers (nurses and domestic workers) and those who are *better* than others. Just as a car manufacturer would attempt to market its competitiveness by promoting its top-of-the-line automobiles, brokers attempt to secure their credibility as foreign labor providers through the added export value of their labor commodities. I argue that the representation and hypercommodification of Filipina workers as ideal care workers is a product of a highly coordinated process that brokers initiate through the construction of their added export value, a unique Filipina labor power that serves as their global comparative advantage.[1]

"MARKETING A PRODUCT IS ALL ABOUT
MARKETING A PERCEPTION"

Employment agencies define the contours of the Philippines' labor export arena by positioning the country as a site with a lucrative labor resource. The mere presence of the agencies, along with a state infrastructure that facilitates the country's overseas employment program, makes it easy for labor-receiving nations to procure labor from the Philippines. Further, a neoliberal ethos of labor migration shapes many Filipinos' enduring professional aspirations, which are projected to be fulfilled through overseas employment. Employers, however, are not seeking to obtain any type of labor but workers who are suited to the former's labor processes. Therefore, a critical job for brokers is to figure out ways to meet the demand at the same time that they address emergent global competition. To this end, how they perceive Filipinos (and how they market such perceptions) is crucial in building their reputation of credibility. They must be seen as capable of providing jobs to Filipinos as well as supplying "ideal" labor to prospective employers. What becomes "ideal" is not simply about why Filipinos would be good workers but how they would be *better* than workers from other ethnic groups, such as Canadian nurses or Indonesian domestic workers. Regardless of their labor niche, the brokers' strategies reflect a general view of marketing upgraded labor commodities as a way to build Filipinos' comparative advantage in the global marketplace, much in the same way that the state discursively constructs Filipinos as heroes, entrepreneurs, and ambassadors of goodwill.

In the case of nursing and domestic work—care work that is constructed as in the realm of "women's work"—marketing Filipinos as upgraded commodities takes the form of selling a type of racialized productive femininity that is supposed to constitute the women's added export value. If "femininity is a trope—a structure of meaning through which workers, potential and actual, are addressed and understood and around which production itself is designed" (Salzinger 2003, 15)—then Filipinas' added export value is this type of trope, one through which foreign employers come to view women in the Philippines as workers who are "better than" others, who represent a "superior" labor commodity in the context of the Third World.

It is this understanding that undergirds the brokering process, as is revealed in a remark made by a labor broker from Tricorder

Enterprises: "Marketing a product is all about marketing a perception." The ways in which he represents Tricorder's nurses create a perception that Filipinas are better: their labor power offers employers more than what is typically available in the labor market. But what he believes makes this process difficult to realize is the perception of the Philippines as a place that is *only* able to supply domestic workers, and he adamantly calls for the government to stop the deployment of domestic workers. "We should be known for doctors. . . . When foreigners think of Filipinos, what comes to their mind are 'domestics,'" he asserted. He believed that the government should "remarket and reposition the product they are selling" in ways that build an image of the Philippines as a source of highly skilled and highly trained workers. He suggested that the state either put a ban on deploying domestic workers or "remarket" Filipino workers by finding ways of assigning a higher price to them, thereby increasing their market value. "In Europe—France or Italy—Filipino domestics are highly priced. It is a status symbol [there] if you have a Filipino nanny. They are expensive." He believed that providing training would be a key strategy for remarketing these workers (interview by the author, October 16, 2001).

Labor brokering Filipino workers' added export value also reflects the attempt of brokers (and the state) to address what they see as the perception of the Philippines as only able to provide low-skilled work. Marketing Filipinos' added export value as their comparative advantage permits them to pitch a professionalized image of the Philippines. It allows them to parade Filipinos as prized commodities who will not only offer *more than* the typical labor required of a particular job but also do so in ways that can subsequently redress the image of the Philippines as a source of only nonprofessional workers. More important, this allows brokers to ensure their profit goals as they manage their global competitiveness. They do this by describing Filipinos' readiness to migrate and, in the case of nurses and domestic workers, the unique labor that Filipinas offer.

Ready-to-Leave Filipinos

A central concern of foreign employers in doing overseas recruitment is how workers will adjust and adapt to new living and working environments. This concern partly drives how agencies promote their workplaces as having an established "Filipino community" that will serve as a social support system and perhaps mitigate any pain caused by family separation. This is especially crucial given the presence of transnational families and continued public anxieties about an emergent "care crisis" in the Philippines (Parreñas 2002a), which is claimed to be a leading cause of juvenile delinquency among Filipino youths and marital dissolution among Filipino couples. In this care crisis discourse, children of migrants suffer from the absence of a parent, usually the mother, who is often held to be the culprit. Transnational parents are well acquainted with the difficulties of separation and the estranged relations they have with the children they leave behind (Parreñas 2001a).[2] Numerous exposés have revealed the plight of Filipino workers who became victims of unscrupulous recruiters or employers, who subjected them to physical, sexual, and emotional violence, violence that is sometimes made all too visible by the number of coffins containing workers that return to the Philippines every year.[3] Thus, the Filipino public, as much as its consciousness is shaped by a strong desire to partake of the material benefits of working overseas, is also keenly aware of the not so glamorized aspects and possibilities of this journey.

This same awareness also influences labor brokers' work because it affects the ambivalence and scrutiny that workers express through questions they ask and those that employers may construe as indication of their readiness to leave. Like that of Philippine state officials, the response of brokers is to promote the notion that Filipinos possess a natural capacity for migration through their so-called innate sense of adventure or to attribute workers' readiness to leave to overseas career aspirations. A broker from Tricorder explained that when British foreign employers inquire into the readiness of Filipinos to go overseas and be separated from their families, his immediate response is to say that this is not an issue, because "fortunately, Filipinos, especially nurses, when they are in school, they are already prepared to leave, they are already psychologically ready" (interview by the author, October 16, 2001). He was also promoting the readiness of Filipino nurses by reflecting an emerging general public critique that held that Filipinos were pursuing nursing as a ticket to leave the Philippines and often as a pathway to working in the United States—a pursuit that was made possible by another wave of nurse shortages that the country faced.

During a 2001 conference organized by the Philippine Nursing Association and the Philippine Nursing Association of America in Manila, this critique was particularly apparent: the role of Filipino nurses in alleviating the global nurse shortage was a central issue.[4] One speaker highlighted the changing dynamics of the educational instruction and training that Filipino nurses were receiving, characterizing the transformation as the "internationalization of the Philippine nursing curriculum." These changes have been brought about by the increased presence of "foreign visitors" who have become influential in altering the structure of the Philippine curriculum in ways that they claim meet global demands for nursing practice and, in turn, contribute to the competitiveness of Filipinos."

Meanwhile, the celebrated view of Filipino nurses as playing a prominent role in filling global labor shortages prompted some panicked and disappointed responses from other nurses at the conference. At one point during an open forum, a self-proclaimed female nurse bravely stepped up to the podium and asked, "What is being done to keep Filipino nurses in the country? Where is the virtue of serving one's country rather than thinking of going abroad?" She then exclaimed, "The labor-receiving country is the only one benefiting from this! Are these nurses returning anything to the Philippines in terms of their contribution to [the] education [of other nurses]?" (field notes, December 21, 2001). Such critical assertions, however, quickly faded away as others clutched onto the rhetoric of "opportunity" and "choice," reminding each other that overseas employment was a product of people's freedom to do what they believed was necessary for survival. Given the predominance of such a muted reaction, it may not be surprising that brokers such as the one quoted above not only capitalize on the idea that pursuing overseas employment for Filipinos is a natural desire but also claim that it is a familiar idea, one that stems from a degree of calculated social and educational preparation.

References to the schooling of Filipinos as a key site for preparing them for overseas employment and nurturing this desire also reflects how an ethos of labor migration is cultivated in the Philippines. In the schools, Filipinos learn the skills for becoming nurses as well as dream of providing this service to other nations. Representing Filipinos as "already psychologically ready" allows brokers to appease foreign employers about Filipinos' awareness of and ambivalence about the difficulties of working in a foreign environment, especially in the absence of any familial support. The factor of psychological readiness can be interpreted as an added bonus for foreign employers, whose principal concern is to find workers who are ready to work with minimal supervision, support, and mentoring.

Brokers also promote Filipinos' readiness to leave as stemming from the economic power that the workers derive from their overseas earnings. While some brokers believe that overseas Filipino workers endure the pain of family separation, isolation in a foreign country, or oppressive work situations because they envision these situations as temporary, the reality dictates otherwise and some end up renewing their labor contracts. A broker from Troy International reasoned that Filipino workers may decide to work overseas not solely to fulfill their desire to make a living wage. She opined that it could pertain to the fact that they did not save any money, a phenomenon sometimes characterized as the fault of the spouse. It could also be that they "enjoy the country they went to." In most cases, she explained, it was perhaps the case that they wanted to maintain the material rewards of working overseas. "When Filipinos experience earning a lot of money, they don't quit," she asserted. "Once they've built a house, they won't just be content with that. Next would be another piece of land, a car, a store. Sometimes, as is common in the Filipino culture, they go out of the country out of envy. They say, 'My neighbor has a lot of these things so I need to go abroad so I can buy those too' " (interview by the author, January 30, 2002).

She offered a different rationale for understanding Filipinos' sense of readiness, claiming that it was fundamentally shaped by economic forces in ways that cannot solely be attributed to their family's economic dependency on their earnings. Rather, it might also stem from a resulting desire to support and maintain new lifestyles. In her narrative, Filipinos experience a newfound class identity that drives them to pursue a kind of consumerism that some brokers attribute to workers' addiction to the buying power of their earnings or, at times, a result of their envy of other people's material possessions. Using a culturally essentialist logic, this broker painted envy for the consumption of material goods as an innate cultural trait of Filipinos.

Filipino workers' readiness to work abroad is also often attributed to a lack of preparedness to and ambivalence toward returning to the

Philippines. Brokers argue that Filipino workers' experiences overseas have transformed the latter's everyday lifestyle expectations in ways that make it difficult for them to go back home. Constable's (1999) study of Filipina domestic workers in Hong Kong revealed just such an ambivalence felt by workers about returning home that was born out of a sense of estrangement from their families. Brokers capitalize on this factor but emphasize that returning workers become estranged from Philippine culture. A labor broker from Tricorder, who exemplified those making this observation about overseas workers, explained that Filipino workers who return to the Philippines after many years of working overseas end up experiencing a bittersweet homecoming because they have difficulty adjusting to a lifestyle and environment that have become foreign to them. He reasoned, "When they get here they just die of boredom. They can no longer tolerate the heat, the pollution, because they are used to a certain lifestyle." A worker from Saudi Arabia, he went on, may actually find the lifestyle there easier in terms of everyday living. But in the Philippines, "You have the traffic, pollution, and heat. You have to commute, you have to fight your way through the streets. Some die of high blood pressure because they have become 'soft.' This is the real life. They suffer a lot here. So they go back" (interview by the author, October 22, 2001).

Brokers often add this kind of rationale as a factor that also explains why migrants may not necessarily return home to permanently settle in the Philippines. Using a discourse of suffering, brokers deploy and rely on a construction of foreign nations as places of comfort, luxury, and the so-called good life and the Philippines as a place of hardship. In this discourse, befitting the culture of sacrifice that the Philippine state promotes, Filipinos are again portrayed as suffering migrants but whose anguish is caused by a harsher environment—the "real life"—that no longer can accommodate their newfound sensibilities. Any difficulties that workers may face overseas are rendered invisible in a narrative that creates a glamorized and idealized facade of working and living abroad. This situation, in turn, enables brokers who must defend Filipinos' preparedness to work abroad to pitch their comparative advantage as derived from the workers' unpreparedness to return, which employers are supposed to interpret as a good indication of Filipinos' commitment to succeed and thrive overseas.

Educated Nurses with Tender Loving Care and Flexibility

While brokers market a perception of Filipinos as ready-to-leave workers, they also further specify their added export value based on the occupation they will perform. How they construct the desirability of Filipino workers depends on their perceptions of a given occupation and the individuals most suitable for performing this work. In the case of nursing recruitment, a central task of brokers is to market a perception that Filipinos offer a kind of value that will readily identify them as ideal nurses who can maintain and adapt to their specific health care standards.

The packaging of Filipino nurses' value relies on a combination of factors. First, all nurse brokers identify the source of nurses' fundamental worth and typical qualifications as a four-year bachelor's degree in nursing training, U.S.-patterned education, and English-language competency. It is a kind of representation that is made possible through the country's colonial history, which has left the Philippines with an educational system that is a legacy of U.S. occupation. As Choy (2003) illustrates, the colonial presence of the United States in the Philippines and the establishment of a U.S.-based nursing curriculum that emphasizes a U.S.-oriented work culture and English-language proficiency became preconditions for creating a labor force suitable for the United States. This colonial legacy defined the late twentieth century mass migration of Filipino nurses to the United States and continues to enable brokers to package Filipinas' professional competence.

Alongside the aggressive promotion of a Filipino workforce with the basic value of professional competence, brokers emphasize Filipinos' added export value on the basis of a characterization of nursing as essentially women's work and, by default, foreground women as the primary providers of this labor. Even though they do not necessarily exclude men from the pool and in fact do send men to perform nursing work, they insist that nursing is exclusively in the realm of women's work and that Filipinas are exceptionally suited to providing it. Some would go so far as to reason that men are qualified to the extent that they can be effeminate or model qualities that are believed to be innate to women. A broker from Tricorder had this to say:

> The perception is that nursing is really a more feminine type of work because it is a job that requires caring. Males are not as inclined to

provide caring to other people, unlike females, who are intrinsically caring people. There are also quite a bit of males [in nursing] but of this group, there are only a [few] "real men" . . . as in they are gay. The staff here can confirm that. A majority of them are gay men. It's a profession where you have to show a lot of caring and that is not a normal thing for male Filipinos (interview by the author, October 22, 2001).

In providing this explanation, the broker wanted me to understand that his perspective is not unique, that this is a sentiment shared by other brokers. Certainly, it is a sentiment that reflects gendered norms about care work. This is evident in his characterization of nursing as being feminine because "it requires caring" and that women, as opposed to men, are naturally better in providing this service because caring is intrinsic to womanhood. However, this logic allows him to make a rather problematic claim that Filipino men who participate in this occupation are not living up to culturally appropriate norms of masculinity and to attribute their desire to do nursing as indicative of homosexuality. Meanwhile, he also invoked *appropriate femininity* by imposing heterosexuality on female nurses. Grounded in this ideological framework, the added export value that brokers ascribe to Filipino nurses is necessarily gendered and heterosexual, illustrating the productive femininity that they will provide foreign employers.

Specifically, brokers market Filipinas as "ideal" nurses by virtue of the latter's perceived innate capability to do care work with a degree of *tender loving care* (TLC), which they illuminate variously. One way they do so is by characterizing this TLC as Filipinas' intrinsic sense of compassion. A broker from Tricorder noted, "Filipinos have been trained to take care of [their] elders, unlike those from other countries. When you go to another country, it is very natural for the Filipino to take care of patients because they do that at home, they do that with [their] relatives. Filipinos will be trained to be more compassionate, to be more caring. . . . That is why it is very natural" (interview by the author, October 16, 2001).

This imputed natural capacity to provide tender loving healthcare that grows out of a culturally prescribed duty to provide elder care is what brokers often claim has instilled in Filipinas skills that are easily transferable to nursing work and thus, defines their competitive edge. Along with this sense of compassion, this TLC also originates in what brokers describe as Filipinas' patience and uninhibited dedication to their work. A broker from Holodeck insisted, "Our nurses here in the Philippines are much more patient. You know how Filipinas are when it comes to domestic types of jobs—they give it everything they've got. Some of the feedback that we get is that when you send Filipina nurses overseas, they do not have these inhibitions when it comes to work. They don't [make so many] demands, unlike other nurses like the North Americans—Canadians" (interview by the author, October 27, 2001). Similarly, a broker from Exocomp remarked, "Even when it is difficult or they [Filipina nurses] are suffering, they still work. We require female nurses because they say that females are more efficient in setting up the hospital" (interview by the author, November 9, 2001).

The racialization of Filipinas' added export value becomes evident here as brokers sell this TLC as their comparative advantage over another group such as Canadians. This sentiment of being better than another group was echoed in a recruitment seminar featuring hospitals in New York and California. At the seminar, an immigration lawyer working on behalf of the hospitals repeatedly declared to a group of ten nurses, "You are needed. You are needed everywhere; isn't that nice to be needed? Filipinos are loyal and ethical, unlike Canadian nurses, who will break a contract and go to the next better offer. Filipinos are not like that" (field notes, November 13, 2001).[5] In this proclamation, this broker aimed to construct Filipinos as compassionate and caring not only toward their patients but also toward their employers, to whom they responded with loyalty and the commitment to completing their contracts.[6]

This TLC can also be attributed to Filipinas' supposed hospitality and their pleasing and comforting nature. As a broker from Tricorder stated, "Unlike Brits [British nurses], who are rougher, our nurses have TLC. *Pinays* [Filipino women] are sweet, hospitable, smile a lot. They are hygienic and clean with their bodies" (interview by the author, October 22, 2001). Similarly, a broker from Holodeck insisted that "the female touch is just different when it comes to caring" (interview by the author, October 27, 2001). As is reflected in these narratives, when brokers discursively construct Filipina nurses' comparative advantage through their capacity for TLC, they also promote a highly sexualized representation.

Not only do Filipinas provide a much gentler and welcoming "touch," they also offer a sanitized physical body that may strategically mask their foreignness to the extent that it is "fit" for public consumption.

This racialized and sexualized discourse of Filipina nurses' productive femininity can be read as being indebted to the country's long history of colonization, which depicts Filipinas as subservient and compliant service providers, not only in domestic labor but also in sex work (Chang and Groves 2000; Eviota 1992). The thriving sex industry in the Philippines is a remnant of the presence of U.S. military bases, which created the so-called rest and relaxation (R&R) industry, in which young and poverty-stricken women emerged as "hospitality girls"; "go-go dancers/entertainers"; "comfort women"; and most recently, "guest relations officers" (Sturdevant and Stoltzfus 1992). The kind of "caring" nurses that brokers promote can be interpreted as a crucial product of this history and not so much of Filipino women's culture, per se.

Another way in which brokers rearticulate this image of Filipinas' subservience is by pointing to their perceived flexibility and durability as another added export value. By *flexibility*, brokers refer to an innate willingness of Filipina nurses to assume multiple work responsibilities with minimal resistance. A labor broker who worked as a nurse in Saudi Arabia and is now the operations manager of Riker Manpower Services enumerated that "some of the Westerners, particularly the nurses, only want to be managers. They don't want to work at the bedside. It's mostly Filipinos who work at the bedside and on site. Non-Filipino nurses want to manage, meaning [they want to assume] higher positions so they cannot be like Filipinos who can do all the jobs [in the hospital]" (interview by the author, November 20, 2001). Following this logic, Filipinas are made to be "better," because they can perform a wide variety of tasks and their lack of aspirations for occupational mobility allows them to assume these tasks—many of which are undesirable—willingly.

Brokers also capitalize on the fact that Filipinos' flexibility as workers results from their trainability, which is a cost-effective factor for employers. A labor broker from Holodeck proudly pointed out that that "Filipinos are easy to [teach]. All they need is a little bit of training and they already know what to do. . . . With very little time, they could easily adjust. . . . Sometimes, even when the skills required for the job do not match the capability of the Filipinos hired for that job, they make it a point to deliver the kind of work and service that employers want" (interview by the author, October 27, 2001). This adaptability and self-initiative, according to brokers, help constitute Filipino's added export value. They also build on characterizing a certain kind of flexibility whereby Filipino nurses can act as responsive automatons who can readily mold themselves into the type of workers that their employers want, able to fulfill their varied expectations.

Obedient and Overqualified Maids

Some brokers, especially those who recruit professional workers such as nurses, often scorn continuing state support for the recruitment of domestic workers from the Philippines. Agencies such as Tricorder claim that this support only reifies the traditional conception of the Philippines as a source of low-skilled workers, downgrades the image of the country, and hurts the ability of brokers to market Filipino nurses. On the other hand, domestic work brokers profit from and count on this image. Historically, foreign employers naturalize domestic work as the work of Filipinas, so they use the terms *domestic helper* (Constable 1997a, 1997b) *nanny* (Pratt 1998), and *Filipina* interchangeably. Thus, domestic work recruitment revolves around the notion that domestic work is "women's work" and that Filipinas are especially fit to perform it.

Even if brokers are aware of men working as domestics overseas, they hold on to the premise that women are more suitable for this kind of work. "A DH [domestic helper] position is only for women," remarked a broker from Troy International. She explained that the one reason why men may be seen employed as domestic workers may have to do with accommodating to the physical demands of patients whose bodies may be too difficult for women to lift. She added that the preference for women domestic workers had to do with the following factors: "Women are much more organized and detail oriented in the house compared to men. Women have less desire to go out [to see friends or sightsee]. They cannot court people, unlike men, who go out courting girls" (interview by the author, January 30, 2002). Brokers like her put forth the gendered notion that women possess the kind of inherent discipline that is required in order to deliver domestic labor efficiently. In this case, not having any desire for leisure or romantic pursuits make them ideal domestic workers

for employers who prefer, and oftentimes expect, their maids to be readily available at all hours of the day.

Unlike in the case of Filipina nurses, the way that brokers market the
"basic" value of Filipina domestic workers revolves around behavioral
traits that are ideal for domestic labor. Their basic selling point for all
Filipina domestics is that the latter possess the qualities expected of and
preferred in a servant: obedient, hardworking, God-fearing, loyal, cooperative, and compliant. As a broker from Troy International put it,
"Filipinos have this very strong stress tolerance. Most Filipinos don't
know how to complain and they just keep on saying, 'Yes, yes, sir,
madam,' just to be able to finish the contract without any fights or conflict" (interview by the author, January 30, 2002).

These qualities highlight workers' subservience and submissiveness
to authority, which accord with the typical employers' most often preferred hierarchy in the household. Similar to what Hondagneu-Sotelo
(2001) found in her study of Latina domestic workers and their employers, these are also qualities that reify employers' perception of their role
as consumers, rather than employers, of domestic labor. These characteristics assure employers that the labor commodities they purchase will
provide optimal service as round-the-clock automatons and will do so
with minimal disruption in the intimate space of the household into
which they will be incorporated. Moreover, their so-called high tolerance of stress makes them ideal servants insofar as they relieve employers
from worrying about how the isolation and foreignness of their work
situation can potentially affect their job performance.

However, brokers explained that the competition from countries
like Indonesia and Sri Lanka and the varied and rigorous demands of
employers for highly skilled domestic workers threaten the position of
the Philippines as a leading provider of domestic labor, thereby increasing the need to emphasize Filipinas' added value as maids. Brokers
attempt to accomplish this task of emphasizing workers' added value by
representing Filipinas as educated, multiskilled, and trainable servants—
all of which are qualities that seemingly contribute to "upgrading" them,
much in the same way that reflects the Philippine state's efforts to professionalize their domestic labor recruitment. As the owner of Starfleet
boasted, "Filipinos are the Mercedes Benz—they are educated, literate,
English speaking, possess a good work ethic. They don't complain, they

are quiet, and they keep to themselves—and they are trainable." And by this he was referring to the fact that most of his agency's applicants were college graduates and not individuals who were already employed as domestic workers. In fact, he claimed that many were nurses or teachers. "Nurses would rather work as a DH [domestic helper] in Hong Kong than as a nurse in Saudi because of the pay of working as a domestic worker there," he reasoned (interview by the author, February 26, 2002).

Filipina domestic workers' added value as educated, skilled, and trainable servants are often attributed to their "two-for-one" value. Noel Josue, executive director of Kaibigan ng OCWs (Friends of Overseas Contract Workers), an NGO providing social and legal services to migrant workers, summed it up by saying that with these qualities, "You have a [maid] and a tutor at the same time" (interview by the author, April 25, 2002). By this he was alluding to the capacity of many Filipina domestic workers to provide employers with additional tutoring services for their children who may need assistance with their schoolwork or for family members who may want to learn English. Indeed, as Lan (2003b) demonstrates in her study of Filipina domestic workers and their employers, the English-language proficiency of Filipina domestic workers contributes to elevating the status of their employers, who boast that they have hired "educated" maids. With employers in the role of consumers, the seemingly top-of-the-line labor commodity that they have purchased (the "Mercedes Benz" of domestic workers) serves as the family's status symbol, to be paraded by the family and envied by other employers.

Unlike in the case of Filipina nurses, whose added export value is based on a kind of feminized trait such as TLC, for Filipina domestic workers, the added export value is just the opposite. Filipina maids challenge the perception of domestic work as a job that is performed by uneducated and unskilled individuals. Brokers market them aggressively as individuals who are overqualified for doing domestic work, thereby making it seem as if an employer would be lucky to have one of these workers. A Filipina maid becomes a fetishized commodity (Marx 1867/1978) or a prized acquisition that provides employers extra services without the additional costs. The comparative advantage that Filipinas may gain in the global market as highly sought out maids because of their representation as educated and overqualified for domestic labor does not necessarily entail salaries that are commensurate with their added export value and, therefore, does not pose any additional costs to employers. And that is the bitter rub of it all.

SATISFACTION GUARANTEED

If brokers are going to painstakingly represent Filipinas' desirability as care workers, then they must ensure that they can, indeed, generate them. Mohanty (1997, 5) notes that "global assembly lines are as much about the production of people as they are about 'providing jobs' or making profit." Labor brokers are in the business of not only marketing perceptions about Filipinos' added value, but more important, also guaranteeing that they can obtain workers who would fulfill whatever kind of work processes and organization they wish to implement. They are in the business of selling "high quality" labor commodities, and a principal way of doing so is through the practice of "manpower sourcing/pooling."

The goal of manpower sourcing/pooling is to generate a sufficient lineup of workers following receipt or in anticipation of an overseas job order request.[7] Many agencies place advertisements in newspapers, on television, or on the radio to lure applicants to their offices. But in most cases, they rely on word of mouth and on the reputation of credibility that they build with applicants, whom they are able to successfully and quickly place overseas. But generating a sufficient labor pool is only the first step. In order to ensure that they have ideal candidates who possess the added export value of which they proudly boast, agencies employ strategies that best suit the type of labor they are marketing, those of which are best represented by activities such as headhunting, household work training programs, and applicant coaching.

Headhunting

Agencies that market nurses rely heavily on "headhunting"—the practice of going to particular places to find candidates who are believed to possess the qualifications that employers are likely to find attractive. In some cases, the term refers to activities in which an agency, through its internal contacts and connections, makes informal visits to hospitals to announce job openings by distributing fliers or holding informational seminars. A labor broker from Holodeck Placement explained that going to "strategic areas" to find the workers the agency needed was the best way to fill job orders that often required specialized training. For example, if a job order required nurses with specialized cardiac care training, the agency then recruited from hospitals that were known for providing this specialized care. The visits sometimes become more regular, as in the case of Tricorder, which employs a group of recruitment specialists who regularly makes hospital visits throughout Manila in order to make their recruitment services visible and who proudly boasted that they typically obtained their nurses from two of the main private hospitals there and those who were nursing graduates of top Philippine universities.

But typically, headhunting happens more formally, as provincial recruitment activities (PRAs). Through PRAs, labor brokers travel to various provinces to conduct recruitment seminars. Unlike in the case of informal headhunting techniques, agencies who conduct PRAs must first secure an authorization from the Philippine Overseas Employment Agency (POEA) and from local government units. PRAs are important because of what brokers perceive are differences between provincial and city applicants and the ease with which they can often market a particular job. A labor broker from Riker Manpower explained that its PRAs took it to the southern Philippines, where there is a predominantly Muslim population, in order to obtain nurses for its Saudi Arabia market. The broker explained that the nurses the brokers find in Manila most likely were dead set on going to the United Kingdom or the United States. She suggested that this could be attributed to the "modern mentalities" of Filipinos. "So if you want to get nurses going to Saudi Arabia, definitely, you have to go to the far provinces," she stated (interview by the author, November 20, 2001).

By "modern mentalities," she was referring to the preference of most Filipinos to work in urban and cosmopolitan instead of rural areas (in this case, the desert) overseas. This is compounded by their knowledge of the cultural customs and laws in Saudi Arabia that impose restrictions in clothing and public conduct of women in ways that lead Filipinos to interpret these differences as an "unmodern" way of living. Many of them would opt not to work and live there. More immediately, this labor broker had just spoken to two applicants who did not want to work in Saudi Arabia because of their perception that its hospitals were not "modern enough" in the technologies they used. Such labor brokers often claimed that it was easier to convince applicants in the provinces because their technical expectations would not be as high as those of nurses in Manila who had worked in more "modern" hospitals.

But perhaps this is not the full story. Labor brokers themselves commented that nurses who work in the provinces earn as little as 2,500 pesos ($62) a month compared with about 12,000 pesos ($298) earned by those working in Manila hospitals. Going to the "far provinces," then, makes it easier for labor brokers to guarantee the availability of workers who can settle for lower compensation packages than what they would have to offer Manila-based applicants. It also supports their claim that Filipina nurses do not have "too many inhibitions" or "salary demands" because they are already underpaid in the Philippines. PRAs function as a practical means of meeting brokers' ideological constructions of Filipinos as ideal nurses.

Creating and Displaying Well-Trained Maids

While headhunting and PRAs are key nurse recruitment strategies, domestic placement agencies are able to deliver and produce domestic workers who offer more than the typical service by requiring their applicants to undergo a rigorous household work training program. Similar training programs exist in other labor export countries such as Indonesia (Rudnyckyj 2004), where prospective domestic workers are not simply taught these household skills but are trained in how to behave as a servant. This was the case even before POEA's series of policy changes that now require every domestic worker to obtain a certificate of competency in household work from TESDA. At the time of my fieldwork in 2001–2002, many domestic placement agencies already required their applicants to obtain the needed competency in household work and caregiving from one of the many training centers in the Philippines. This requirement was in response to the then escalating complaints of foreign employers about workers' household work skills such as the inability to use particular household appliances or provide infant and elderly care or simply the inability to provide a level of household maintenance that would meet with the desires of employers. Starfleet is one of these agencies that is particularly proud of the "quality" of its applicants, all of whom have undergone an intensive live-in one-week training. Starfleet's

owner explained that this training is especially crucial for their applicants, a majority of whom are college graduates and are, therefore, "not
accustomed to being a domestic helper in a foreign land" (interview by
the author, February 26, 2002).

In nurse recruitment, prospective employers and applicants typically
have an opportunity for face-to-face meetings; domestic work recruitment operates differently. Domestic work agencies rely on representing
their applicants on "biodata" and personalized videos, both of which
they send to their foreign brokers, who make them available to prospective employers.[8] Personalized videos range from four to six minutes; their
production typically follows the scene I described at the beginning of the
chapter. Domestic work classified ads routinely highlight secondary education as a minimum requirement alongside behavioral attributes such as
"hardworking, trustworthy, humble, and obedient," all of which coalesce
in those personalized videos. Labor brokers tell me that the videos
mainly function to allow prospective employers to see, scrutinize, and
evaluate the physical characteristics and communication skills of prospective maids. Foreign employers typically have the following questions:
Do they speak "good English" and with minimal accents? Do they have
any facial deformities that would be considered "bad luck" in the family?
Are they "too fat?"—this last characteristic being one they equate with
laziness.

Starfleet takes these questions seriously and into account when they
produce the personalized videos and attempt to showcase the skills and
added value of their applicants. On the videos, employers hear applicants
describe their educational background, their domestic work experience,
and the reason why they are applying for overseas work. But the videos
also describe, in minute detail, the applicants' strategies for managing a
household from the time they wake up to the time that they go to bed,
sometimes highlighting any unique expertise they can provide families,
such as infant care. This "scientific management" of work tasks would
make Frederick Taylor (1911) proud, mirroring what he believed was
key to the success of any labor process—controlling *who* performs the
labor and *how* the laborer delivers the work.

To this end, Starfleet's applicants receive a scripted narrative that
contains a detailed description of what they need to project on screen.
Not only are they instructed to memorize and recite this narrative

verbatim on video but they are supposed to do it without blinking, smiling, or stuttering. Then, the video features them responding to questions they receive verbally from the videographer that aim to feature their notable skills, education, or work experience. Since many of the applicants are college graduates, the agency strives to represent this background as bonus qualities by asking relevant questions, for example, "As a college graduate, what can you contribute to your employer?" The applicant is supposed to show that this added value will not hinder her ability to perform domestic work. Thus, a typical applicant responds by describing how her education can be an asset to her employer because she can provide additional tutorial services to children in the household. "I can help your children do their homework or learn English," they may announce in the video.

Starfleet believes that it is not sufficient to simply say that it has well-trained applicants; it must show exactly how. It does this through what it calls "action shots," which it incorporates in the videos. The action shots feature an applicant performing a household task (such as bathing a baby, cleaning, or cooking) depending on what best highlights her expertise and attests to her training. In one such shot, an applicant appeared in a bathroom to demonstrate the myriad ways that she will clean each section of this space. In another, an applicant showcased her infant caregiving skills by appearing in front of a washbasin holding an infant doll and describing the ways in which she will bathe, clothe, and feed the infant. In yet another shot, an applicant appeared in a kitchen and displayed her skills in preparing Filipino and Chinese food. These action shots complete the process of ensuring employers a docile workforce as well as modeling labor commodities who are capable of reproducing a disciplined labor process.

Agencies such as Starfleet count on the quality of images represented in these videos and therefore, depend on being able to represent well-trained and skilled commodities and, more important, disciplined subjects. The meticulous process through which the videos are produced indicates the effort that agencies place on ensuring the construction of workers' docility at every stage of the recruitment process. Some employers, for example, prefer applicants who meet a particular weight because of the perception that it is directly correlated to food consumption and energy level. As a result, when Starfleet gets applicants who do not have this ideal body weight, the applicants often engage in informal agreements to lose weight prior to their departure and monitor their progress to ensure a successful outcome (see also Constable 1997a).

Through the personalized videos, labor brokers sell a diverse pool of workers with varying expertise on household and caregiving work and offer foreign employers an opportunity to make individual assessments of and "handpick" the labor commodity that best suits their needs. Labor brokers rest on the fact that they are lining up the most qualified, top-of-the-line candidates—a product of the rigorous recruitment process that they have implemented, whether by scouring different locations to find their workers, by requiring specific kinds of skill-based training, or by meticulously ensuring that their workers are represented in the best possible way. Employers are clearly treated as consumers, who if for some reason find themselves dissatisfied with their selection, can be comforted by the ninety-day guarantee that agencies provide them. With this guarantee, they can request another worker—a pricey promise that agencies hope never to have to fulfill.

Coaching Applicants

Being able to coach applicants into becoming the ideal worker they project is central to the work of labor brokers. A good deal of their work revolves around socially conditioning and training prospective workers to adhere to a specific mindset as a means of successfully finishing their contracts. It is in this process that brokers designate applicants as being primarily responsible for their success by promoting amicable working relations with their employers. The "social support" they offer workers in order to help them cope with difficult work relations or employers privileges the interests of employers. As Marx (1867/1978) noted, the labor process and its products belong to and are the property of the capitalists who purchased the materials that underlie this process. Filipino workers are the labor commodities that foreign employers purchase and whose labor power they own and control. And in a competitive global marketplace where foreign employers receive other bids (and possibly lower ones), how workers accept this reality wholeheartedly is instrumental to their survival and success overseas.

Coaching Filipino workers so that they understand and accept their subservient positions undergirds the social support that brokers provide them. This is a conceptualization that I certainly did not expect. Given that POEA holds agencies "jointly and solidarily liable" for the workers they recruit, I expected that brokers needed to assist applicants in potentially dealing with employers who may exploit and violate their labor contracts by imposing unreasonable or inhumane working conditions. But what became apparent was that brokers regard employers as their primary client and therefore, any support they provide applicants privilege the interests of their employers. A labor broker from the Exocomp Staffing Services nursing agency, remarked:

> During [our] pre-departure orientation seminar, I always inculcate in the [minds] of the applicants that when they reach their destination, [they] are there to work. [I tell them], "If you have any problems, you can write to us. If you are having problems, like your employer is strict or you don't like the system of your company, it's the same thing in the Philippines, there is *no guarantee* that you will have a good employer, a good system. Otherwise, you can just come back here and put up your own business and have your own system. There is no guarantee that your employer will have this kind of good system. You have to adjust and you should be flexible" (interview by the author, November 10, 2001; emphasis in the original).

Just as brokers complain that the labor export field is unlevel because of the power that the state holds over the private sector, it is also unleveled from the perspective of workers. If employers are dissatisfied with a worker, they have tremendous bargaining power through which to receive a replacement. However, if workers are dissatisfied with their employer, they are reminded that their only option is to return to the Philippines; and they are left with primary responsibility for resolving conflicts with their employers. Brokers generally explain that their overseas workers could correspond with them by letter, e-mail, or phone when problems arise, but with the understanding that they, the workers, first need to work through the difficulties on their own, before contacting the agency.

This becomes problematic particularly in cases in which labor brokers are fully aware of the increasing prevalence of sexual harassment and abuse in the workplace, especially in the Middle East. In one instance, a labor broker from an agency marketing nurses to Saudi Arabia commented off the record that in recognition of this "reality," he tries to prepare nurses during their pre-departure orientation seminars how to "watch out" for such possibilities. However, I was disturbed to find out that not only does his agency fail to offer them any protective mechanisms for dealing with these issues, he also seemed to find these instances somewhat amusing and not worthy of serious consideration or critical intervention from the agency.[9] This same broker had previously remarked that one of the most desirable qualities of Filipino workers was their capacity to "endure difficult situations." Thus, conditioning them to rely on themselves as their primary means of social support and holding them responsible for their relations with employers is precisely how this labor broker can claim that Filipino workers have a capacity to endure and tolerate difficult situations. By training them to be "flexible" and to "adjust" to their employers' work standards, authority, and power, labor brokers can fulfill their guarantees to their foreign clientele of a docile Filipino workforce.

Moreover, nursing labor brokers, aware of the fact that some of the nurses they send may be overqualified for the kind of work that they will actually perform overseas, must also condition applicants to make sure that they do not undermine their supervisor's authority. The president of Tricorder Enterprises, which markets Filipino nurses to the United Kingdom, explained that Filipino nurses are generally "better" than British nurses primarily because of the quality of nursing education in the Philippines, which offers a bachelor's degree, as noted earlier, unlike the United Kingdom. Upon the arrival of the nurses in the United Kingdom, a typical feedback he receives from Filipinos is that they are far more "advanced" in their training than what might be expected, given the kind of work that their British supervisors instruct them to carry out. In order not to threaten their supervisors' authority, this labor broker remarked, the nurses practice "a self-imposed discipline" in which "they tell themselves not to act better [than their supervisors]" and simply defer to their authority (interview by the author, October 22, 2001). To the extent that this has become a "self-imposed" discipline, it is a result of the fact that it is precisely how labor brokers have conditioned the workers to behave. Filipino nurses are supposed to internalize the notion that while one of their primary objectives in working overseas is to grow professionally, regardless of their training and knowledge they have to abide by their supervisor's rules and practices.

For domestic workers, the notion that they are their employers' property is even more emphasized. They are supposed to understand that their employers have purchased them as household servants and, as consumers, the employers have certain "rights" over the workers' livelihood. A conversation that I had with the operations manager of Troy International about the support they offer to their employers and workers best exemplified this view. As with other domestic placement agencies, Troy works with a local broker who is supposed to monitor the working conditions of the workers the agency sends overseas, so a worker going to Hong Kong, for example, is supposed to be managed by a Hong Kong–based agency.[10] In cases in which problems arise between employers and their workers, this local broker is supposed to relay the case to Troy, which will then intervene and attempt to resolve the problem; according to this operations manager, this often entails requesting employers to "give the worker another chance."

Troy also fields complaints from workers, which often culminates in situations in which brokers must reaffirm the nature of the work itself. As this broker told me, "Workers might tell us that the employer is cruel or unkind. And what I tell her is that the cruelty or unkindness of the employer is *natural*. It is the *privilege* of every employer to be mean and cruel. If they yell at you or scold you every day, you have to accept it because that is part of your job. When you have your own housemaid, then you can do the same thing" (interview by the author, March 18, 2002; emphases added). Characterizing this statement as a form of "counseling," she admitted that sometimes her job requires her to find ways of lightening up difficult employment situations in which workers may find themselves and at times having to intervene when the "workers just cannot handle it anymore." But ultimately, she held the view that while the job of brokers is about helping workers find a job, it is also, and more important, about educating them to accept the nature of domestic work. Simply put, "We explain to all our applicants how hard it is to serve people so they are prepared emotionally."

This particular broker, who also possessed overseas work experience, believed that the problems that workers sometimes experienced grew from their inability to embrace their positions as servants. She interpreted employer guarantees and worker social support as issues pertaining to the ways that workers themselves must single-handedly manage their work performance in ways that honor their employers' authority. It is this logic that allows brokers like herself to impose a greater demand on workers to secure their jobs and relations with their employers. They teach workers to discipline themselves to comply and accept what is supposed to be this "natural" situation, of being maltreated by their employers. It is only when workers "just cannot handle it anymore" that labor brokers feel obligated to intervene on their behalf.

What, then, are the conditions that warrant a response from labor brokers? Do workers have to be sexually or physically abused before brokers will act? Labor brokers simply asserted that workers need to be able to justify their inability to withstand their employer's behavior toward them. They were referring to the fact that they are more likely to honor the workers' wishes of transferring to another work site if they can establish that they are in immediate danger or that there is a clear and present possibility that they are suffering from something greater than verbal abuse.[11] After all, labor brokers believe that such verbal maltreatment from employers and their inability to view domestic workers' personhood is a *natural* occurrence. Some brokers also believe that cases of maltreatment result from workers' laziness or inability to do their job, as in, for example, their improperly using and damaging household appliances, such that costly damages were incurred by employers.

Agencies, like the Philippine state, are quick to remind workers that they are not simply workers but are representatives of the Philippines. Therefore, they are obligated to protect the country's image as a labor provider. The owner and president of Troy International complained about the dissatisfaction and disappointment he felt toward those he perceived as *misbehaving* Filipino workers who engage in illicit activities such as gambling, theft, and prostitution. This is a sentiment he echoed in a pre-departure orientation session his agency provided to individuals leaving for Hong Kong and Israel to work as domestic workers as he strived to remind them of their moral "obligation" to uphold the image of the Philippines. "When you are in Hong Kong and you end up behaving unfavorably, the name of Filipino workers will be marred, especially that of the Filipina. When you steal and kill, the name of the Filipino worker is blemished," he said. He encouraged them to "take pride" in

their country by reexamining the way they work. He offered a cautionary view:"If the only reason you went overseas is because you envied the
appliances that your neighbors own, then, of course, that envy which
motivated you to work will not be enough because you are not determined to face the hardships there. But if you go there because you want
your child or family to be economically uplifted, then you will sacrifice.
This is a sacrifice. Therefore, when you become homesick for your family,
you will think about how you want your child to attend a better school"
(interview by the author, February 16, 2002).

He explained further that adopting this kind of mentality would not
only make the workers "good" Filipino citizens but would also help mitigate the sadness and loneliness caused by their being separated from their
families. The issue here is not so much that brokers uphold the state's
framework of labor diplomacy by promoting overseas Filipino workers as
ambassadors of goodwill, but that their aim is to protect the agency's
image and profits. A worker who cannot deliver the expected work or
finish her contract because she cannot develop a good working relationship with her employer or because she becomes homesick for her family
affects the agency's reputation. By invoking overseas employment as a
form of "sacrifice," he strived to mold them into workers who could
carry out their work duties with ease and dedication because their family depended on their success.

The gendered dynamics of coaching applicants how to be "ideal"
workers is also present in this brokering process. This same broker
exclaimed at one point, "If you are married here, do not get married
there," and vehemently reminded the workers about their responsibilities
to their families, especially their spouses (field notes, February 16, 2002).
He explained to me afterward that he was merely responding to an escalating global concern about Filipina women's promiscuity, citing activities such as engaging in sex work, having extramarital affairs, and
seducing male employers. The perceived promiscuity of Filipinas is again
part of a looming discourse of the Filipina as "prostitute," a representation born of a colonial history that created a thriving sex industry. Filipina domestic workers become subjects of brokers' "disciplinary gaze"
(Foucault 1979), which insists on emphasizing the characteristics of obe-
dience, honesty, loyalty, and responsibility, which in turn are ultimately
meant to allay employers' fears of Filipinas' perceived sexual unruliness.

Similarly, Troy International features its applicants on screen by having them answer questions such as, How will you fight homesickness in a foreign country? Can you work without a day off? If given a day off by your employer, what will you do and where will you go? These questions respond to the oft-cited concerns of employers about the psychological readiness of applicants to thrive successfully in a foreign country and among strangers. In these videos, applicants can be found narrating their family's dire financial hardships, their obligation to support an elderly and ailing parent, or their aspirations of having their children attend school. Employers are supposed to see the applicants' determination to uplift their families economically as a guarantee of docility. The questions also seek to appease employers who have concerns and fears about the potential "unruliness" of Filipina domestics who congregate noisily in public, conduct "sideline" businesses, work additional jobs, or engage in illicit sexual relations during their days off.[12] Since their employers regard them as their property, they perceive these activities as tarnishing their social standing and respectability in their communities. Thus, the series of questions outlined above attempted to respond to these concerns and concurrently establish domestic workers' subordinate positions vis-à-vis their employers.

Labor brokers can also begin to train prospective workers to become those marketable commodities they commonly boast about by presenting themselves as adaptable to and cooperative with their employers' demands. They train them to envision their success overseas as one that is dependent on their ability to view themselves as service providers to foreign employers who have control over their everyday activities, both inside and outside their households. Given that employers regard them as their property, labor brokers have to train prospective domestic workers to behave "properly" and engage in only activities that will not mar the image of their employer.

Brokers also coach applicants to be "all-around workers," a construction that allows them to fulfill their claim that Filipinos are teachable and uninhibited about assuming multiple work responsibilities. As one broker noted, an "all-around worker" is one who focuses on assuming one aspect of a given job as well as realizes the eventuality that employers can demand other tasks from them. And they must acknowledge and do the work without contesting what is asked of them.

An all-around worker is someone who takes the initiative to acquire additional skills and training that allow them to assume work duties that are not automatically part of their jobs. Although this labor broker was referring to the fate of Filipino workers whom the agency sends to the United States as nurses but who end up working as nurse aides, this label best captures another aspect of this coaching process.

During their interactions with nurse applicants, brokers specifically ingrained the notion that more skills would mean greater chances of being selected for overseas employment. In an orientation for U.S.-bound nurses that was organized by Exocomp in affiliation with a U.S.-based nursing registry, the registry representative reminded applicants of the importance of viewing themselves as "knowledge workers." According to this representative, "knowledge workers are those who continuously learn and train and therefore increase their employability" (field notes, November 18, 2001). Given that this registry and Exocomp do not shoulder the costs of taking the required nursing entrance examinations and hospital training, he argued for them as worthwhile investments for the applicants. Not only will these efforts show foreign employers that they are committed to working overseas, they will also prove that they can work in a variety of health care settings (hospital, clinics, nursing homes, and rehabilitation centers). This is especially relevant for this nursing registry, whose work is doing just that. Therefore, an applicant who may have had work experience in different units of a hospital or an applicant who may have worked in both hospitals and rehabilitation centers are the ideal all-around candidates.

Nurse applicants I met in the Philippines are quite aware of the preference for workers who can demonstrate this flexibility. Myrna, whom I met at the 2001 joint Philippine Nursing Association and Philippine Nursing Association of America International Conference in Manila, worked in Saudi Arabia for four years and is again applying for a nursing position in the United States, Canada, and the United Kingdom. She attended the conference to network with other nurses but primarily because of the sessions that provided educational credits that she can put on her curriculum vitae. At this time, she was also taking specialized training classes in cardiovascular care to increase her marketability and to widen her job options overseas. She understood that an ideal applicant must show this all-around-worker potential by carrying a variety of skills and being comfortable to work in any hospital unit. This is important because becoming a "floater"—someone who moves from one unit to the next—happens more often than what applicants are told.

Similarly, Pilar, another a former nurse from Saudi Arabia, whom I met in the lobby of Exocomp, explained that some applicants in the Philippines become overly selective about the units in which they want to work, without understanding the realities of the market. She recounted stories about nurses she knew in Saudi Arabia who expected to work in operating rooms only because that had been their position in the Philippines. She told me that this mentality may only be to their disadvantage because there is no guarantee that one's dream job will be attainable. She added, "It is better if a nurse knows every section [hospital ward]. I know pediatrics. I know how to be in the psychiatric ward. I can also go to the oncology department. I can go to the ICU [intensive care unit] because I had participated in rounds in the Philippines" (interview by the author, April 3, 2002).

Like Myrna, Pilar recognized that an ideal nurse applicant is one who has the knowledge, experience, and flexibility to fulfill the demands of different work settings. Her mobility in different hospital units gives her an edge over other nurses and that which she claimed guarantees her indispensability in any hospital. While labor brokers explained that Filipina nurses' desirability as a workforce stems from their natural willingness to assume different work responsibilities or go beyond their call of duty, nurses such as Myrna often qualified this generalization as a survival tactic and not so much an inherent trait. Myrna explained that moving up to a supervisory position often means being able to impress one's employers, and this often has to do with becoming a "superwoman" who is willing to assume additional work responsibilities without any added cost to the hospital.

Similarly, for domestic workers, the notion of the all-around worker is a given. When workers prepare to leave for overseas employment, labor brokers do not outline the former's specific duties but only give them a basic idea that their role is to "manage the household." In reality, what falls within this category of household management is much more demanding and rigorous than what the category implies. Thus, domestic work applicants specifically mention their capacity to manage a household—from cooking different cuisines, to caring for both the elderly and infants, to being able to assist children with their homework. Two applicants who were applying to work as caregivers in Israel and who had prior experience in Taiwan corrected my assumption that caregiving is synonymous with domestic work in terms of the need to become an all-around worker (field notes, March 23, 2002). They reasoned that caregivers are *only* supposed to take care of one individual in a household, unlike domestic workers, who are responsible for myriad tasks. For this reason, these two applicants were specifically applying for a caregiving position, hoping that they would be able to take care of an elderly individual who would be far less demanding than an entire family, and therefore, the applicants would "have more opportunities to relax."

While brokers do a fair amount of coaching their applicants in how to maximize their marketability as global workers, their success depends on their ability to get workers to take them seriously. As I show in the next chapter, many of them do. The case of Myrna and Pilar indicate that coaching may not always be necessary insofar as their prior work experiences have made them quite aware of the importance of adaptability and flexibility as a form of job security. But what coaching does is to reify this importance by orchestrating a process of self-disciplining that will not only allow them to secure a job but also allow agencies to secure their reputability that they can, indeed, deliver workers with added value.

Conclusion

As partners of the state in constructing the Philippines as the home of the Great Filipino Worker, employment agencies seek to broker an image that can fulfill this social imaginary. Their activities challenge the oft-cited claim that an economic logic—poverty and the country's inability to provide viable employment opportunities—is the only actor driving labor migration from the Philippines. This chapter showed a key aspect of the labor-brokering process that rests on selling Filipina nurses and domestic workers as ideal care workers by highlighting their added export value. This racialized form of labor power and "productive femininity" represents Filipina nurses as not only educated but also loving and Filipina domestics as obedient but also overqualified. This added value is supposed to act as Filipinas' *brand name* as care workers—the racialized and gendered trope of productive femininity—through which foreign employers are supposed to imagine the value of Filipinas.

Not only are they determined and committed to working overseas but they are supposed to offer *more* skills than other workers in the global marketplace. While simultaneously claiming these traits as unique to Filipinos, they are the ideological constructions that labor brokers are determined to fulfill through myriad calculated techniques. From head-hunting in workplaces that yield their desired nurses, to requiring rigorous training of prospective domestic workers, to psychologically coaching them to embrace their docility, they attempt to secure their positive reputation. Therefore, labor brokering is about securing job orders for Filipinos but also about disciplining and governing Filipinos' conduct in order to stress their comparative advantage and meet the agencies' financial bottom line.

However, this representation also reinforces class and gender inequalities. First, these agencies behave as patriarchal social institutions that (re)produce gendered ideologies about work and Filipinas that in turn, act as a form of labor control and social discipline.[13] They construct Filipinas as capable of doing nursing and domestic work because they are women and their added value gains them a comparative advantage; in addition, brokers devise strategies that ensure the production of such labor power. Thus, they are able to condition the types of workers that get incorporated in specific labor processes. Second, promoting the notion of Filipinas' added export value creates their vulnerabilities as workers by generating a standard upon which foreign employers determine the "ideal" worker, in general, and formulate their expectations of Filipina workers, in particular.

CHAPTER 6

Living the Dream

You will be able to buy everything that you want [in America]. But it is a lonely place.
> —Gabriela, a nurse working in Arizona

IN 2006, I met Gabriela, a thirty-one-year-old nurse living in a growing suburban enclave in Arizona.[1] She and her husband had just bought a single-family home in one of the newest KB Home communities, so new that their house address had not yet appeared on MapQuest.[2] The novelty of their home was complemented by strikingly matching furnishings, from the dark wood–tone tables, coordinating lamps, and even banana-leaf-shaped ceiling fan blades, all of which were seemingly carefully selected to evoke a kind of hybrid British colonial/tropical-theme home. Indeed, the living room could have easily been a model room right out of the Bombay Company, a popular retailer of traditional English-style furniture in the United States.

Similarly, Kitty, a twenty-five-year-old nurse in Gray Meadows, Texas, whom I met in 2004, while not owning a new home, proudly pointed out the new Toyota Camry she had bought for herself.[3] She had also just purchased a Toyota Corolla Altis for her mother in the Philippines. Kitty is a frequent consumer of personal services pertaining to hair and facial care. In fact, she was late to our interview because she was getting her hair done. My interviews with both Gabriela and Kitty, which happened during one of their days off, were rare occasions. While nurses typically work thirty-six hours a week on twelve-hour shifts, Gabriela's work week is forty-eight hours, of which twelve hours are specifically overtime. Kitty puts in considerably more overtime hours and so frequently that she has earned the reputation in her unit of having "fat" paychecks. During our interview, she recounted banking twenty-four hours of overtime in a given week. When we spoke in 2004, she had accumulated fifty-two overtime hours for the month. While news abounds of nurses being forced to work overtime because of staff shortages, this situation is not the case for Gabriela and Kitty. They both prefer to work "extra," as they put it, using work as a mechanism to ease the loneliness of being home and away from their families and friends in the Philippines. Most important, the material luxuries they enjoy reflect this labor.

Gabriela and Kitty would certainly make President Arroyo proud. They are poster children for Arroyo's newest proclamation of nurses as the "new aristocrats." They are no longer tagged as simply *bagong bayani*, modern-day (economic) heroes, whose earnings boost the country's foreign exchange reserves. They now also possess a prodigious buying power and investment potential. This new representation prompts us to imagine nurses as *more* than just workers; they are also consumers with an economic power that enables this transformation.

A few examples are noteworthy. In a 2007 *New York Times Magazine* news article, we meet Rosalie Comodas Villanueva, a Filipina nurse working in Abu Dhabi who has relieved her migrant worker father from being the family's primary breadwinner, a position he had held for almost two decades. Not only does she dutifully remit four hundred dollars a month to her parents; in addition, through her generosity her parents have a home equipped with luxuries atypical of the average Filipino household: a patio, tiled flooring, two kitchens, and flushing toilets. The pages of a new magazine, *Philippine Nurses Monitor,* which professes to serve the Filipino nurse communities in the United States, are filled with information about the many ways that nurses can enjoy the economic fruits of their labor. From taking advantage of the "special no down payment package for OFWs [overseas Filipino workers]" to buying a luxury condo in the Philippines, to receiving tips for leisure and travel from their peers, to learning how to become "nurse entrepreneurs," readers can dream or, perhaps, *fantasize* about the things they can consume or business ventures they can pursue.[4]

Similarly, nurses I interviewed in Texas and Arizona such as Gabriela and Kitty boast the material rewards of working overseas and the pleasures of owning and purchasing commodities of which they can only dream in the Philippines. Being able to own a home or to purchase a car produces celebratory images that reflect the very promises that the state and employment agencies broker to the nurses I interviewed and those that govern their professional consciousness as overseas workers seeking employment in the United States. But these images hide the contradictions and tensions in those promises—the simultaneous gains and losses behind a professional consciousness rooted in chasing the American dream of consumption.[5] America may encapsulate their dream opportunity when it comes to material acquisition, but often, behind these representations is loneliness and estrangement, which this pursuit often veils.[6]

In this chapter, I discuss the professional consciousness that materializes among Filipino nurses, one that is inextricably linked to the ideology of the American dream, of Americanized consumerism, and their embrace of this. I show how this consciousness shapes their aspirations as workers and immigrants and as "success stories" in the eyes of their families in ways that often become reduced to the value of the U.S. dollar. But what does the focus on American-dreaming Filipinos have to do with political economy? How they *imagine* the American dream and their potential to be Americanized subjects is crucial not only in defining the moral economy behind their professional pursuits but also in illuminating how institutional actors (the Philippine state and employment agencies) can create the image of the Philippines as the home of the Great Filipino Worker. After all, as Tadiar (2004, 4) explains, "imagination as culturally organized social practice, is an intrinsic constitutive part of political economy" and "capitalism and state rule and not only nationalism are suffused with imagination."

In this chapter, I highlight how workers incorporate this social imaginary and dream of "America." As Gabriela's quote above highlights, Filipinos imagine/fantasize about the U.S. as their prime destination because of the perceived economic power it bestows. But what their narratives veil, as Gabriela signals, is a simultaneous disappointment and estrangement. That is, they may embrace the American dream and its material rewards and even support the ethos of labor migration that characterizes the country's national consciousness, but ultimately, they seemingly stand outside the dream that they claim to chase. Nurses such as Gabriela and Kitty revel in the commodities that their earnings can buy at the same time that they believe that "the good life" is in fact in the Philippines and long to return home.

CULTIVATING AMERICANIZED
NURSING SUBJECTS

Gabriela and Kitty's presence in the United States defies the kind of economic logic of poverty and any global labor market rationale that labor recruiters proclaim are the driving forces for pursuing overseas employment in the United States. The two women came from middle-class families and did not pursue nursing simply as a mode of economic survival. Rather, nursing was their ticket to work in the United States, a place they perceived would reward them with earnings commensurate to their training and endow them with an elevated social status—an issue I take up later. But this pursuit was made possible by colonial relations between the United States and the Philippines.

Choy's (2003) seminal work illustrates how these relations have contributed to the institutionalization of nursing, creating a foundation upon which Filipinos became technically and socially suited to work in U.S. health care settings. The implementation of an Americanized nursing training, the use of English as the language of instruction, and the promotion of an Americanized nursing work culture provided the necessary historical "preconditions" (41) driving the mass migration of Filipinos to the United States beginning in the mid-1960s. Colonial relations between the two countries led to educational and training opportunities, such as the *pensionado* and the Exchange Visitors Program (EVP), that had been a vehicle for Filipino nurses to go to the United States since the 1950s.[7] These programs served as tools for establishing the cultural and intellectual supremacy of U.S. institutions (Espiritu 2007) and ultimately were instrumental in shaping familiarity with the Filipino nursing workforce on the part of contemporary foreign employers.

Indeed, an unintended consequence of these colonial relations, as Choy (2003) argues, is the mass migration of Filipino nurses to the United States in the second half of the twentieth century. Between 1956 and 1969, following implementation of the EVP, more than eleven thousand Filipino nurses left for the United States; nurses made up more than 50 percent of the total number of exchange visitors from the Philippines (Asperilla 1971 cited in Choy 2003). The momentum was maintained by the 1965 Immigration Act, which provided two occupa-tional preference categories reserved for highly skilled migrants, which

TABLE 6.1

H1-B and J Visa Distribution in 1966–1978

Visa type	Total issued	Philippines	Canada	U.K.	Ireland	Korea	India
H1-B	15,291	9,158	3,034	1,325	504	143	26
J	9,729	5,053	93	141	41	244	201

SOURCE: Ishi 1987.

Filipino nurses were able to use as a means for entering the United States (Ball 1996, 2000; Bergamini 1964; Choy 2003; Ishi 1987; Liu, Ong and Rosenstein 1991; Ong and Azores 1994). They also took advantage of the H1–B visas that allowed them to come as temporary workers. As Ishi (1987) noted, in 1966–1978, of the total number of H1–B visas that were distributed, approximately 60 percent went to the Philippines, outnumbering those that were awarded to Canada, the United Kingdom, Ireland, Korea, and India (Table 6.1). Such trends help explain the widespread presence of Filipino nurses in the United States; in turn, they shape neocolonial relations between the two countries and the persistent dependence of the United States on the Philippines to supply much needed nursing labor during times of shortage.

"WE ARE SO FAR INTO THE PIT": THE CURRENT NURSE "SHORTAGE"

The labor that the nurses I interviewed provide reflects the ongoing recruitment of Filipino nurses to the United States—a quick-fix strategy for the nationwide nurse shortage in a country unable to meet current and projected demands for a qualified registered nurse workforce. The size of the U.S. registered nurse workforce will decline 20 percent below national requirements by 2020, according to Buerhaus, Staiger, and Auerbach's (2000) landmark paper. It is an alarming projection that has sent health care institutions and policy makers clamoring for both short- and long-term solutions.[8]

In Arizona, Governor Janet Napolitano convened a nurse shortage task force in 2002 to evaluate the impact of this shortage on the state and to make recommendations. The task force's report addressed how to attract more people to nursing, increase the capacity of registered nursing education programs over the following three years, improve the work environment of nurses, and remove regulatory barriers to nursing practice and education (Arizona Governor's Task Force 2004–2005). Patricia Harris, director of health care education at Maricopa Community College and a member of the task force, stated, "We are so far into the pit" in not having an adequate supply of registered nurses for current and projected staffing demands that action needed to be taken. She described the current nursing shortage as, while not the first in U.S. history, by far the worst she had experienced.

Given the numbers of upcoming nursing graduates, the supply of nurses is still far below what is needed. Why is this the case? Harris, along with other health care experts, attributed the problem to several factors.[9] The baby boom generation (those born between 1946 and 1964), who make up a large proportion of the nursing workforce, will reach retirement between 2005 and 2010, at the same time that they will also require health care services. There has been a concomitant steady decline of nurses entering the profession since the 1980s. This phenomenon can be explained by the availability of employment opportunities for nurses that take them away from bedside nursing to pursue administrative work, which is likely to be better paying. Another cause of the decline is a growing dissatisfaction on the part of nurses with the hospital work environment. The demanding workload, stagnant wages, lack of opportunities for career mobility, forced voluntary overtime, presence of a business model of health care delivery, and stress-related illnesses are some of the sources for this dissatisfaction.[10] To top this off, some nursing programs actually have a waiting list of places for entering students as a result of a shortage of nursing educators.

While hospitals have attempted to remedy the situation by offering attractive hiring packages to U.S.-trained nurses or by relying on a contingent workforce such as traveler nurses, those who work on short-term contracts, foreign labor recruitment is one viable alternative or stopgap measure. Even though the same health care institutions do not acknowledge foreign labor recruitment as an official remedy for this labor shortage, it is, nevertheless, a subject of a sizeable funding consideration. That is, what they are willing to offer to foreign recruits via hiring packages contributes to their success and to the ability to capture the interests of Filipinos to go to places that may not initially be desirable, such as Texas and Arizona, because of the smaller proportion of Filipinos residing there. This is an issue to which I now turn.

FROM PROVIDING LAVISH RECRUITMENT
PACKAGES TO CREATING FILIPINO ENCLAVES

As I described in Chapter 4, in the recruitment seminars that U.S.-based employers conduct in the Philippines, Filipino nurses are already bombarded with images that suggest that working in the United States will lead to a significant transformation of economic status. They are reminded that this employment opportunity is not only about immigrating to the United States and attaining the rights and privileges afforded to all its permanent residents, but also about partaking in the material rewards of their earnings. The tourist-directed brochures that recruiters distribute and the token Filipino representatives who are paraded as economic success stories and who attest to the glamour of working overseas are supposed to ingrain in the minds of Filipino applicants the reasons why working in the United States is *the* ultimate opportunity.

To further reify this point, recruiters effectively promote an enticing "hiring package" to their applicants. In contrast to earlier waves of foreign nurse recruitment in which H1-B visas were used, in present recruitment efforts many hospitals offer immigrant or green card visas in the form of employment-based visas such as the EB-3, which ultimately carries the promise of U.S. citizenship. Unlike the H1-B visa, the EB-3 allows employers to sponsor a nurse job applicant (and her or his family) for permanent residency (that is, give her or him a green card).[11] Once they are permanent residents, nurses are eligible to apply for U.S. citizenship, after five years of continuous residency in the country. All the nurses I interviewed fit into this pattern, which set them apart from the nurses who had come before them. They had left the Philippines with the express intention of becoming permanent U.S. residents and, ultimately, U.S. citizens. Whether this notion stays with nurses permanently is an issue that I take up later.

Nurses I interviewed in Texas and Arizona earned between thirteen and thirty-four dollars an hour. Notwithstanding the cost-of-living indexes in these two places, and the cut that agencies take from nurses' pay, as in the case of some of the nurses in Arizona, their wages seemingly depend on their employers, years of work experience, and the type of specialty care provided (wages of emergency room nurses and cardiac care unit nurses are slightly higher than those of medical oncology nurses). They perceived this salary to be well above anything they could possibly earn in the Philippines and therefore found them sufficiently enticing. According to Pia, a nurse with five years' nursing experience, the 5,000 pesos a month ($116) she would be earning in a provincial hospital in the Philippines could not compare with the $18 an hour ($1,152 a month) offered to her in Texas.[12] Michelle, another nurse in Gray Meadows, recounted that her initial contract offered $13 an hour, an amount that seemed low given that she had been working as a nurse for ten years. However, this rate, upon conversion to Philippine pesos, would allow her, as the eldest daughter, to fulfill her family obligations to put two of her siblings through college. As is clear from this example, employers benefit from the power of the U.S. dollar conversion in the Philippines and the relative competitiveness of U.S. nursing salaries compared with those that Philippine hospitals can offer.

Many Philippine-based agencies that work with U.S. hospitals or staffing registries are able to secure packages (called a surety bond) that include the stipulation that employers pay for the exams required of nurse applicants, airfare and other travel costs for the journey abroad, and all other immigration-related fees. This was the case for one of the employers of nine nurses I interviewed in Gray Meadows. The attractiveness of this employer was based on its ability to shoulder what is typically the costly aspect of a job application to the United States (see Table 6.2).[13] A typical contract for the nurses employed by this employer included other perks, such as three months' "free" housing in a fully furnished apartment, a relocation bonus of $4,500, a sign-on bonus of $2,000, a $225 gift certificate to purchase hospital uniforms, and a transportation allowance of $4,500. This kind of package has become a source of tension for Filipino nurses in Gray Meadows who work for another employer or who came at a different period, when such perks were not yet offered. While nurses in Arizona did not have the same kind of extensive package, they also received one month of free housing.

Both groups of nurses recounted that upon their arrival in the United States, they were assisted by a representative from their employers who helped to process numerous types of employment-related paperwork, including that needed for their Social Security cards; took them to

TABLE 6.2

Typical Recruitment Package ("Surety Bond") for Nurses in Gray Meadows, Texas

Item	Cost to employers (dollars)
Immigration fee	115
CGFNS	325
TOEFL/TWE	110
TSE	150
CGFNS exam review	150
NCLEX registration	200
Air/hotel for Guam (to take NCLEX)	580
Visa application	260
Visa documentation	65
Medical exam	85
State license application	265
Endorsement to Texas	125
Visa screen application	325
Total	2,755

NOTE: Data is based on the package offered to nurses in 2003–2004 and is designed for a two-year employment contract.

the bank to open an account; and generally oriented them in affairs of daily living. Above all, however, what was especially helpful for these nurses was the strategic ways in which employers created a sort of mini-Filipino enclave by placing similar workers in the same housing complex. For example, in Texas, I found that one apartment complex was home to all the newly arrived nurses and to a few "old-timers"—those who had been in Gray Meadows for at least two years and who decided to stay in that housing complex. The apartment complex was not only located about two to three miles from the two hospitals where the nurses worked but also situated two blocks from the only Filipino restaurant in town. This restaurant was the heart of this Filipino nurse community. Its owners provided much needed familiar hospitality and its food had become essential for nurses who stopped by before or after their shifts to pick up home-cooked meals that their schedules do not permit them to prepare at home. Similarly, in Arizona, the nurses I interviewed were placed in an apartment complex with a significant concentration of Filipino nurse residents who were working for the same hospital, which was located in close proximity.

This strategy of creating a Filipino nurse mini-enclave is advantageous for employers, who can take credit for fulfilling their promise to nurses—to give them a kind of home away from home where newly arrived nurses can feel that they are in an environment with other nurses who are their peers but at the same time can provide them mentorship and emotional support. This is precisely what has happened in both Texas and Arizona. Filipino nurses themselves have created a support system that at least tries to mitigate the transportation problems that they all face. In both sites, employers provided nurses, in their initial few months, with a financial allowance or a bus card that they could use for public transportation. However, taking public transportation to work became cumbersome for the night shift nurses, who did not feel safe waiting at a bus stop alone, or for those who did not feel comfortable facing the oppressive summer heat. Grocery stores, churches, and shopping centers were not within walking distance from the apartments. Therefore, nurses who owned their cars often reached out to newly arrived nurses either by offering free rides to places to which they were going to already or by establishing official carpooling services for a fee.

Such a community of support is instrumental in relieving the homesickness that many nurses encounter and in alleviating their fears about a new work environment. During one of my visits with Marife and Jan, newly arrived nurses in Arizona, one of their friends stopped by before her work shift to drop off a household item she had borrowed. As she expressed her nervousness about going to work and her ability to navigate a new environment that may demand skills she thought she did not have or interaction with a new group of people, Marife and Jan showered her with comforting statements of "You can do it!" They kept reminding her that such nervousness was "natural" and that she possessed the qualifications needed to perform the job. Even though she did not appear to believe them, their moral support seemingly brought her the kind of push she needed to survive another day of work.

Thus, when Filipinos arrive in the United States as nurses, they come with and benefit from a robust recruitment package that sets them

apart from other Filipino workers similarly pursuing overseas employment and from nurses who preceded them. They also benefit from their
employers' efforts at cultivating a home away from home by strategically
placing them in locations that are transformed into a sort of enclave of
support for Filipino nurses. In some ways, as I describe later, these efforts
also reflect the fact that sites where the nurses are placed, such as those in
Texas and Arizona, are not Filipinos' "first choice" or "ideal" destinations because they do not reflect the kind of big-city "America," with its
skyscrapers, that are embedded in their imagination or these locations are
devoid of the vibrant Filipino communities they know about. These
packages attempt to compensate for this.

However, the accommodations can also be viewed as responses that
are tailored to this professional class of workers. They come with particular material and career aspirations that recruiters seek to address in
exchange for the labor they supply as a quick remedy to the continuing
nurse shortage crisis. For nurses themselves, such recruitment packages
complement their vision of a seemingly bountiful America that they
embrace and of which they are determined to become part, an issue to
which I turn next.

"WE ARE BORN TO HAVE THE AMERICAN DREAM"

Eureka Incognito, a nurse working in Arizona at the time of
our interview in 2005 (she is now in San Diego) began her work in
1997 as a nurse in Dubai, where she was for two years, and then worked
in Jeddah for four years,. She chose to work in the Middle East to
save money for what she ultimately dreamed of—a job in the United
States. Not wanting to waste any time, during her vacation time
she studied and took the exams required for working as a nurse in the
United States and then eventually put in her application to work there in
2000. Justin and Mabolo, whom I met in Gray Meadows, abandoned
their dreams of pursuing careers in mass communication and business,
respectively, in order to pursue nursing. Gabriela and Kitty left their
loved ones in the Philippines to work in places lacking much-needed
familial support. These individual journeys represent the typical stories
I heard from nurses I met in both Texas and Arizona. That is, while
nurses I encountered possessed varied work and life experiences, one

thing they seemed to share was a determination to live and work in the United States.

This determination enables and supports the ethos of labor migration held by the Philippine state and employment agencies and their discursive construction of the United States as the "ultimate" dream opportunity. While the particularities of the journey to the United States may differ, there is a common perception that being a nurse in the United States affords the opportunity to partake in the American dream. The American dream, for Filipino nurses, boils down to an idealized image of "America" as a place that provides unlimited economic and social opportunities—an image they believe has been naturally ingrained among Filipinos. As Justin simply noted:

> We [Filipinos] are born to have the American dream. Since I was young child, I thought that America is a good place to live, everything is free, there is democracy, and you have freedom. The value of dollars is different to you. Here you can acquire things. You can pay for them in installments, unlike in the Philippines, where you cannot think about buying a car. I was able to have a car already in less than a month. In the Philippines, I could only dream of it. When you see an Expedition [a type of automobile] you think to yourself, maybe I can buy one like that in another lifetime [laughs]. But here, America is making my dreams a reality. I always wanted to have a car and in less than a month, I was able to acquire one (interview by the author, January 1, 2004).

Justin, as with many of the nurses I met, espoused an Americanized dream that revolves around material acquisition and a heightened power to consume material goods. Whereas owning a car such as an Expedition is something she could only fantasize about in the Philippines, this idealized American dream not only makes this possible but also delivers it instantly. This seemingly innate predisposition of Filipinos to desire and articulate the American dream is something that other nurses express is instrumental in cultivating their determination to work in the United States. While some nurses refer to it as emblematic of a kind of "colonial mentality," a byproduct of the U.S. colonization of the Philippines, others refer to it as originating in popular culture and the idyllic images of the United States that appear on their television and movie screens.

Thanks to transnational corporations, globalized media, and migrant transnational social networks, the images that travel and get imported globally portray the United States as a place of wealth, cosmopolitanism, and limitless opportunities. Another nurse, who will be called HB and who works in Arizona, recounted how as a young child in the Philippines, she perceived her aunts and cousins who worked as nurses in the United States as being able to "buy whatever they wanted" by virtue of the things they brought back on their trips home to the Philippines. The United States is supposed to be *the* place to satisfy one's career and educational aspirations.

But working in the United States is also about having a "voice." Thus Pia, a nurse working in Gray Meadows, observed, "People seem to have more voice here. Whatever they want to say, they can say it. Your rights prevail. In the Philippines, whoever has money, they are the one with rights" (interview by the author, January 20, 2004). For Pia, the American dream is a promising response or alternative to the stark social inequalities that pervade the Philippines and render many powerless and voiceless. The American dream then becomes what Grewal (2005, 5) describes as "a search for a future in which the desire for consumption, for liberal citizenship, and for work came together to produce a specific subject of migration." Pia and Justin are emblematic of these subjects insofar as they embraced this ideal at the same time that they did not see themselves as part of building this dream through the invaluable labor they contributed to the U.S. economy and the well-being of Americans.

But other nurses, such as Kit, also define the American dream as being about the U.S. dollar's conversation rate in the Philippines. She interpreted work in the United States as providing her with earnings that expanded her buying power in the Philippines. The initial contract she signed in the Philippines stipulated that she was to earn twelve dollars an hour—an amount that seemed low given that she possessed seven years of nursing experience. However, at the time, she and her colleagues did not think of the amount as being low; she explained, "We were so happy because when you convert that to pesos, that is a lot! I like to read girlie [fashion] magazines so I thought, how many magazines can I buy with that money? I can buy two pocketbooks [paperback books] or magazines!" (interview by the author, January 20, 2004). Although she was going to spend these dollars in the United States, the standards by which she measured the value of her earnings were based on her ability to purchase what in the Philippines were "luxury" items. Interestingly enough, during our interview, I couldn't help but notice the stacks of *In Style*, a popular women's fashion magazine, piled up high in the living-room area. Kit's earnings obviously afforded her the ability to buy not just one issue of a "girlie" magazine but a whole year's subscription.

HEROES TO THEIR FAMILIES

When I met Mabolo in 2004, she had been working in Texas for about four months. During our meeting, she was particularly jovial because of the increasingly real possibility that she would finally be reunited with her husband and four children. She had left them behind because she had not had money then to finance the cost of processing their visas and airfare, a cost that employers typically do not cover. Now, she had saved enough money from the overtime hours she had put in to bring them to the United States, buy a minivan to drive them around in, and even plan to purchase a home before they arrived. Indeed, Mabolo was strikingly proud of her newfound class status, which was defined by her ability to provide her family a new lifestyle. For Mabolo, being able to work in the United States allowed her to shower her children with "luxuries" that they never had in the Philippines, a new dress for one of her daughters to wear on her first communion, a pair of Converse-brand tennis shoes for her son, a pair of roller skates for her younger daughter. Coming from a poor family and having experienced financial hardships, she felt that her children had been deprived of such luxuries, as their requests for clothes or toys were often denied. "Before," she elaborated, "when they asked me to buy things for them, I would have to explain so much about how we need milk first. My husband and I have explain to them that we only had this much money left for their jeepney [a form of public transportation] fare and their food allowance. I was [always] telling them how tight our pockets were so that little by little, they knew that we couldn't get anything extra. Everything went to food, milk, and basic daily necessities (interview by the author, January 27, 2004). Mabolo's ability to provide her family with these kinds of lifestyle changes redefined her position as her family breadwinner, through her ability to purchase material goods, at the same time that the gratitude that she receives from her children alleviated her sense of guilt and pain that was brought on by familial separation.

Kitty's case is similar to Mabolo's. The car that Kitty purchased for her mother was a useful distraction to help the latter through her separation from her only daughter. The car, according to Kitty, not only eased her mother's loneliness, which Kitty measured in the decreasing frequency with which her mother phoned her in tears since receiving the car, but also provided her mother physical and social mobility with which to get out of the house and socialize. From her mother's perspective, she had a car that she could proudly parade and boast about as a luxury item that her daughter had purchased after only a few months of working in Gray Meadows. For Kitty, who is the youngest daughter in her family, providing her mother with what was considered an extravagant gift was empowering, even though it meant sacrificing her days off so that she could put in overtime hours. For other nurses, the potential power of their earnings and the mere fact of working in the United States elevate their status and "value" within their families. As Eureka explained, "I am the very first person in our family to get here successfully. Even my relatives see me differently. My mother's sibling already went to my parents' house to borrow money to help pay for someone's surgery and that is because I'm here already. So my mother loaned her money and she said that she will pay me back (interview by the author, August 1, 2005).

The power given by the convertibility of the U.S. dollar in the Philippines is not only in the items it can buy; it is also about the kind of transformative power it carries for reconfiguring the social positions of Filipino nurses with respect to their families. Like the Vietnamese men in Thai's (2008) study whose U.S. dollar earnings allow them to move from a status of "low worth" (in the United States) to one of "high worth" (in Vietnam), these Filipino nurses enjoyed new roles of being economic providers, gift givers, success stories in their families. Their earnings became their social capital, from which they derived some measure of empowerment that brought them fulfillment for making what had become a long, and often painful, journey for many.

Most of the nurses I interviewed had not embraced, or even heard of, the state's designation of them as *bagong bayani*, modern-day heroes of the country. They either found the term unfamiliar or amusing because they did not see their decision to work overseas as having anything to do with helping an economically ailing country. Mabolo stated that the real heroes were the people who stayed in the Philippines to "serve Filipinos" despite the meager salaries that they earned. She and other nurses defined any sort of heroism they may have possessed *only* with respect to their family. As Justin noted, "When I came here, I did not think of our government. I went here for my family" (interview by the author, January 16, 2004). For them, the notion of heroism signified a type of patriotic commitment to the country, which many did not believe was reflective of leaving the Philippines. Joen, a nurse in Gray Meadows, described overseas workers such as herself as "rebels" who ended up "serving" others first instead of Filipino compatriots. She felt guilty for leaving but rationalized her decision as a pragmatic response to a state that could not provide viable employment.

Another nurse—Michelle—shared Joen's sentiments and explained that her desire to earn more and to make decent earnings was her primary motivation. "You wouldn't even be working here if nurses were getting good compensation in the Philippines. Maybe we do become heroes! Maybe in terms of my family, I become their hero," Michelle surmised (interview by the author, January 20, 2004). Thus, while the notion of state heroism made many of the nurses, like Michelle, uncomfortable, they accepted being regarded as their family's heroes. They knew that their sacrifices were made primarily to improve their lives and those of their families. They realized that their earnings might also lift up the Philippine economy, but to be rendered the state's heroes assumed that they had left for and in service to the Philippines.

At the other end of the spectrum, there were nurses such as Barkada, who had worked in Arizona for three years when I met him in 2007. He believed that he bore no guilt whatsoever for leaving. He claimed to have "served the Philippines" as a volunteer nurse for two years, after which he worked as a nurse, earning only 7,000 pesos ($163) a month. Thus, he felt justified in his decision to leave and did not believe that he owed the country anything beyond what he had already put in. He not only saw the *bagong bayani* proclamation as just another "gimmick" of the state, but also insisted that his decision to pursue nursing was in the service of his children, announcing, "The American dream is for the kids, not for me" (interview by the author, March 15, 2007).

They Think You Are Smarter

One of the most surprising things I discovered was the number of nurses I met who possessed overseas work experience, having worked in countries ranging from Libya, Saudi Arabia, and Singapore, to the United Kingdom. These nurses often used these jobs as stepping-stones for an eventual job in the United States. While some used their experience to build clinical work experience, others used it as a way to save money. Most important, these jobs offered salaries that were far greater than what the nurses could earn in the Philippines. On the other hand, other nurses, while waiting for their U.S. employment applications to go through, opted to stay in the Philippines but decided not to practice nursing and instead pursued jobs in retail, in the corporate world, or in the pharmaceutical industry—all of which offered better salaries than working as a nurse. But regardless of their work experiences, they were all working to fulfill one aspiration—to eventually make it to the United States.

For Gabriela, working in the Middle East in places like Saudi Arabia was for the "die-hard nurse" who was willing to put up with what she perceived to be culturally restrictive societies. Saudi Arabia was also not a viable option for her because of the reputation it has gained as a place of sexual promiscuity that results in illicit romantic relations and out-of-wedlock pregnancies among Filipinos. She agreed that while working in Saudi Arabia would be a cost-effective choice because a contract came with untaxed housing and earnings, she was not willing to venture to a place that had such a reputation. She also knew that while salaries in the United Kingdom were competitive and that the conversion of the British pound in the Philippines was higher than that of the U.S. dollar, the cost of living and taxes reduced the desirability of the United Kingdom as a place of employment. Thus, while she concurred with the notion that Filipino nurses basically had two options—to go to the United Kingdom or the United States, she did not wish to put in time in a place that she knew she would eventually leave anyway. "Why go to the Middle East or the U.K. when you know that those who go there end up going to the U.S. anyway?" she reasoned (interview by the author, December 19, 2006). Similarly, Rosalie Comodas Villanueva, the nurse working in Abu Dhabi who was featured in a *New York Times Magazine* article on April 22, 2007, declared, "The U.S. is the Ultimate. If you make it to the U.S., there is no place else to go."

How has the United States attained a much greater social currency than that of the United Kingdom or the Middle East? While the American dream for these nurses is specifically tied up with practices of consumption, it isn't the only element that adds to the desirability of the United States as a place of employment. It is also about the promise of citizenship. For example, while working in the United Kingdom would have afforded nurses such as Justin decent earnings with a similar, if not greater, currency conversion in the Philippines, the ability to become a permanent resident of the country is not available. Justin remarked, "Filipinos usually have only two choices—the U.S. or U.K. Unlike the U.K., you can come as an immigrant and after five years, you can become an American citizen. So it seems more secure here" (interview by the author, January 16, 2004). For Justin, U.S. citizenship is job security, insofar as it provides her and her family access to the economic privileges and social rights afforded to U.S. citizens.

In addition to the promise of citizenship, the perceived intellectual merits and higher clinical standards attached to working in the United States seem to add to its social currency. Nurses described their application process as akin to "passing through the eye of a needle," (*dadaan sa butas ng karayom*) because of the amount of bureaucratic paperwork they need to fill out and process and the series of costly nursing competency and licensing exams—CGFNS, NCLEX, TSE, TOEFL[14]—that they need to take. Marife, the nurse in Arizona described above, explained that having passed the exams required to work in the United States definitely adds to the perception of one's intellectual capacities. This is because whereas only one exam is required to go to the United Kingdom, the United States demands much more. "So, in a sense, the perception is that you are smarter because you passed all of the requirements. For example, in our hospital, there were twenty of us. Everyone went to London and I was the only one who was able to come [to the United States]. So they think that I am really smart and talented because I passed the CGFNS, NCLEX, TSE, and TOEFL" (interview by the author, August 1, 2005).

All the nurses similarly expressed the difficulty they experienced in taking these exams and, for some, the frequency with which they had to retake them. This was the case for Alberto, a nurse working in Arizona who jokingly compared his experience to getting a master's or doctoral degree. He put in his application for the United States in 2000 but did not actually leave until 2004 because he, like many nurses I interviewed, had to retake the two exams (TOEFL and TSE) that test for written and oral proficiency in the English language. In most cases, employers will only cover the cost of taking one exam, so the cost of retaking them is shouldered by the applicants. Therefore, the social prestige that comes from being able to secure an employment contract for the United States pertains not only to the practices of consumption that the U.S. dollar can enable but also from mastering the varied U.S. nursing practice requirements (see also George 2005). This prestige contributes to a sort of social tiering of employment destinations for Filipino nurses, with the United States occupying the top tier, followed by the United Kingdom, and then the Middle East, a phenomenon that defines how overseas Filipino nurses' success become articulated and recognized by their peers.

THE GOOD LIFE

The same nurses who feel empowered by their ability to financially help their families also struggle with the misconceptions that come with their economic power. They may have become heroes to their families, but such heroism presents them with a number of expectations. This becomes particularly evident during their homecoming to the Philippines. For example, Joen, who had been working in Arizona for three years when I first met her, described a surprising and overwhelming first trip back home. "People [in the Philippines] were saying how my salary was so high that I'm like a millionaire. I have to explain to them that I earn in dollars but I also spend in dollars. I don't just pick money out of nowhere. I work there and life is also hard in America. . . . I have to explain to them that I have bills to pay for—phone, cable, apartment, car, insurance. But they don't believe me. They just look at my salary" (interview by the author, January 19, 2004).

Despite the insistent and endless explanations that Joen provided to her family about her financial obligations and the kind of overtime hours that were required to make her trip possible, she was perceived to possess limitless economic resources. Like the American-dreaming nurses themselves, the people they leave behind imagine America as a land of milk and honey, and they, too, cannot fathom the material reality attached to the dream. For Joen's family, she has become *their* American dream. But in some ways, she is also their investment. Joen commented that when she ran out of money because of the cost of taking the NCLEX in Guam, her sister and father borrowed money from various people to help finance this important trip. Thus, she herself saw how she was an investment for the family and in light of this they were only right to expect particular payoffs. The sense of pride that nurses express about becoming such providers often masks their longing for some level of understanding of the labor that they have to perform in order to maintain these roles and their desired lifestyles in the United States.

What nurses also seemingly expressed at the same time that they contemplated their own successes was the cost of pursuing this dream. As was the case with Joen, who enjoyed her car, financial independence, and savings account, these material rewards come with demands for adopting and embracing a lifestyle that she claimed to be more culturally individualistic. Learning to be alone and living independently are key to what she believed were necessary for surviving in this American dream land. Behind the so-called glamorous lifestyles that employment agencies sold the nurses was a sense of loneliness and alienation that gave pause about whether this dream was worth pursuing after all. As Gabriela noted, "You can buy everything you want in America. But it is a lonely place. Although I feel full from the things that I buy, I still feel unhappy. . . . In the Philippines, while you have very little money, you are happy" (interview by the author, December 19, 2006). Gabriela left the Philippines for Arizona with much trepidation because it meant an indefinite separation from her mother. She felt that she had abandoned her mother, who was then just recently widowed and had to face losing her only daughter as well.

Ironically, it was her mother who encouraged her to pursue employment in the United States. Gabriela herself felt that she and her husband already had decent-paying jobs in the Philippines. The pain of this separation became very much heightened in anticipation of the arrival of their first child, who would be her mother's first grandchild. As we sat in her finely appointed living room, none of the niceties displayed in this middle-class household could have concealed the overwhelming discontent she felt with her current situation and her longing for her family and the life she had left behind in the Philippines. "Life is much simpler there," she reiterated as her eyes welled up with tears.

Leaving the Philippines is also about abandoning one's "comfort zones." Many of the nurses in the United States declared that contrary to popular perception, life in the Philippines is enjoyable and more relaxed. They attributed this to their not having the same kind of demanding work schedules and being able to hire domestic workers easily. Unlike in the United States, it is not atypical to see households, regardless of class status, to employ the service of domestic workers; this is possible because of a highly unregulated wage system that makes hiring domestic workers "affordable." For example it is not uncommon to hire domestic workers at two thousand pesos a month (approximately forty-six dollars). The inability to find a similar arrangement in the United States makes it difficult for nurses who have young children and need child care. They are driven to negotiate with their spouses about one parent's postponing entering the paid labor force immediately upon settling in the United States.

This was the case with Marife's husband, Jan. While Marife worked the night shifts and also put in overtime hours, Jan, also trained as a nurse, stayed home and took charge of most domestic household responsibilities, including child care, during their first year in Arizona. This eased their worries about their children's adjustment to a new environment as well as eliminated the cost of procuring child-care services. For Marife, this meant enjoying a supportive partner who was proud of his ability to "pamper" and "spoil" her with home-cooked meals. I, too, benefited from this, as on my visits to their home I was often showered with food he had prepared; and he made sure that I did not go home empty handed.

But the "easy living" in the Philippines that nurses describe is not simply about the ability to afford domestic help; it also encompasses the social relations they cultivate. Many say, *Masarap ang buhay sa Pilipinas* (Life is good in the Philippines) as a way of expressing a sense of pride and longing for a place that they seemingly did not always appreciate as such. They express disdain for the fast-paced world of work that the United States demands and because of which few moments are left for leisure. They are disappointed with how friendships develop and the formal arrangements needed for social gatherings. They all learn very quickly that in the United States, time is like gold and that Americans are obsessed with managing and protecting their time. They also feel socially constrained in workplaces that they think discourage casual and informal conversations on the job and contribute to the social distance they feel from their colleagues.

While there are certainly some nurses who do not wish to return to the Philippines because they have become accustomed to the U.S. lifestyle, most whom I interviewed discussed plans of returning and retiring there. Juxtaposed with their determination to chase the American dream was a fundamental longing to return "home." Many were especially fearful of what they observed was a lack of respect for the elderly, who they saw facing the fate of ending up in a nursing home instead of being under the care of their family. Mabolo, who seemed quite content with settling in the United States, and even in a small town such as Gray Meadows, wished to retire eventually in the Philippines. She remarked, "The Philippines is a good place of retirement. Here, you will just end up in the nursing home. You are just a figure in the population here. When you are old, you will be in a nursing home. In the Philippines, you will still have a life there even if you are old. You can have a comfortable life there to your own specifications. You can have a caregiver there and still maintain your social life. Here, when you are old, you end up in the nursing home" (interview by the author, January 27, 2004). While acknowledging the various permutations of nursing homes that attempt to mask the institutionalization of care and aging, Mabolo adamantly expressed her disdain of growing old in any setting that was devoid of family and one that she perceived robbed individuals of their autonomy. "In the Philippines, you can at least maintain some sense of dignity and can still live independently but with some assistance," she insisted.

For nurses such as Mabolo who have lived their lives chasing this dreamland of opportunity and wealth suddenly find themselves disillusioned and disheartened by a clash between their value system and that of the United States, a source of discord that in this case revolves around caring for the elderly. Perhaps realizing these clashes between value systems allows them to imagine the Philippines differently and behave like cultural ambassadors in ways that would make President Arroyo proud. Contrary to the general perception that agencies promote Filipinos working overseas, many workers are actually committed to returning to the Philippines and see it as their ultimate home. As Justin noted, "Life is good and enjoyable in the Philippines but life is nicer here in America [in terms of material rewards]. These are two different things." This kind of realization and distinction challenges the notion of immigrants as being driven by the desire for material consumption; it paints a richer and more complicated picture of what comes to be defined as "the good life." That is, the promise of the American dream, the good life that nurses imagined they would find in the United States falls short of their expectations, and for many nurses, this unexpectedly propels them back to the Philippines.

Conclusion

These stories tell us that Filipino nurse-migrants are not exceptions in terms of how the American dream and its economic and social payoffs are a fundamental element that defines immigrants' determination to leave for the United States. This chapter shows that the economic power and prestige that the American dream promises to Filipinos contribute to their professional consciousness as nurses in the United States. The empowerment they derive from their U.S. dollar earnings and their reclassified position as both breadwinner and hero of their family underlie the moral economy of their migration. That is, they understand their position as Filipino nurse-migrants through the values of Filipino familial piety intermixed with Americanized consumerism and materialism that institutional actors such as the state and employment agencies instill. But their stories also show the social costs of internalizing an ideology that has been the basis of their career aspirations. Toward the end of our interview, I asked Gabriela to reflect upon her life and career in the United States thus far and offer some "words of wisdom" for nurses who wished to take a piece of this American dream: "Life is good here in terms of the fact that you can do what you want. Just work hard and don't let your emotions take over you. You need to be brave. You come here to get wealthy so don't think of anything else; otherwise, why come here at all? Just work hard. Pray and don't forget why you came here. You will get what you want" (interview by the author, December 19, 2006).

The statement that Gabriela made, imbued with notions of promise and prescription at the same time, bears a striking resemblance to what labor brokers themselves pitch to prospective migrants. But as Gabriela's story has revealed, the cautionary tone behind her statement also unveils the disappointment, estrangement, and loneliness that come with living this dream. The American dream may guarantee economic advancement, but it does not guarantee that Filipino nurses in the United States will live happily ever after.

CHAPTER 7

Securing Their Added
Export Value

You can call Filipinos anytime and they will work—
even if they have not had any sleep. However, I maybe
hardworking but it is also because I have a goal. *I want
to earn extra money.*

—Eureka Incognito, a nurse in Arizona

On October 3, 2005, I received a startling voice mail
message from Eureka Incognito, a nurse I had met in Arizona seven
months earlier. "I am now in California," she said in her usual upbeat and
excited voice. She was staying temporarily at her father's friend's house as
she looked for jobs in Los Angeles and San Diego. She spoke with a sense
of hope and happiness that I had not heard in a long time and especially
not in the past few months. Our usual conversations had revolved around
her daily complaints about the unfair distribution of workload, in which
she was at a disadvantage, and the inability of the employment agency
managing her contract to intervene on her behalf or to entertain her persistent requests for a job transfer. This was coupled with the fact that she
also felt terribly isolated from other Filipino nurses, as she was one of the
few who had ended up in a hospital unit devoid of any other Filipinos.
As her work situation worsened and it became increasingly clear that she
was not going to get any relief from her agency, she decided to tap into
her savings to buy out the remainder of her contract and pursue employment in California on her own.

Eureka, like many nurses from the Philippines, possessed the nursing
skill, education, and work ethic that are desired by any employer looking
to benefit from the so-called added export value—the unique Filipino
labor power—of Filipina nurses. However, she also behaved in ways that
defied the expectations of her employers. Far from being "quiet," she

pointed out her higher patient load, compared with those of her colleagues, during her work shifts, which often rendered her unable to take
breaks. She demanded assistance from her colleagues whenever she
became overwhelmed with her patients. She once reported a technical
error that her colleague had committed as a matter of procedure and
patient protection, even though it meant suffering a backlash from other
nurses. She asked her agency why her paychecks did not correspond to
the amount of overtime hours she had put in, only to find out that this
agency pocketed half of her overtime pay. Needless to say, Eureka is not
the marketable ideal—docile—worker who is the dream of foreign
employers. As a result, her supervisors wrote her up as being "combative," "unfriendly," and "not a team player" while the employment agency
that was supposed to also advocate for her frequently dismissed her complaints as a product of homesickness and suggested "personal counseling"
as a remedy.

In this chapter, I address Filipino nurses' understanding and internalization of the quality of their work in ways that echo what agencies
have been pitching as their added export value as nurses. That is, nurses
also believe that they offer a unique form of labor power that they
racially brand as distinctively Filipino. I highlight Eureka's story because
she is one of these nurses. But she is also an exception and behaved in
ways that challenged the very ideals that she embraced that made Filipino
nurses desirable—the capacity and willingness to assume multiple
responsibilities, flexibility, and unrivaled loyalty and commitment to
their employers. Therefore, her experiences also very importantly reveal
the inherent vulnerabilities that Filipino nurses face as foreign contract
workers who have very limited recourse to take action against their
employers.

In this chapter, I provide the rationale and motivation behind this
internalization and the vulnerabilities that the nurses possess in ways that
explain their own understanding of themselves as model workers or the
readiness to embody this discursive construction even though it may
consequently portray them as docile and passive. This simultaneous
empowerment and disempowerment that they derive from internalizing
the notion that Filipinos are "different" and "better" nurses may not necessarily ensure job security and may even undermine worker solidarity.
But it provides them with some measure of self-satisfaction and pride.

It also alleviates their professional insecurities about their technical competence and their everyday fear of losing their job. Embodying the notion that they are "better" and that they offer a unique form of labor power as Filipinos serve as social and cultural capital (Bourdieu 1980/1990, 1984), allowing them to acquire a form of power to manage their disadvantaged positions. Just as brokers have a role in manufacturing the kind of nurse that will be marketable in the global economy, these nurses act in ways that will mitigate their vulnerabilities as contract workers. In addition to their vulnerabilities, as Eureka's quote above suggests, their material realities and aspirations underlie their attempt to capitalize on the discursive constructions that they assert will provide them a comparative advantage.

DISTINCTIVELY FILIPINO

"Filipino nurses are different," nurses explained to me repeatedly. They claimed that this was clearly observable in how they, as opposed to their "American" or "white" colleagues, approached and provided nursing care.[1] While they were aware of the political and economic realities that propel foreign employers such as those in the United States to recruit nurses from the Philippines, they hardly, if at all, attributed it to colonial relations between the two countries. Before they left the Philippines, their understanding of why employers recruit Filipino nurses was shaped by what foreign employers relayed to them is the reputation of Filipinos as competent nurses who possess the educational, technical, and English-language proficiency to deliver health care in the United States.

For example, when Cherry was applying for a job at Gray Meadows, her recruiter simply told her that the reason why these employers were going to the Philippines was because they had "heard about" Filipino nurses. Although they had no prior experience with hiring Filipinos, the fact that they had heard about the quality of their service created a sufficient basis for hiring them. For Filipino nurses themselves, the discursive construction of Filipinos as ideal nurses acts as the frame through which they perceive their comparative advantage. And if, as Foucault (1972, 49) noted, "discourses are practices that systematically form the objects of which they speak," then these discursive constructions can also regulate the conduct of individuals that they seek to govern.

In other words, the ability of labor brokers to succeed in marketing Filipinos as members of a top-quality workforce and the ability of foreign employers to procure this labor that they have heard so much about depend on how Filipino themselves display this and deliver it.

Remarkably, Filipino nurses do uphold their unique approach to nursing care, which, for many, becomes evident when they see their work in relation to non-Filipino colleagues. Their sense of Filipinos' added value becomes clearly defined and to some extent even changes a bit. While they also agree that the English-language proficiency and the bachelor's degree in nursing add to the desirability of Filipinos as workers, this is not their only primary explanation. Many attest to the capacity of Filipino nurses to carry out work responsibilities with minimal direction, assistance, and complaints. This is what Gabriela saw as Filipino nurses' "self-sufficiency," which she herself provided to her Arizona employers. "So long as I can handle the work, I will do it. I don't want to rely on other people. I will only ask for help if I cannot do the work on my own or I am too busy," she explained (interview by the author, December 19, 2006).While Gabriela's approach may easily be tagged as a marker of passivity, she claims it with pride insofar as she sees it as a sign of strength and, as I describe later, a way of garnering respect from her colleagues.

Similarly, Joen characterized Filipino nurses as being "willing to do everything" in terms of taking on more patients and not complaining despite being handed patients who may require more care. She simply viewed this as an innate characteristic of Filipinos that she embodied. "For us, you know how we are. We are patient. We are hard workers. So it is okay for us to be given this much work," she reasoned (interview by the author, January 19, 2004). While Joen's assessment is based on having worked in Gray Meadows for three years, newly arrived nurses such as Justin also quickly observed this as a characteristic that makes Filipino nurses distinct compared with the "unruly and complaining" American (white) nurses. She remarked that if Filipinos complained, they did so in private and with other nurses but never in front of the employer. With certainty, Justin simply stated, "It is inherent in us that we don't talk back to the employer so that even if we want to demand for a higher salary, we just keep quiet" (interview by the author, January 16, 2004). She said this matter-of-factly, almost as if to indicate that there is a time and place for Filipino nurses to speak up and not deferring to authority would be out of character, even if the consequences may be much more detrimental such as not being able to discuss their desires for a wage increase.

In addition to being self-sufficient, Filipino nurses claim that their work ethic involves taking pride in their work by making sure that the tasks assigned to them during their shift are completed, even if it involves not taking breaks or clocking out past their shift. As some nurses recounted, they want to end their shift by creating a smooth transition for the group that follows them. Therefore, they become extremely critical when they observe that their white colleagues (primarily) do not do the same. And this is what sets Filipino nurses apart from their White colleagues, according to Mabolo: "Filipinos have a different mentality. In the Philippines, when you have a job to do, you do it and you don't pass it on to the next shift. Here, sometimes, whites avoid assuming these responsibilities and just say that this and that happened, like "The IV is leaking," but in the Philippines, you don't do that because the next shift will get angry. If that happened in your shift, you should fix it in your shift. But here, I see that they pass it on to the next shift" (interview by the author, January 27, 2004).

While Mabolo expected a certain kind of continuity in the care provided across work shifts, she, like other Filipino nurses, believed that a smooth transition was about resolving any problems during a nurse's shift and handing over completed tasks to the colleagues who would follow them. Nurses interpret any deviation from this as an indication of poor job performance and laziness that contribute not only to a poor quality of care for the patients but also to nurses' sense of integrity about their work. Joen expressed it best: "You know how we [Filipinos] are, we just want to do the job right. When I work, I'm confident that it is done well." To this end, Joen relied on her self-sufficiency to carry out her tasks.

Nurses also take on the kind of "flexibility" they believe Filipinos offer to their employers in terms of their work schedules. This often involves assuming work shifts that are typically undesirable for their colleagues, such as nights, weekends, or holidays. Often it is about the willingness to put in overtime hours, which are crucial for units facing staffing shortages. While the primary motivation for Filipino nurses is the "extra" wages that they can garner from working such schedules, this kind of flexibility is cost effective for their employers. Eureka knew that if she worked overtime, it would save her unit from the possibility of securing the costly services of a nurse staffing registry to hire a temporary nurse. Unfortunately, it had also created an expectation that Eureka could work anytime her unit needed her. This materialized in her unit's sometimes asking her to work four nights straight, which, at twelve-hour shifts, can be an excruciatingly tiring schedule. Other times, it meant being asked to come in during her days off with only a few hours' notice. As a result of the reputation she had gained of being available and not turning down requests for overtime, she sometimes found herself screening her phone calls at home out of fear that her nurse manager would call to see if Eureka would relinquish her day off and come in to work a night shift.

Other Filipino nurses I met revealed the same kind of flexibility and tended to make the generalization that this trait was distinctively Filipino. While they understood that working certain shifts offered an easy way of supplementing their incomes because of the financial incentives offered, they also explained that it reflected a fundamental difference in work ethic from that of their white colleagues. It is this difference that perhaps makes visible the kind of added value that foreign labor can provide. That is, Filipinos see themselves as willing to sacrifice their weekends, days off, and holidays in contrast to their white colleagues, who they believe value these times and are less flexible with their schedule.

But the most important aspect of their care that Filipinos believe contributes to the unique care work they offer reflects what labor brokers often tout as the TLC (tender loving care) they incorporate in their work. Diana, who had been working in Arizona since 2003 described the patient care that Filipinos provide as "more sensitive." She elaborated: "You have a patient who is depressed and you will see Filipinos check on that patient frequently as opposed to whites who will leave her or him once they have administered the medicine. If the patient complains, the white nurses will make themselves visibly annoyed. But we [Filipino nurses] will keep talking to that patient. Some agree that we give a different patient care and that we listen to patients and that we provide them comfort. We spend more time with them.

But whites will not allow themselves to spend more time with the patient. *Filipinos are different. They are just different*" (interview by the author, May 3, 2006; emphases in the original).

She described this in relation to her British colleagues, whom she criticized for spending more time taking care of themselves (for example, taking breaks to smoke) than they did in attending to their patients' needs. She expressed disappointment about the fact that she sometimes ended up shouldering the complaints of patients who were dissatisfied with the care they had received from other nurses, most of whom tended to be white. Although she also pointed out that her observations were not applicable to all her white colleagues, she was particularly adamant in claiming that Filipinos provide "different" and better patient care. Moreover, the attentiveness and patience that she described were traits that she reiterated to me were simply "inherent among Filipinos." Using a culturally essentialist logic in the same way that brokers do, she argued for the naturalness of delivering compassionate care work among Filipinos, an approach that is part of traditional patient care in the Philippines.

Similarly, Mabolo, who was firm in saying that she did not consider herself to be in the ranks of the country's *bagong bayani* (modern-day heroes), took pride in being able to provide compassionate care work by having a deep sense of empathy for her patients' pain and suffering. "It is as if we pity and feel sorry for them to the point that if only we can do something good for the patient, we feel that we should do it," commented Mabolo, after recounting a patient's complaints about the care he received from other nurses. Mabolo discovered that the pain and discomfort he experienced came from wearing an ill-fitting body brace, a situation that could have easily been remedied with attentive nursing care. She attributed this poor-quality patient care largely to the inability of her non-Filipino colleagues to empathize with their patients.

In general, as with Mabolo and Diana, Filipino nurses feel a sense of obligation toward their patients in terms of striving for compassionate, "tender-loving" bedside care, which they claim comes easy for Filipinos, who grew up with this care ethic and are trained in providing it. This belief transcends gender; the male nurses I interviewed agreed with this assessment. Ansel, a nurse in Arizona, reasoned, like Mabolo, that unlike his non-Filipino colleagues, he was more responsive to his patients. He claimed that he could not ignore their calls, albeit incessant, because he would feel guilty for somehow neglecting them. Another male nurse in Arizona, Barkada, explained that Filipino nurses were *malambing*, that is, they possess a distinctive Filipino trait that he claimed came from an inherent hospitable and loving nature that enabled them to bond easily and establish good rapport with their patients. Barkada noted that he had this reputation, specifically in terms of his ability to lift up his patients' spirits through his sense of humor. Thus, it is not surprising for him to see why patients often appreciate being under the care of Filipino nurses and why he has gained some popularity in his unit.

THE COST OF BEING BETTER

As the previous narratives show, Filipino nurses perceive themselves as possessing qualities that make them better nurses, and they embrace this difference with pride. This is despite the fact that they themselves notice that their superiority sometimes leads to disparate work responsibilities and assumptions about their work ethic. Joen, who had earlier recounted the notion that Filipinos' sense of patience and self-sufficiency helped them deal with their workload, also noticed the unexpected consequence of having greater responsibilities in their unit, which sometimes resulted in overwhelming and exhausting work shifts. While she understood that this perhaps happened because Filipinos might be reluctant to seek help through a desire to complete a given task or through a lack of trust in colleagues' quality of care, she also admitted that this mentality may not necessarily be beneficial for Filipinos in the long run. "I think that saying that Filipinos are willing to work long hours and assume more work responsibilities have a negative connotation. Maybe they can call us hard workers but not that we can do everything" she said (interview by the author, January 19, 2004). Joen reasoned that the kind of flexibility that has come to define Filipino nurses' work ethic makes them appear "weak" and easily exploited.

Some perceive that if they are self-sufficient and do not require any additional assistance on the job, it can sometimes backfire. This was the case with Diana, who complained about not being able to get any support from the certified nursing assistants (CNAs) in her unit. She gave this as an example of how her colleagues took advantage of the reputation that Filipinos had gained about their capacity to provide bedside care independently and with minimal assistance. However, in some instances, this had come to mean complete withdrawal of support for Filipino nurses such as Diana who may be unable to carry out a task alone (for example, lifting a heavy patient) or should not assume tasks assigned to CNAs (such as bathing a patient). While Diana was also unaware of how hospitals also exploited the labor of CNAs, her assessment was based on observing the disparities in the support they provided in her unit in ways that short-changed Filipinos of the benefits of having this assistance. Thus, at the same time that Diana firmly held on to the notion that Filipino nurses provide better patient care, she also entertained the possibility that this very perception may have created the problems she was experiencing in her unit.

The notion that Filipinos desire and are unlikely to turn down overtime comes with unfair expectations that put them in difficult situations. As noted above, Eureka's willingness to put in overtime came with an automatic assumption of her being always readily available. Other nurses shared this sentiment and although many admitted that they welcomed the financial incentives that overtime work provided, they also felt constrained by the assumption of their readiness to do so. HB, another nurse in Arizona, felt obligated to work overtime, especially during the first few months at her job, because she thought that this was a way to build rapport with her supervisors. However, she eventually realized that the requests she received were not limited to her but were received by all Filipinos in her unit. This overdependence on Filipinos to remedy staffing problems became most visible when her supervisors gave her the role of being the liaison to other Filipino nurses. She was the one who phoned her Filipino colleagues to ask if they could give up their days off and come in to work or perhaps extend their current shift. And because her supervisors also already anticipated that some Filipinos were keenly aware of the possibility of such requests and sometimes tended to avoid them during their days off, they advised HB to use her personal mobile phone to increase the likelihood that they would pick up the call if they thought it did not originate from the hospital.

Like HB, other nurses expressed the thought that even though they welcomed any opportunities for extra pay, they had become disdainful of the overdependence on Filipinos, who employers assumed would be at their beck and call to fill a unit's staffing needs. Filipino nurses serve the dual role of becoming a quick remedy for the overall nursing staff shortages and, as Marx would describe it, the *reserve army of labor* for employers to use for filling undesirable work schedules. As the nurses themselves stated, the perception of their readiness, flexibility, self-sufficiency, and willingness to assume multiple work tasks might certainly enhance their position as ideal nurses, but they also were aware of the effects of these perceptions. Nevertheless, they were not likely to challenge them, but instead continued to accommodate and promote their added value as nurses. If they had already seen how these discursive constructions could disempower them, then how did they rationalize their accommodation of them? This is an issue that I address in the next sections.

"I Don't Complain So Long as They Pay Me"

The reputation of Filipino nurses as unlikely to complain or challenge authority and as possessing high work standards is in place even before they start working. As occurred with nurses I interviewed, the contract negotiation with employers seemed almost nonexistent, if not unnecessary; not one of them attempted to negotiate his or her wages, benefits, work responsibilities, or schedules. But while this response can easily be marketed as an indication of Filipinos' docility and desperation to leave the country, it is only part of the story. While the convertibility of the U.S. dollar in the Philippines shaped their readiness to accept job offers as they were originally presented to them, they also did so purposefully. For example, for Michelle, not only was she aware that the thirteen-dollar-an-hour wage offered to her was lower than what she might have got from another hospital, especially given her ten years' nursing experience, she did not contest this by trying to bargain for more or look for another employer. As Michelle reasoned in an interview with me, she did not necessarily have in mind specific characteristics of an ideal employer but simply strived to find one who could be her ticket out of the Philippines: "For me, I saw that I have an employer and that was the important thing. All I was thinking about was getting an employer who would be my stepping-stone. I did not want to be picky" (interview by the author, January 20, 2004). And even after they found out that other colleagues who came after them got higher salaries and sign-on bonuses, they did not seem to be embittered to the point of demanding some sort of parity from their employers. Rather, they simply pointed to having obtained their ultimate goal of reaching the United States. As Joen put it, "I am already here [in the United States]. I have my green card and I can go anywhere I want to" (interview by the author, January 19, 2004).

This kind of mobility is, indeed, specific to having an immigrant EB-3 visa. This visa allowed Joen to stay in the United States indefinitely and gave her the freedom to look for another employer upon completion of her first contract. But the freedom of mobility she expressed was also about the general relief that she, like other nurses, felt about leaving a place that had, in many ways, stunted her professional growth. That is, the circumstances of nurses such as Michelle and Joen underscore the underlying determination of Filipino nurses to migrate because of what they perceive is the relative low value attached to nursing work in the Philippines. This is reflected not only in the very low wages afforded to them but also in the dismal quality of available employment opportunities.

For instance, Joen, having made it onto the dean's list, was one of the top graduates in her nursing class—a standing that she thought would give her an edge in finding employment. Her naïveté blocked her from seeing that finding work as a nurse in the Philippines is less about one's performance in school than it is about having connections in hospitals. She ended up working as a volunteer nurse in a provincial hospital, joining other nurses who persisted with the minimal stipends offered to them, as they hoped that the training they obtained will help them transition to a permanent employment at a hospital. Meanwhile, she witnessed colleagues who she claimed were less competent and skilled than she was get immediate placement in hospitals simply because they had relatives, friends, or government officials there who advocated for them. This is the "padrino system," according to Pia, another nurse in Gray Meadows, who had had similar experiences to Joen's and was also determined to leave the Philippines. Like Joen, who eventually pursued administrative work for various companies as a more viable alternative to doing volunteer nursing work, Pia worked in the Middle East instead. She refused to work as a volunteer nurse and reasoned:

> Nurses get exploited in the Philippines. From my experience, after graduation, they are looking for experience. But how are you going to gain experience if they do not give you an opportunity? So they

are exploited in the sense that they will take you as volunteer—without pay, without allowance, without nothing! So you have to volunteer first. . . . They said that the ones who volunteer first are the ones who will get "absorbed" [get a job in a hospital]—that is your ladder. That is the trend in the Philippines. I did not do that and I did not want to do that because if you are working, then you should be paid, right? After all, they should also pay you for your exhaustion and toil. You are also eating during that time so you need money for food! So, I am not guilty about leaving the country. It's their fault that nurses leave (interview by the author, January 20, 2004).

Like other nurses, Pia regarded her ability to work in the United States as a way to escape a place that devalued and took advantage of her labor without proper wage remuneration and as a place that institutionalizes and reproduces social inequalities within the profession. Working successfully as a nurse in the Philippines becomes an issue of *who* you know instead of *what* you know and leaves many nurses unable to compete and thrive in this unjust system. The embittered response that Pia expressed can help explain the underlying drive of Filipinos to migrate or their readiness to accept job offers without much contestation. Perhaps they also help give meaning to the ways in which they approach their work and deal with racialized work expectations and distribution of workload. That is, the perception that they are willing to work any shifts or assume a greater workload is a result of the material realities they face. As Pia herself stated, "It is in Filipinos' nature not to offend their employers as much as possible. In a way, I guess they take advantage of that but that is work. You came here for the work" (interview by the author, January 20, 2004).

Mabolo, a nurse who admitted to having found it difficult to adjust to a twelve-hour shift and who was always working the undesirable work shifts or putting in significant overtime also rationalized them as acceptable to her because she was getting paid for the work. Although the work schedule was a particularly hard adjustment, knowing that she got additional pay for those shifts led her to think that it was a sufficient exchange for the flexibility she gained. "I don't complain so long as they pay me," she reasoned as she recounted her willingness to volunteer for and pitch in to meet the staffing needs of her unit. As with many other nurses, Mabolo came from a work setting in which financial remuneration is not always guaranteed for performing this kind of labor. Thus, the material incentives that came with night shifts or overtime allowed her to negotiate the inconvenient and exhausting aspects and demands of doing the work.

This was also the case with Eureka, whose colleagues found her willingness to do overtime to be excessive. But for her, besides the fact that working acted as a cure for the loneliness and isolation of living in Arizona, she could earn additional income: "You can call Filipinos anytime and they will work—even if they have not had any sleep. However, I may be hardworking but it is also because I have a goal. I want to earn extra money" (interview by the author, August 1, 2005). Thus, while she did not contest this work ethic, she also made it very clear that it was not an addiction to work or some extraordinary trait that spurred her to perform this labor. Rather, it was simply a practical desire to earn more.

Similarly, the monetary value that nurses' work represents in general serves to mitigate patient care challenges that come up and sometimes allows them to mask negative feelings toward their work. For example, in speaking about the differences between the work of Filipino and white nurses, Gabriela explained, "You give whites a needy patient and they just say that they are 'PIA' [pain in the ass] and would complain. But Filipinos will not do that and will be at the patient's beckon call, even though deep down, you are cussing [the patients] out. You cuss them out and then you remind yourself that that patient represents the dollar that you are working for (interview by the author, December 19, 2006).

Gabriela's observations provide a way of countering the oft-cited notion that Filipinos are always already innately patient and have a non-combative demeanor that makes them ideally suited for withstanding the grueling aspects of their work. Gabriela offered an alternative interpretation of the level of work performance that easily leads to depictions of Filipino nurses as submissive by highlighting the nature of the emotional labor that they deliver to deal with the same difficulties faced by their colleagues. In this case, Filipinos' seemingly accommodating response to "needy" patients makes sense, especially given the consumerist framework that dominates service-oriented industries, in which the security of one's job depends on consumer satisfaction.

For Filipino nurses whose dollar earnings not only go toward their own livelihood but also supplement those of multiple members of their families, the satisfaction of their patients is their job security. This is also not to imply, however, that Filipino nurses are simply grateful for the opportunity to provide this care; rather, it reflects the pragmatism with which Filipinos navigate their vulnerability as immigrant and contract workers and their determination to fulfill their goal of attaining a decent livelihood, if not prosperity.

"WE ARE AFRAID OF GETTING SUED": MANAGING A CULTURE OF FEAR

A significant difference that Filipino nurses observe in their transition and that they appreciate is the respect that they derive from being a nurse in the United States. Besides the living wage they earn, they have an increased sense of autonomy with respect to their nursing practice. Many of the nurses I interviewed mentioned the remarkable degree of responsibility they had in providing input on their patients' care and the close partnership they had with physicians in assessing a patient's needs. This is unlike what they were accustomed to in the Philippines, where their role was merely to assist and to be available at the whim of physicians. Pia described the relationship this way: "Nurses in the Philippines are dependent on doctors. . . . The nurse is just the hands of the doctor and is the one who will do whatever the doctor tells her to do. But here, it is different. Sometimes the nurse also has to make patient assessments. And because you are the one assigned to the patient, you are the one who knows more about that patient. Therefore, you are the one to report to the doctor and then you can suggest a course of treatment" (interview by the author, January 20, 2004).

Nurses like Pia are shocked to learn that their responsibilities in the United States go beyond simply supporting physicians; they engage in a kind of partnership with physicians, one in which their opinions and their assessments of patients are sought and highly valued. Many of the nurses I interviewed did not speak fondly of their experiences in the Philippines, where the exploitation of nurses is seen in their wages as well as in their everyday interactions with colleagues who devalue their work. During a group conversation, Marife, Jan, and Ansel, all of whom were working in Arizona, complained that being a nurse in the

Philippines is often a demoralizing experience when it comes to relationships with physicians (Interview by the author, August 1, 2005). They claimed that physicians there not only undermine the skills and training that nurses possess but also use them to assert their authority. That is, nurses are constantly reminded that they are *just* nurses and cannot act without the direction of physicians. Their collective experiences reveal that nurses must not only put up with the meager (if any) wages they get but also manage the powerlessness imparted to them in their practice. They are always already presumed incompetent and unable to provide any patient care without the expertise of a physician, which in turn creates an environment and working relationship in which physicians can freely denigrate or humiliate nurses. Such disrespect, is, according to Ansel, simply a result of the fact that "doctors there do not trust nurses to assist patients."

Thus when nurses come to the United States, they are astonished by their new status and the expectations that their colleagues hold for them. They realize that although there is still a hierarchy of authority in their units, they do not have the same diminished position vis-à-vis their superiors. They take note of the ability to work as a team and be regarded as a valuable team member. This was the case for Kitty, who for the first time could finally identify herself as a nurse. She was pleasantly surprised about the relatively high value attached to the work of nurses, unlike in the Philippines, where being a nurse was seen as an undesirable, low level job, primarily because of the low wages.

And unlike in the Philippines, where Kitty was not given any responsibilities that had anything to do with directly managing the well-being of a patient, in the United States, she said, "you have to think." That is, while doctors made the final decisions, as a nurse she was now able to also evaluate the state of her patients' health and make appropriate treatment recommendations to physicians. She remarked that this was always the way she had envisioned nursing work or how she had seen it portrayed on American TV shows such as *ER*, but it had not matched her own experience until now. Another nurse, Kit, with seven years' nursing experience when I met her in 2004, shared Kitty's assessment. She saw this autonomy as about having professional growth; not only did she feel integrated in the hospital in terms of providing patient care but she was also remarkably surprised about the availability of continuing education courses that allowed her to obtain additional training and skills.

At the same time that this was a welcome change for the nurses, their newfound role and autonomy was quite intimidating. Because they administered a significant number of medical procedures to their patients and worked in close partnership with physicians, they also saw themselves as being on the front lines when it came to patient complaints and mistakes. They quickly learned about the proliferation of lawsuits in U.S. health care delivery and the looming possibility of losing a job as a result. Many were not accustomed to a working climate in which health care providers are fundamentally at the mercy of their patients' satisfaction. As Ansel pointed out, "Every time you go to work, you feel nervous. You don't know what will happen or what kind of patient you will have. Will the patient tell on you or complain about you? That is always my worry. What if I do something wrong and then this patient complains to my manager? What if they sue you? That scares me" (interview by the author, August 1, 2005). Unlike in the Philippines, where nurses find the work more "relaxing," nursing work in the United States is downright intimidating. As Ansel alluded to above, the anxiety for nurses behind the ramifications of getting sued and losing their job takes away from their enjoying their work in the same way that they did in the Philippines. They may have gained a certain degree of autonomy in their practice here but this empowerment also comes with a price.

For nurses, making mistakes, having dissatisfied patients, and being sued have all created a *culture of fear* that hovers over their nursing practice and I contend that this also influences the way that they approach and provide patient care. During my second interview with Marife, who just finished her first year with her Arizona employer, she firmly observed that Filipino nurses like her had a much greater responsibility and a heavier workload than other nurses. She reasoned that their charge nurse, who essentially supervised the entire unit for a given shift and managed the distribution of workload had always expressed to her that Filipinos were preferred because they rarely complained or contested their assignments, even if some disparities resulted. Marife admitted that she often got more patients and those who required greater attention in comparison with her white colleagues. Although she initially claimed that she didn't know why this was the case, she also reasoned that part of this seeming passivity had to do with the culture of fear: "Of course, we [Filipino nurses] are afraid of being sued [and] that is why we are cautious. White nurses are so argumentative and they would fight with patients on the phone. We let it go" (interview by the author, August 27, 2006). Marife, like other nurses, was fearful of the power afforded to her patients, which she interpreted as requiring a certain level of emotion management that might undoubtedly make them appear more accommodating. That is, Marife's reasoning provides an alternative, if not additional, explanation for the patience and tolerance that Filipino nurses may display toward their patients.

This is not to say that they are merely impostors or that any tender loving care they provide is fake or superficial. Rather, her explanation sheds light on how their actions and approaches to their work function to allow them to mask their vulnerabilities and fears of failure. The newfound autonomy that seems to bring them a sense of empowerment is the same autonomy that is the source of intimidation and fear as a result of the potential liabilities that their new responsibilities bring to them as nurses in the United States. For many of them, keeping patients content and satisfied is their pragmatic response and allows them to deal with this tension and gain some measure of control over their fragile employment situation.

"I WANT TO BE GOOD LIKE THEM": FLEXIBILITY AS MOBILITY

When U.S. employers pursue hiring Filipino workers for their hospitals, they are mainly attracted by those workers' four-year bachelor's degree in nursing, their having been trained under a U.S.-modeled curriculum, and their facility in the English language. While the Filipino nurses whom I interviewed affirmed that these factors were the basis of their desirability as workers, they were still left with some feelings of insecurity. This was especially the case with those who were still adjusting to a new system and had been in the United States for no more than five years.

Diana, for example, recalled the overwhelming sense of unpreparedness she felt when she first started working in Arizona. Despite her eleven years of bedside nursing experience in the Philippines, she was astonished by the unfamiliarity of the new system in which she was working: "I felt like I didn't know anything. When I got to the [unit floor], I felt like I was a student again. There are equipment and technologies that we don't have in the Philippines. I know how to provide nursing care but I'm not used to other things [procedures and equipment] (interview by the author, May 3, 2006). Similarly, Justin, while understanding the professional currency of their Bachelor's of Science in Registered Nursing degree also felt inept in terms of her lack of knowledge about delivering procedures and using certain available technologies to manage patient care during her first few months in Texas. This all made for an enormous learning curve for her, which she claimed was not always understood by her colleagues, who expected that her Bachelor's of Science in Registered Nursing degree and the salary it afforded her would produce a nurse who was ready to work with minimal instructions.

Additionally, the threat the nurses felt with regard to their professional competency came from the American patients themselves, whom the nurses perceived to be more knowledgeable than their patients in the Philippines about their health care. Bing, who had had a total of nine years' nursing experience, which included working in Saudi Arabia, believed that this was a contributing factor to the pressures she felt as a nurse. She expressed how her success as a nurse depended on her ability to complete tasks assigned to her as well as her capacity to anticipate the questions that her patients might ask: "People are much more knowledgeable here so you have to be very knowledgeable as well. Sometimes, they know much more about a disease than you" (interview by the author, September 1, 2006). Needless to say, encountering patients who were proactive about their health care was new to her and was a source of everyday anxiety. For her, being able to answer all her patient's questions and provide thorough explanations were ways she could demonstrate her competence as a nurse.

Filipino nurses project flexibility as a way of coping with such insecurities and draw from it as another means of gaining and building technical competence. This is exactly what Michelle thought about in response to the high praise she often received from her supervisors about her apparent docility. "My charge nurse would say that there are so many nurses here who are resistant and that I am good to work with because I am easy to talk to and that I am obedient. . . . I'm open to challenges and

I do not resist." But she found this comment odd. "How can I learn," she asked," if I resist the things that they give me? This is how I learn. And I want to learn. I want to be like them. I want to be good like them (interview by the author, January 20, 2004; emphasis added). Whereas her supervisors interpreted her reactions as an expression of docility, she viewed her situation as offering an opportunity to rebuild her confidence in carrying out certain procedures, confidence that she claimed was rapidly deteriorating during this transition.

Michelle, with her thirteen years' nursing experience, which included supervisory positions, felt unable to keep up the pace in her new position. She was unaccustomed to the rhythm of her unit and to the increased reliance on machines to determine a patient's condition. All this was new to her. She tried to use her assignments as a way of learning and improving her skills and to be ultimately as "good" as her colleagues. Yet another nurse, Sylvia, expressed something similar and believed that flexibility was a way to build "mobility in the profession." Sylvia believed that being flexible and having the willingness to assume multiple responsibilities could lead to job promotions, which might include assuming leadership roles. She recognized this behavior as a possible advantage that Filipino workers could maximize over time.

For many of the nurses I spoke with, one of the key sources of the insecurities that they felt was their level of competency in English. Although they had passed all the English-language exams and evidently could converse and write in English, unfamiliar slang and the speed at which the language was spoken in everyday conversation jarred them. Reflecting some common reactions, Diana felt that she was "running out" of English words to say, while Pia had difficulty understanding accents. The nurses' self-esteem diminished and they felt humiliated every time they had to ask their patients or colleagues to repeat statements or when their colleagues asked them to do so, claiming that they were unable to understand what the nurses had said. Edward, a nurse in Gray Meadows, was one of the many who felt exceedingly self-conscious and intimidated about his English-speaking abilities. He described his strategy, which he claimed was his "secret," of rebuilding his self-confidence. At the end of his shift, he visited his elderly patients and engaged them in casual conversation. He saw them as starved for company and as an abundant source of stories that they could tell about their lives. He argued that this was a symbiotic relationship because they also gained an audience with whom they could share stories and their everyday concerns. So he spent time asking them a variety of questions, about topics ranging from their daily activities, to their families, to their life story. He reasoned that these conversations enabled him to practice his English with individuals who were not likely to scrutinize or make judgments about his fluency. He described this "secret" to me with pride; he felt that it was not only a clever way to befriend and gain the admiration of these patients but also an effective strategy, which cost nothing and required little effort, for improving his confidence in speaking English.

The image of competence that Filipino nurses project to their supervisors and employers becomes especially crucial. Like Michelle, Eureka faced an overwhelming number of tasks, which she readily assumed in order to prove herself. She stated that her white colleagues often took advantage of Filipinos for being so compliant and flexible, and she provided an explanation for this. During one of her night shifts, she was given four patients—infants—all at once, which caught the attention of another nurse, who pointed out the unfairness of being given such a large patient load. Eureka, however, felt that the other nurse's reaction was unnecessary. "If it were just me, I wouldn't have said anything. One of my coworkers told me that I should have just said no, that I cannot do the work anymore. But I can't say that, unless I'm not confident I can do the job. It wasn't the right time then to do it and I didn't want to risk losing my license" (interview by the author, August 1, 2005).

Eureka explained that working in the neonatal intensive care unit was difficult because she was dealing with patients who had already been fragile before their present condition had occurred. Having more than two infants to manage was especially challenging when it came to their feeding times because each infant needed close individual attention. Having four infants for one nurse in a given shift is quite excessive. But Eureka's choice not to complain or seek relief from her supervisors was motivated by fears of her being evaluated as incapable of doing the work and therefore, unfit to be a nurse. She was afraid of losing her license and, as a result, her job. She thought that proving she could handle a workload that was considered excessive would create the perception that she did not shy away from challenging tasks or become intimidated by them.

Outside her work hours, Eureka spent the little free time she had reading about and reviewing medical procedures. She used overtime assignments to practice new techniques. She viewed professional competency through skill building as the surest form of social capital for Filipino nurses. She had advice to impart to nurses who were planning to make the same journey she had taken: "They need to prepare themselves and make sure that they update their skills. We [Filipinos] are competitive in terms of knowledge but not in terms of practice. [Whites] are boastful. They won't consider you an equal unless they know you are capable and that you will speak up. So you really need to know your work. You need to be confident. If you are confident, then they cannot take advantage of you. You are your only defense" (interview by the author, August 1, 2005). Eureka believed that Filipinos were qualified to practice nursing and provided a more compassionate type of care, which would always give them an edge over others. However, she also recognized that because of the number of nursing schools in the Philippines that were simply "mass producing" nurses for immediate deployment abroad instead of allowing them to receive additional training first, the nurses who would come to the United States would experience the same sense of unpreparedness.

Justin would agree with Eureka insofar as the former also struggled through her transition, trying to learn procedures, such as preparing patients' laboratory tests, that were not traditionally carried out by nurses in the Philippines. But she asserted that "once we get to know all of these things, we will be better than Americans. Touchwise—Filipinos are different" (interview by the author, January 16, 2004). Justin, like other nurses, believed that she was already competitive because of the type of care and rapport that Filipino nurses shower on their patients and that once she acquired these skills, she could see herself as being on par with her colleagues. Nurses like Eureka and Justin leave the Philippines with minimal preparation for the work that awaits them. Meanwhile, their employers provide them with minimal orientation and assume that their Bachelor's of Science in Registered Nursing degree means exactly the same thing as in the United States and that they are already equipped with the knowledge and skills they need to navigate a new work environment.

"Do They Think That We Are Robots?"

As the nurses accommodated and tried to make the most of the disempowering situations in which they found themselves, they also showed how they could and did fight back. While they were evidently ruled by a disciplinary power that turned them into seemingly docile subjects, this does not mean that they did not challenge what they faced, despite the consequences that resulted. Eureka's story best exemplifies this.

Although Eureka's willingness to work overtime and her apparent flexibility may lead one to believe that she was always noncombative, her story reveals otherwise. She actually perceived that she might be an exception to what her employers expected of Filipino nurses. In her everyday practice, she claimed to violate rules, which she believed were illogical and insensitive. For instance, she discussed the ways in which she, along with other Filipino nurses, often defied workplace norms about catering to the families of the infant patients, whether it be in spending extra time with them or sneaking them items like water or a stuffed toy for their infant. Her colleagues saw this as going beyond their job but Eureka felt that these were minor things that did not require any additional energy or labor on her part. Over time, her supervisors and colleagues learned that she was not who she appeared to be. "People have to complain once in a while. You cannot just be taken advantage of all the time. You should stand up for yourself. If you know it is not fair, then you need to raise that as a problem in order to formulate action," Eureka affirmed to me.

True to her words, she did exactly that when her workload became unbearable by taking it up with the employment agency managing her contract. "Do they think that we are robots?" she exclaimed as she recounted pushing her agency to investigate her case because she felt that her supervisors treated her as an object to be controlled at will, as someone they did not envision would question authority, let alone file a complaint. But she defied their assumptions and relentlessly pursued her case with this staffing agency. Unfortunately, the results were not favorable to her and the agency did not mediate in the way that she expected. This is the same agency, referred to earlier, that was already weary of her questions about the significant amount of deductions that it took from her paycheck. Since Eureka had already been labeled a "troublemaker," whose homesickness the agency had claimed made her psychologically unstable, she was left without much recourse but to find a way of escaping her oppressive situation. She bought out her contract and sought another employer in San Diego—a place where she had a family friend who could provide her support.

While Eureka's case is indicative of the vulnerabilities faced by foreign contract workers, it also highlights how they are finding points of resistance, even as they simultaneously accommodate the same power that seeks to weaken their agency. Another nurse, Kitty, also refused to keep quiet and tried to protect herself from being taken advantage of by her employers. In a same conversation in which she affirmed that Filipino nurses tended to be noncombative, shy, and quiet, she also described herself as an exception to this. She diligently took note of the number of patients assigned in the unit and unhesitatingly called out any disparities to her charge nurses.[2] If her charge nurse insisted that Kitty take on another patient, she refused and told the charge nurse that she could not provide "total patient care." She was aware that her charge nurses would be responsive to this reasoning, especially since too many patients might affect quality of care. Unlike other nurses, Kitty wasn't bothered if she was perceived as inflexible or uncooperative. She acknowledged that she was given a greater number of patients because of the reputation she had gained for finishing her work quickly. "I work fast. When I'm done working, I sit down to do the charting so they think I don't have any work. So sometimes, I just work slower! I don't want them to think that I'm hurrying with my work so I can get another patient. I just work slower. I get this work habit from my white colleagues. Filipinos are not like this," she described (interview by the author, January 27, 2004).

Kitty is atypical of the nurses I met insofar as she not only openly expressed her dissatisfaction with workload distribution but also articulated her preference for working with white colleagues. For one, she believed that working with other Filipinos was often distracting because of the idle chatting that happened keeping her from concentrating on her work. Second, her Filipino charge nurses were sometimes just like her white colleagues and would often assign her patients who needed very close attention. She attributed this to the fact that she was among the younger nurses on duty (Kitty was twenty-five-years old) and therefore was perceived to have more tolerance for handling difficult patients. Finally, she seemed to enjoy working side by side with her white colleagues because it allowed her to pick up nursing techniques that she believed they had the expertise to impart, thus contributing to her professional advancement. This was evident when Kitty praised these colleagues for particular skills and also for their assertiveness. As she mentioned previously, the knowledge that working more slowly was her best protection from being overloaded with work was a "habit" that she learned from them. Thus, not only could she learn about bedside care from her white colleagues, but she also could learn about how to maneuver through labor processes that could easily become exploitative, especially in the midst of discursive constructions about the docility of Filipino nurses.

Like Eureka and Kitty, Gabriela noticed that her supervisors took advantage of Filipinos' self-sufficiency by assigning them heavy workloads, against which some Filipino nurses asserted themselves. But Gabriela was not one of them. She found solace in an understanding that this oppressive situation was only temporary. She rationalized that being assertive came with being familiar with and having the confidence to do the work. She also believed that her supervisors were likely to honor her requests once she had proved herself worthy of their respect. "Eventually, when they see that you do good work, they give you respect. I get their respect first and then I assert myself. Once you get their respect, they respond to you," she explained (interview by the author, December 19, 2006).

It was this type of advice that she dispensed to incoming nurses whom she often found crying and anxious because they were experiencing the same difficulties with their patients and their workload that she was. Gabriela's understanding of her situation made it appear that the challenges they faced as foreign-trained nurses were part of their rite of passage in coming to the United States. She reified the notion that they were presumed to be incompetent—one's "worthiness" to practice nursing in the United States was not a given but had to be proved. This is what nurses such as Gabriela believe.

The logic that surrounds Gabriela's understanding mirrors a general perception that all the nurses I met had of their employers. As some expressed earlier, they regarded their first employer as their stepping-stone to the United States and to other employers. They knew that all they needed was an initial sponsor and that after their two-year contract ended in, they were no longer bound to the same employer. This was the case for three nurses—Joen, Kit, and Eureka, who have all relocated to pursue their California dreams and are now working in San Francisco, Los Angeles, and San Diego, respectively. The sense of rootlessness that Gabriela described is not only about the demeanor that nurses fashion in doing their work but also about their employment prospects and options once they finish their initial contracts.

CONCLUSION

On May 24, 2006, the *New York Times* featured an article that discussed the ongoing dependence of the United States on the Philippines for nurses and the consequential effects on a country that is losing thousands of its nurses each year as a result. In response to this article, the letters to the editor section, under the headline "America's Nurses and the World's," featured an image by Hope Larson that depicted a hunched-over nurse, perhaps Filipina, carrying children in her arms and older adults on her back, all of whom seemed to be in pain or even dying. The nurse's face and posture revealed a caregiver who was strong, determined, and able to withstand any challenges. This is certainly the type of image that brokers use to meet the expectations of prospective employers who come to believe that they are supposed to get not just any nurse but one with added value and, perhaps, extraordinary qualities. The image also aptly captured the ways that the Philippines rests on the backs of workers like this nurse, individuals whose remittances save and sustain a weak economy. She sacrifices not only for her family but also for her nation.

But perhaps the most important aspect of the image is its exposure of the moral economy that governs how Filipinos approach their work and that which illustrates their determination to succeed at all costs. In this chapter, the stories of a number of nurses reveal the ways that Filipino nurses abroad manage their vulnerabilities and the contradictions and tensions behind their embrace of their added value as workers. While they believe and take pride in the idea that they are good, if not better, nurses than others, they also seemingly act in ways that perpetuate the perception that they are docile workers. However, as with the image that

Larson's cartoon projected, the nurses I came to know were not docile or weak; but rather, their self-sacrifice and unwavering strength reveal individuals who are determined to succeed.

They may be "America's nurses and the world's" but they are also their family's economic heroes, and their families' livelihood depends on their success. This is the moral economy that sustains them and governs how they accept their added value as workers, even with awareness of its consequences. They are pragmatic actors who learn to harness the power they derive from it at the same time that they manage the simultaneous ways that this same power renders them vulnerable. Their stories unveil not only the unique structural realities that shape the employment status of these nurses but also their fears and anxieties of failure—both of which inform their action or reluctance to take action. Their job is their life and without it, all their sacrifices will have been made in vain. This is, perhaps, what underlies what Eureka told me during the end of one of our interviews as she continued to offer some parting wisdom to those who might come after her. She wanted to remind them to keep in mind one single thing in the face of adversity: "You came here to work. You didn't come here just to live." Eureka was well aware that while nursing may have been the ticket to the United States, it was also the only ticket to her survival and that of others like her.

CHAPTER 8

Conclusion

THE YEAR 2007 was a good year for the Philippines' overseas employment program. With more than one million workers deployed globally, the country celebrated being ranked fourth among developing countries for its global remittance flow of $14.4 billion (POEA 2008). The increase in the number of highly skilled professionals (nurses, information technology personnel, engineers) and the corresponding decrease in the number of domestic and construction workers deployed did well to fulfill the state's project of "upgrading" its image as a labor provider of "high-value jobs." The opening and expansion of new markets in Canada, the United Arab Emirates, Azerbaijan, and Taiwan following the "aggressive" marketing of Filipino workers continued to secure Filipinos' employment opportunities. As POEA administrator Rosalinda Dimapilis-Baldoz explained, these accomplishments were a tribute to the "world's number one worker, the Overseas Filipino Workers" (POEA 2008, 7).

How these "number one workers," these "great Filipino workers," are produced is the focus of this book. In a globalized economy that is heavily sustained by the labor of immigrants, we are prompted to ask how certain places come to be defined as possessing "ideal" labor resources or how certain groups come to dominate a particular labor force. In this book I tackle these questions by using the Philippines as a case study. I have unraveled the social production and commodification of overseas Filipino workers as ideal labor commodities and the Philippines as the home of the Great Filipino Worker. I have described the institutional and cultural forces that enable this social imaginary through the process of labor brokering—a form of labor control and neoliberal capitalist discipline that sustains the country's labor migration and *brands* Filipinos in ways that aims to transform them into a highly coveted workforce. It is a transnationally coordinated process that is carried out on multiple levels—that of the Philippine state, of employment agencies, and of workers—all working together to keep vibrant the country's labor export economy.

This book intervenes in the often essentialized explanation that designates economic logic as the primary factor driving "Third World" nations such as the Philippines, to explore such programs of development as overseas employment. That is, while the lack of economically viable employment may create a surplus of "ready-to-go" workers, how employers come to imagine Filipinos and how Filipinos come to perceive working abroad are defined through this brokering process. The Philippine labor export economy is unique certainly not because it is the only one that exists in the world but rather because of the coordinated and institutionalized processes that enable it to steadily send Filipinos to capture a sizeable portion of the global economy as a labor provider.

To this end, this book has four goals. First, my intervention in migration discussions shows how labor migration is not a simple linear, bureaucratic process, as it is defined by scholars such as Tyner (1996, 2000) in their descriptions of how the Philippines carries out its labor recruitment process. The ideological and cultural dynamics of this process are integral mechanisms that give meaning to the creativity imbued in marketing Filipinos and overseas employment. Filipino workers themselves also define their migration pathways, as in the case of America-dreaming nurses who pursue alternate routes as stepping-stones to an eventual job in the United States. Second, this intervention provides a more complex picture of the driving force for Filipino migration that is not limited to an economic logic of supply and demand. In this scenario, the outflow of labor is merely the result of an impoverished country that cannot provide viable means of livelihood for its citizens and leads to a creation of a surplus of skilled workers that can readily address the needs of a globalizing economy. I agree with Choy's (2003) contention of the presence of a culture of migration in the Philippines that supplements or deprivileges this economic logic. But extending Choy's claims, I show how institutions such as the state and employment agencies act as social bodies that coalesce to generate ideologies and produce an ethos of labor migration unique to a contemporary period shaped by neoliberalism and a global division of gendered *and* racialized labor.

Thus, a third goal of this book is to show how the commodification of Filipino workers as "ideal labor" reflects a neoliberal form of government that focuses on ruling a citizenry through ideals of entrepreneurship, self-regulation, and "freedom," all of which influence the kind of state-led transnationalism the state carries out in defining Filipino workers' relation to their families and nation. As I have shown in this book, this strategy allows the state, with the support of employment agencies and even NGOs, to "manage" labor migration and profit from it at the same time that it absolves itself of any responsibility for the workers it rewards as its modern-day heroes, ambassadors of goodwill, or potential investors.

The fourth goal of this book is to show that not only gender but also *race* matters in the global division of labor and the ways that these dynamics influence the Philippines' ethos of labor migration. Race matters specifically in how Filipinos are branded to have what I refer to as their *added export value*—their comparative advantage as workers in this global playing field. Using the recruitment of care workers such as nurses and domestic workers, I show this added export value to be about a racialized form of productive femininity and unique Filipina labor power that the state, employment agencies, and workers themselves use to promote not only how they are good, but also how they are *better* workers than others. Salzinger (2003) and other feminist scholars remind us that global production systems are very much informed by a "trope of productive femininity" that is transnationally produced and results in the iconic woman worker whose docility is supposed to be "ideal" for capitalism.

In this book, I specifically point out the actors who enable these tropes to materialize and circulate, and in doing so, I underscore the gendered and racialized moral economy of the Filipino migrant—a market-oriented value system that defines the social positions of labor migrants. For one, this moral economy illuminates how the state and employment agencies seek to define Filipinos' relationship with their nation and the role they should embody as labor migrants. As "model" and "great" Filipino workers, they are asked to be not only entrepreneurial and competitive but also socially respectable. It also captures the determination of Filipino workers for survival and social mobility as it gives meaning to how they rationalize their work, navigate unjust relations, and even embrace their "added export value" when upholding it becomes disempowering.

I illustrated that this gendered and racialized moral economy informs how institutions define their role not only in carrying out this program of development but also in the immigrant identity formation of Filipinos. As in the case of professional workers such as nurses, how they resist and accommodate the ways that they are supposed *to be* as workers is governed by their attempts to mitigate their vulnerabilities as foreign migrants. This is important to acknowledge because their stories allow us to explore a different way of seeing class struggles and, perhaps, suggest a more nuanced depiction of their struggles and their social agency. That is, they show the simultaneity of their experiences—how they can both be oppressed and at the same time empowered and how they can embrace and at the same time challenge the powers that govern their lives. This is a kind of picture that is often missing in worker or immigrant narratives.

Most comprehensive estimates put the number of world migrants at approximately 191 million in 2005 (International Organization for Migration 2005). The Philippines represent a huge piece of this global landscape, cited as the top-third migrant-sending country after China and India (International Organization for Migration 2005). The Philippine state is certainly not alone in enacting transnationalism; other developing nations are also committed to reconnecting with their diasporic communities and tapping into the resources that they offer. For example, the Indian state created the Non-resident Indian (NRI) category to capture their citizens who are living overseas and encourage them to be connected with their homeland by providing them the opportunity to maintain financial accounts in India or to buy properties. In Mexico, organizations such as hometown associations (HTAs) serve as bridges between overseas migrants and their local hometowns of origin through fund-raising activities, which are often about encouraging migrants to support community development projects back home.

With globalization and the resulting and continuing widening disparities in income among groups, migration for the purpose of employment is likely to continue. And labor-exporting economies such as the Philippines will likely persist in supporting it because of the invaluable gains to be harnessed from workers' remittances. Other economies will likely follow their lead. During my fieldwork in the Philippines, state officials often mentioned upcoming visits of representatives from other labor-exporting countries who sought to emulate or learn from the successful institutionalized system the Philippines had created to manage labor migration. Meanwhile, some employment agency brokers relayed their fear that the Philippines would not always have the prominence it occupied as a labor provider. For example, U.S. employers are venturing to India for nurses, given the country's recent focused efforts on revising their nurse education and training programs to increase Indian nurses' global marketability. Other countries, among them Sri Lanka, with its Bureau of Foreign Employment, a state body overseeing the country's labor export program, operates much in the same way as the Philippines' POEA by facilitating Sri Lankans' ability to work abroad. It works with private employment agencies as a leading provider of domestic workers, primarily to the Middle East, and sets up household-training programs to orient applicants for work overseas.[1] Similar training programs also exist in Indonesia, another provider of domestic labor that is considered to be a competitor of the Philippines.

Thus, how the Philippines maintains its comparative advantage as a labor provider through the quality of the workforce it generates is key to managing this reality. While I do not see the Philippine state completely abandoning the deployment of such vulnerable skills categories as household or entertainment work because of the economic gains from it, it will likely continue on the trajectory of professionalizing its image as a source of highly skilled workers or "supermaids." In fact, in POEA's 2007 annual report, the state proudly exclaimed that the 6.7 percent increase in the number of "high-value jobs" (health care, engineering, information technology) accounted for 75 percent of the new jobs for that year, while the number of newly hired household workers and construction workers decreased by 50 percent and 30 percent, respectively. Nevertheless, along with employment agencies, it will continue to promote the distinctiveness of Filipino workers and continue to brand them as "ideal," just as the nurses I met will likely do the same for their survival. The choreographed brokering process between these institutional actors and workers ensures that the Great Filipino Worker can continue to be globally reproduced. Perhaps, in a post-9/11 world contained by xenophobic anxieties, this representation can continue to secure the passage of Filipinos through tightening global borders, even if they are faced with the reality that how they fare on the "other side" is not guaranteed. That is, their added-value qualities may temper (often unfounded) anxieties about the role of immigrants in displacing local labor if it means that they can offer *more* for *less*.

Ultimately, the labor-brokering process is not just about defining or providing employment opportunities but is fundamentally about image building, whereby the aspects of Filipino workers that give them the moniker of *high value* are accentuated when they are promoted to foreign employers and where the imperfections about overseas employment that defy the dreams of the very same workers are hidden or minimized. The nurses I met had spent most of their lives planning to leave the Philippines, only to find themselves disenchanted and entertaining the possibility of returning. Marketing dreams and manufacturing heroes are not just about commodifying human lives but also about the creative, albeit problematic, process of managing people's needs, desires, and aspirations.

NOTES

CHAPTER 1   HOME OF THE GREAT FILIPINO WORKER

1. Although the state typically refers to them as heroes, I call attention to the fact that women constitute the bulk of the overseas workforce deployment. At the time that the "modern-day hero" label was coined, then-president Corazon Aquino spoke before an audience of domestic workers in Hong Kong, to whom she referred as the *bagong bayani*—"modern-day heroes" of the Philippines. I argue that this increased participation of women forced the state to incorporate "gender-sensitive criteria" in its overseas employment framework (Guevarra 2006b).

2. Choy (2003) argues that a culture of migration helps explain the mass nurse migration of Filipinos to the United States and that this was made possible by critical exchanges between the media, travel agencies, the state, and nurses, all of whom contributed to constructing the United States as a promised land and migration as the most lucrative means of survival. Maruja Asis (2006) also attributes the desires of Filipinos to migrate overseas to a culture of migration in the Philippines. I extend their concept by illustrating concretely the political economic and cultural mechanisms that enable this national sentiment to proliferate through various levels of analysis (of the state, of the employment agencies, and of the workers). I also show how Filipinos themselves respond to, accommodate, or challenge this social imaginary.

3. I am not arguing that there is or should be a gendered and racialized moral economy but that this is a good description of how the Philippine state and employment agencies are trying to govern Filipinos as workers and citizens by infusing Filipino "moral" values regarding the family and femininity with Westernized notions of economic competitiveness in order to construct a particular kind of unique Filipino work ethic that the state can parade as one of the country's trademarks (see Guevarra 2006b). Other scholars follow in this conceptualization, among them Aihwa Ong (2006), who describes the "moral economy of the female migrant," and Rhacel Parreñas (2008), who writes about the "moral economy of the Philippine state." I differ from their conceptualization in that I'm highlighting not only the ways that this moral economy is a gendered system but also how it is racialized through the work of various actors not limited to the Philippine state but also employment agencies and workers themselves.

4. Sassen (1996) explains that the partial denationalization of territory occurs through specific corporate practices that can involve the operation of activities beyond the regulatory umbrellas of nation-states so that firms are able to avoid local taxes and regulations. Hence, an actual piece of land becomes denationalized. Examples of such partially denationalized territories are the

export processing zones and free trade zones that have been established in many developing nations to house various garment manufacturing and electronic industries (see Fernandez-Kelly 1983; Kelly 2000; Ong 1987).

5. Basch, Glick Schiller, and Szanton Blanc (1994, 269) refer to as a "deterritorialized nation-state," "in which the nation's people may live anywhere in the world and still not live outside the state."

6. I differ from her (Rodriguez 2005, forthcoming) in that I examine *labor brokering* not only from the perspective of the state but also in its partnership with other actors such as private employment agencies and workers. The brokering process I highlight is also specifically focused on the production of care workers and the gendered and racialized processes embedded in this.

7. See Barry, Osborne, and Rose, 1996; Burchell 1996; Foucault 1991; Rose and Miller 1992; Rose 1999.

8. Lee Kuan Yew (cited in Ong 1999, 72), senior minister of Singapore, stated that the Philippines, despite of its democratic structure, was unable to become an economic superpower primarily because of its "American style constitution," which does not emphasize social discipline, and also because of its lack of Confucian values of hard work, filial piety, thrift, and national pride.

9. All dollar figures used in this book are in United States dollars, unless noted otherwise.

10. See, for example, Acker 2004; Ehrenreich and Hochschild 2002; Mohanty 1997; Mohanty, Russo, and Torres 1991; Nash and Kelly 2001; Ong 1991; Salzinger 2003, 2004; Sassen 2002; Ward 1990.

11. For production work, see Fernandez-Kelly 1983; Freeman 2000; Hossfeld 1990; Mies 1982; Ong 1987; Pellow and Park 2002; Safa 1995; Salzinger 2003; Samper 1997; Wolf 1992. For care work, see Anderson 2002; Bakan and Stasiulis 1997; Chang 2000; Chin 1998; Choy 2003; Constable 1997a; Hondagneu-Sotelo 2001; Lan 2006; Momsen 1999; Parreñas 2001b; Pratt 1997, 1998, 1999; Romero 1992; Rudnyckyj 2004; Stasiulis and Bakan 2003.

12. See, for example, Anderson 2002; Bakan and Stasiulis 1997; Chang 2000; Chin 1998; Choy 2003; Constable 1997; Espiritu 2007; Hondagneu-Sotelo 2001; Lan 2003a and 2006; Momsen 1999; Parreñas 2001; Pratt 1997;1998;1999a; Romero 1992; Stasiulis and Bakan 2003; Tung 1999.

13. See, for example, Bakan and Stasiulis 1995; Stasiulis and Bakan 2003; Pratt 1997.

14. Taglish is a mixture of Tagalog and English; it has become a colloquial language in the Philippines.

15. A jeepney is a hybrid commuter passenger vehicle used for public transportation and known for its fairly inexpensive fares compared with those of other modes of transport. Its construction was inspired by World War II U.S. Army jeeps that were left behind in the Philippines.

16. Gray Meadows is a fictitious name for the town.

17. See Abu-Lughod 1988; Baca Zinn 1979; Beoku-Betts 1994; Narayan 1997; Ong 1995; Villenas 1996; Zavella 1997.

18. PAEF is the binational commission in charge of supervising the Fulbright program in the Philippines.

19. POEA is the state-appointed administrative body in charge of regulating the overseas employment program by accrediting private employment agencies and foreign employers and conducting overseas marketing missions.

CHAPTER 2   CULTIVATING A FILIPINO ETHOS
OF LABOR MIGRATION

1. In the preceding epigraph, *Pinoy* is a term used for Filipinos; RP is the abbreviation for the Republic of the Philippines.
2. This advertisement featured a Filipino worker (chef and server) in an upscale restaurant who was juggling several tasks, readily responding to customer's demands; during this action, the ad flashes the message "highly skilled" on the screen.
3. The breakdown of this number is as follows: temporary migrants, 4,133,970; permanent migrants, 3,692,527; irregular migrants, 900,023. *Permanent migrants* refers to "immigrants or legal permanent residents abroad whose stay do not depend on work contracts." *Temporary migrants* are "persons whose stay overseas is employment related, and who are expected to return at the end of their work contracts." *Irregular migrants* are "those not properly documented or without valid residence or work permits, or who are overstaying in a foreign country" (http://www.cfo.gov.ph). The problem with this classification system is that some overseas Filipino workers are also under contract but carry immigrant visas, such as the EB-3, which is offered to many nurses working in the United States. A worker on EB-3 visas technically enters the United States as a temporary migrant but is eventually eligible to become a permanent migrant.
4. Those determined to be poor are "individuals and families whose incomes fall below the official poverty threshold as defined by the government or cannot afford to provide in a sustained manner for their minimum basic needs for food, health, education, housing, and other social amenities of life" (National Statistical Coordination Board 2008).
5. For a comprehensive account of the role of Pasyon, narratives that take the form of poetry and that celebrate the death and resurrection of the Catholic figure Jesus Christ, in colonial Philippines, see Ileto 1979.
6. For a full text of this proclamation, see United States Adjutant General of the Army 1902.
7. This was also the time that the first set of educational exchanges took place with government scholars known as "pensionados" who left for the United States in 1903–1914. The goal of the program was to fund Filipino scholars in the fields of medicine, education, engineering, and law so they would receive further educational training and then later return to the Philippines as teachers or government administrators.
8. Import substitution is an economic strategy that involves focusing on producing commodities or services that had previously been imported but could now be produced locally. For products intended for the American market, see Agoncillo 1990; Bello, Kinley, and Elinson 1982; Eviota 1992.
9. For a good synopsis of Hawaii's plantation economy, see Liu 1984.
10. Although native Hawaiians initially supplied the labor needed to (re)produce these plantations, plantation growers needed a specific kind of labor that could provide an extensive round-the-clock supervision suited to the nature of sugar production and cultivation (Liu 1984). In general, the sugar growers did not have sufficient local labor to exploit. Between 1876 and 1885, Chinese workers became the primary source of plantation labor, followed by Japanese workers, who constituted the plantation workforce until the early 1900s. They also recruited workers from Germany and Portugal but

in the interest of cost, they preferred recruiting workers from Asia. For one, it was cheaper to transport Asian laborers to Hawaii because of geographical proximity. Also, Asian laborers were cheaper to support because they migrated alone, unlike Europeans, who brought their families with them. During this period, as a consequence of European and American expansion, there was also a rapid decline of the indigenous population because of the influx of certain Western diseases, alcoholism, and warfare (Liu 1984).

11. See Cordova 1983; Liu, Ong, and Rosenstein 1991; Sharma 1984; Takaki 1998; Villegas 1988.

12. Although a small number of women with and without children also migrated at this time, single male laborers were primarily recruited. Also, although laborers were recruited from the Visayas region, Ilocos was HSPA's primary source of labor. From the perspective of HSPA, the Ilocos region became a lucrative source of labor for a combination of reasons. First, it was one of the least economically developed regions in the country because of the degradation of its textile industry as a result of the Spanish shift to agricultural export trade of tobacco, sugar, copra, hem, and abaca, none of which can be grown in Ilocos. The only commodity that can productively be grown in Ilocos is rice and although it showed promise for rice cultivation, this was not developed there at all. Therefore, it was a region believed to have a surplus of laborers who Ilocos could not accommodate. Second, Ilocanos gained the reputation of being hardworking, thrifty, and psychologically prepared to migrate (Sharma 1984).

13. See Cordova 1983; Liu, Ong, and Rosenstein 1991; Takaki 1998.

14. See Chant and McIlwaine 1995; Cortes, Boncan, and Jose 2000; Lichauco 1982.

15. Abaca (known as "Manila hemp") is a plant belonging to the banana species and is indigenous to the Philippines, its largest producer.

16. Many food producers in the Philippines are actually tenant farmers under the control of landlords who have rights over an enormous percentage of their cultivation yields and control over their financing (via credit) and access to technology (Bello, Kinley, and Elinson 1982). See also Rocamora and O'Connor 1977. For more recent discussions on this topic, see Lindio-McGovern 1997.

17. The immigration preference system is broken down into categories as follows: first preference: unmarried children (over twenty-one years old) of U.S. citizens; second preference: spouses and children of permanent U.S. residents; third preference: professionals, scientists, artists; fourth preference: married children of U.S. citizens; fifth preference: brothers and sisters of U.S. citizens; sixth preference: skilled and unskilled workers in occupations in which labor is in short supply; exemptions: spouses of U.S. citizens, children (under twenty-one) of U.S. citizens, parents of U.S. citizens (Liu, Ong, and Rosenstein 1991).

18. The role of private sectors in overseas placement of workers was reinstated by the 1978 Labor Code amendment because of the inability of OEDB and NSB to handle alone the skyrocketing demand for Filipino labor (Asis 1992). Sea-based employment is work that takes place on board maritime shipping vessels (for example, work done by seafarers) or cruise ships.

19. The state-mandated taxation of remittances varied depending on the category of worker: 80 percent for seafarers; 70 percent for professional workers

(doctors, nurses, engineers, teachers) who received free board and lodging; 50 percent for professionals who did not receive free board and lodging; 50 percent for household workers and other service workers (Asis 1992; Nolledo 1992).

20. I am following Kelly's (2000, 17) framework for understanding the Philippines' socioeconomic "place in this world" as one that is rooted in particular historical colonial experiences. Kelly argued that the "country's historical context has left it peculiarly susceptible to arguments that prioritized the global scale and that this is inscribed upon the landscapes in the types of development it experiences." Building on his framework, I also argue that not only have these colonial legacies and "interactions with global processes" defined the Philippines' "place in the world" but they have also intensely reconfigured the nature of Filipinos' citizenship to their nation-state.

21. While *remittances* refers to the "transfers, in cash or in kind from a migrant to household residents in the country of origin," the Bangko Sentral ng Pilipinas (Central Bank of the Philippines; BSP) calculates and records remittances in its balance-of-payments computation by following the IMF's broader definition of *remittances*, which includes (1) workers' remittances or cash transfers from migrants to resident households in the country of origin, (2) compensation or wages to employees paid to individuals working in a country outside their legal residence, and (3) migrant transfers involving capital transfers of financial assets when workers move to another country and are there for more than one year (Asian Development Bank 2004). However, the remittances BSP calculates take into account only money sent through official banking channels.

22. I selected the figures for 2006 because they provide a better breakdown of the skill categories by gender. The total "new hire" deployment for 2006 was 308,142, of which 184,454 were women and 123,688 were men.

23. The current monthly salary of domestic workers in Hong Kong is HK$3,670 (approximately $472).

24. Forms of migration that transpire outside the legal channels can include employment under false pretenses or trafficking workers for prostitution or other types of labor without workers' consent.

25. Based on POEA's Memorandum Circular 11, the age limit applies except in countries where the age requirement for domestic workers is higher or where the minimum employable age is eighteen (for example, Hong Kong, Canada, the United States, Japan, Italy, Spain, Switzerland, and Sweden). Promoters are individuals who act as "agents" of entertainers.

26. Each prospective worker must go through a PDOS, either through the agency that is processing their paper, through POEA itself, or through one of the NGOs accredited by the state.

27. All figures in pesos are in Philippine pesos unless noted otherwise.

28. Given the increasing out-migration of nurses from the Philippines, it would seem to make sense that hospitals would more likely be willing to hire new graduates to help ease the shortages instead of simply requiring them to volunteer. I can only assume that this action may be explained by the fact that many of the nurses leaving are those who have significant nursing and hospital experience. Therefore, they are not easily replaceable. As some nurses recounted to me, it may also have to do with the fact that there are more new graduates than there are staff positions available, especially in provincial locations where there are only a few health care facilities available.

29. I thank Luis F. B. Plascencia for helping me think through this insight.
30. The actual pay that domestic workers receive varies. A random survey of domestic workers in Manila indicated that they earn between 2,000 and 2,500 pesos; for those who work in affluent districts, it is as much as 5,000 pesos (see Visayan Forum Foundation 2006).
31. This is in Hong Kong dollars.
32. It is noteworthy that the 9/11 attacks on the World Trade Center had already happened at the time of this interview. While his statement may have reflected a mistake on his part, it also signified the business-as-usual stance that I observed in the industry in the midst of the 9–11 tragedy. This is not because brokers did not care about the United States but more about the reality that it only represents one of many labor markets for Filipino workers.
33. For an excellent synopsis of POEA's marketing program, see Tyner 2000 and Imson n.d.
34. POLOs are distributed as follows: Middle East: (Riyadh, Al Khobar, Jeddah, Abu Dhabi, Dubai, Bahrain, Kuwait, Unaizah, Libya, Oman, Qatar, Israel, Lebanon); Asia and the Pacific: (Hong Kong, Macau, Tokyo, Osaka, Singapore, Kuala Lumpur, Brunei, Taipei, Kaohsiung City/Taiwan, Taichung City/Taiwan, Seoul); the Americas and trust territories (Saipan; Washington, D.C.; Ontario); Europe: (Rome, Milan, Netherlands, Geneva, Madrid, London, Athens).
35. The Association of Southeast Asian Nations was established in 1967 to promote regional cooperation between Brunei, Cambodia, Indonesia, Laos, Malaysia, Myanmar, the Philippines, Singapore, Thailand, and Vietnam in the economic, social, cultural, technical development of these nations and in the maintenance of peace and stability in this region.
36. I thank Gloria Cuadráz for this key insight and for helping me conceptualize the ethos of labor migration.

Chapter 3 Governing and (Dis)Empowering Filipino Migrants

1. Yamzon refers to the vulnerability of workers overseas, especially women, in terms of the violence and possible death that they face.
2. Interestingly, the title of the Philippine Overseas Employment Administration's (POEA) newly released 2006 annual report is *Empowering the Global Filipino*.
3. Burchell (1996, 23) provides a useful characterization of neoliberalism as one in which "the rational principle for regulating and limiting governmental activity must be determined by reference to *artificially* arranged or contrived forms of the free, *entrepreneurial*, and *competitive* conduct of economic-rational individuals" (emphases added).
4. The Philippine state issued the first set of awards in 1984 but temporarily stopped them between 1986 and 1989 after the EDSA People Power revolt and resulting changes in administration.
5. The BBA categories include (1) BBA for outstanding employee; (2) BBA for Community and Social Service; (3) BBA for Culture and Arts; and (4) Blas F. Ople Award for the Natatanging Bagong Bayani (most outstanding hero).
6. Earlier versions of this award (pre-2005) used to specify "regularly remits money to the Philippines through established Philippine banks" or "has been

involved in promoting the Philippines as a business or tourism destination" as qualifying criteria.

7. While the 2007 awardees have also been named, I cite the 2005 winners instead to illustrate the range of "skills" and "deeds" that this award is supposed to recognize.

8. Dr. José Protasio Rizal was an intellectual and revolutionary who launched the first set of subversive acts against Spanish imperialism. His writings and organized propaganda movement culminated in the infamous Katipunan revolution of 1896–1897. The Spanish made several attempts to suppress him by forcing him into exile and imprisonment. Charged with a crime for inciting rebellion against the Spanish government, he was sentenced to death and executed by firing squad.

9. The terms *OCWs* and *OFWs* often are used interchangeably. I argue that the increasing use of *OFWs* signals an attempt to include undocumented workers or the tourists who may not necessarily be on contracts.

10. These are cases that workers file to POEA against their employers and may include physical abuse committed by foreign employers, unsatisfactory working conditions, contract substitutions (getting a different contract upon arrival to the country), illegal recruitment, and excessive placement fees from employment agencies.

11. What the state defines as "adequate preparation" *does not* include setting up specific structures that would help migrants' families in meaningful ways (such as child care and regular social support services for spouses and children left behind) except for their so called family counseling programs. According to OWWA's brochures and Web site, the agency is supposed to provide "psychological and social well-being" programs to OFWs' families in the form of "strengthening the morale of families of the OFWs left behind." However, the program description does not specify how this is done or how frequently it happens. But with other programs it offers, such as loan, educational, and skill development assistance, informational material is very specific in how OWWA makes these services available to OFW families.

12. According to Foucault (1979, 170), the disciplinary gaze or surveillance is an instrument of a disciplinary, panoptic power that "regards individuals both as object and as instruments of its exercise." The use of this gaze trains and regulates its subjects to model a particular behavior and renders them vulnerable to a state of constant awareness.

13. Every time I called to check when and where the next session would be so that I could attend, either I did not get a clear response or some of the staff members at POEA thought these sessions no longer existed. Thus, the frequency of the sessions remained unclear, although the 2001 POEA annual report provided a couple of photographs from them.

14. Flor Contemplacion was a domestic worker in Singapore who was executed in 1995 for the murder of her employer's child and a domestic worker. Her trial and execution generated a massive public outcry in the Philippines about the absence of welfare protection for OFWs.

15. Apolinario Mabini and José Rizal, the latter mentioned above, are two of the many proclaimed national heroes of the Philippines.

16. Casco noted that elementary and high school guidance counselors encourage young people to pursue courses (in computers, science, engineering, and so on) that will make them desirable in the global market as part of this migrant

worker education program. I also learned that many individuals who now pursue certain courses, such as nursing, primarily do so for the prospect of overseas employment and not necessarily out of interest in the career itself.

17. At the time of my fieldwork, there were five NGOs authorized by POEA to provide these seminars: the Center for Overseas Workers, Kaibigan ng OCWs, the National Greening Movement Foundation, the Women in Development Foundation, and Zonta Club International.

18. This is a type of training based on a state-designed module that specifies the required information for these orientation sessions.

19. Most domestic workers are well educated—many have attained a bachelor's degree. One labor broker told me that the common applicant is not a domestic worker but a nurse or a teacher and that is why he said that many employers get a "two for one" deal (for example, get a maid and a tutor at the same time).

20. These reforms materialized in the POEA governing board resolutions (4–7 and 13–14) passed in November 29, 2006, and February 2, 2007.

21. If one fails this skill assessment, she or he must wait one month before retaking the exam, and if one fails it three times, the training becomes mandatory.

22. The current monthly minimum wage set by the Philippine Labor Code for domestic workers (or "house helpers") are 800 pesos (approximately $16) in urbanized areas such as Manila, Quezon, Pasay, and Caloocan cities and municipalities of Makati, San Juan, Mandaluyong, Muntinlupa, Navotas, Malabon, Parañaque, Las Piñas, Pasig, Marikina, Valenzuela; 650 pesos for chartered cities and other first-class municipalities; and 550 pesos for other municipalities (Presidential Decree 442, www.dole.gov.ph/laborcode).

23. Although this television program appears on a local network and President Arroyo addresses overseas workers, she is likely to rely on other circuits of information to deliver her message to these workers (families, friends, newspaper reports, NGOs, and so on). Some overseas television networks broadcast shows from the Philippines, thereby bringing global visibility to her program. She also addresses potential migrants, summoning them to imagine themselves in this new way.

24. However, while the state seems to do well at creatively inventing such morale-boosting tokens for migrants, it is quite incapable of formulating real social interventions to help mitigate the strain that transnational families face. Reforming the very political economic and educational systems that promote this cycle of dependency on migration would be a good start (one suggestion would be strengthening the local economy by aggressively pursuing other means of income generation for the country). The state could also do better by reconceptualizing its notion of the "family" so as to shift the burden of responsibility of family caregiving away from simply one parent (for example, the mother or wife) and instead promote a more egalitarian view of child-rearing responsibilities. In the current system, the state is much more focused on using entrepreneurship as the most crucial social intervention that will ease the strain and pain that transnational families experience.

25. An extended and different version of this section was published in Guevarra (2006b).

26. I cite this from the draft concept paper titled "Towards Creating an Enabling Environment for a Comprehensive Reintegration Program," which was written by the conference organizing committee who are members of NGOs

such as Atikha Overseas Workers and Communities Initiatives, the BaliK Bayani Foundation, the Episcopal Commission for the Pastoral Care of Migrants and Itinerant People, and the Unlad-Kabayan Migrant Services Foundation, in conjunction with the Overseas Workers Welfare Administration. This is the paper on which this conference was based.

27. Spokespersons for NGOs explain that many women pursue overseas employment to escape constraining family situations and abusive relations. For a good illustration, see Parreñas 2001a.

28. Approximately 83 percent of the Philippine population is Catholic (National Statistical Coordination Board 2004).

29. Although the video does not specify that this pertains to their days off, it cannot be otherwise, since it goes without saying that a live-in domestic worker must stay on the premises of her employer during normal working days. Therefore, the notion that workers must ask for permission from their employer for what they choose to do during a nonworking day shows the extent to which employers perceive domestic workers as their property.

30. The term is a play on *homesickness*. Session leaders claim that married women migrant workers suffer from longing for sexual intimacy, which may lead them to have extramarital affairs.

31. This "self-defense" protection included wearing layers of clothing to bed to prevent "easy access" to their bodies, putting objects that make noise around their beds to alert them of a presence in the room while they were asleep, and scolding men making sexual advances.

CHAPTER 4   DELIVERING "OUR CONTRIBUTION TO THE WORLD"

1. Intramuros ("walled city"), built in the late sixteenth century, is the oldest district in the city of Manila. Its historical significance stems from the fact that this walled area is one of the few structural remnants of the Spanish conquest of the Philippines. It is also significant in that Intramuros was constructed to serve as the center of Spanish colonial political, military, and religious activities, as is evident in the presence of schools, churches, offices, and residences within. Only Spaniards and mestizos were allowed to live within the walled city.

2. By "global circuits of labor," Tyner refers to "circuits [that] bind origins and destinations and provide a material linkage between regions of labor-surplus and labor scarcity" (63).

3. In their research examining the discursive and historical constructions of the reproductive technology RU846, Clarke and Montini conceptualized the women users and consumers as "implicated actors" who were not necessarily always present and had a voice in this discourse but were nevertheless affected and defined by it.

4. Through DFA, Philippine ambassadors and consuls are supposed to assist workers in distress and, when necessary, offer means for their repatriation. DOLE, on the other hand, is supposed to manage the entire overseas employment program through the establishment of two sister agencies—POEA and OWWA. While POEA is in charge of formulating an organized system of recruitment by regulating the activity of the private sector through the issuance of registration licenses, accreditation of foreign employers, and overseas placement of workers, OWWA is responsible for providing social support

services to workers and their families and coordinating with host countries for the repatriation of distressed workers.

5. When I was shopping around for agencies, I had an informal exchange with a labor broker from an agency located in this building who told me that although they were competing with other agencies in the same building on the basis of filling their job orders, they also sometimes ended up referring applicants they could not accommodate to other agencies in the same building. Interestingly enough, when some agencies refused to accommodate me with an interview, these agencies would then refer me to others in the same building who might be more likely able to accommodate me. At one point, I was told by a receptionist of one agency that other agencies had "kinder" and "less-suspecting" owners.

6. These official awards include Award of Excellence, Top Performer Award, and Special Awards. In the Special Awards category are the following achievements: highest deployment of land-based workers, highest deployment of seafarers, highest deployment of professionals, highest deployment of skilled workers, and highest foreign exchange earnings. There are also Exemplary Welfare Programs and Services for moral and spiritual values services, employee relations, on-site services, family services, human resource development, and socioeconomic reintegration.

7. Interestingly enough, these seminars were held at a time when the private sector was actually able to obtain a temporary restraining order against POEA's ability to implement the rules. During one of the orientation seminars, state officials explained that it was just a "matter of time" before the new rules will be implemented.

8. On top of paying the 10,000-peso filing fee to obtain or renew their business licenses, agencies are also required by the new rules to prove that they are financially capable by showing a minimum capitalization of 2,000,000 pesos (previously 1,000,000 pesos), paying a 50,000-peso (previously 30,000-peso) four-year licensing fee, posting a surety bond of 100,000 pesos (previously 50,000 pesos), and signing an escrow agreement in the amount of 1,000,000 pesos (previously 300,000 pesos).

9. Personnel pooling means that the agencies are just creating an applicant database so that when job orders come, they will have a personnel pool readily available.

10. These recruitment documents include (1) the master employment contract (indicating guaranteed wages, which should not be lower than the minimum wage in the host country or the minimum wage standards set forth in a bilateral agreement or international convention; free transportation to and from the work site; free food and accommodation; and conditions for termination of contracts); (2) special power of attorney to the licensed Philippine agency that will serve as their agent; (3) personnel request outlining the position and salary of workers to be hired; and (4) valid business license, registration certificate, or equivalent document (POEA 2002). In countries where there are no POLOs, POEA will then handle the accreditation of foreign employers.

11. Although these revised policies also contain punitive measures for erring workers and foreign employers, based on the number of listed offenses and nature of penalties, it is evident that the primary subject of such punitive measures are the private employment agencies.

12. All the agency names are pseudonyms.

13. Some markets (such as the United Kingdom, the Netherlands, Hong Kong, and Singapore) do not allow the collection of placement fees from workers but the brokers in these countries demand payment from Philippine agencies. In order to pay them, Philippine-based agencies then incorporate the foreign brokers' charges into the placement fee they collect from workers. This is the case for domestic work placement.

14. PASEI (the Philippine Association of Service Exporters Inc.) is a professional association representing more than 650 state-licensed private employment agencies in the Philippines.

15. The ads I use for my analysis do not necessarily correspond to the agencies I studied.

16. A majority of the Filipino nurses recruited for Middle East positions are women because the countries in this region only allow female nurses to attend to and care for both male and female patients. Labor brokers explained that they only get requests for Filipino male nurses for employers of small clinics that only deal with male patients.

17. There are a number of Muslim Filipinas who do apply for Middle East positions because of the familiarity with cultural and religious practices, so some labor brokers conduct their provincial recruitment activities in southern Mindanao, the southernmost region of the Philippines, which is predominantly Muslim, to fill their Middle East job orders.

18. This stereotype about Filipino women as sex objects that continues to circulate is rooted in the country's colonial and historical legacies. The Philippines' involvement in the sex trade was heightened by the American occupation of two naval bases in the Philippines, which facilitated the creation of a sex trade industry (popularly known as the "rest and recreation" industry") in Olongapo City (surrounding the Subic Naval Base) and Angeles city (surrounding the Clark Air Force Base)—primarily serving American military men. In addition, the regime of Ferdinand Marcos encouraged tourism as a developmental strategy, of which sex tourism became an outgrowth and an industry that officially flourished until the overthrow of that regime in 1986 (Eviota 1992; Moselina 1979).

19. This seemingly race-based salary classification goes as follows: first level, Saudi nationals and North Americans; second level, Europeans; third level, non-Saudi Arabs; fourth level, Filipinos (interview by the author, October 20, 2001). For a more comprehensive discussion of the Saudi Arabia labor market and the politics around such wage differences, see Woodward 1988.

20. Although Saudi Arabia was Riker's primary market, like other agencies, it was also trying to diversify its recruitment focus in order to tap into emerging markets such as the demand for live-in caregivers in Canada.

21. Referring to working in the Middle East as an "option" also undermines workers' agency in knowing which labor markets are easier to tap into. Workers who apply to go to the United States know all too well that a much quicker ticket out of the Philippines is to work in the Middle East.

22. At the time of this fieldwork, NCLEX was not yet administered in the Philippines and therefore applicants had to go to either Saipan or Guam to take it; so airfare and hotel accommodation costs were additional expenses that applicants had to shoulder. NCLEX is not always required by employers as a job qualification because it is an exam that nurses can eventually take in the United States. However, some employers prefer applicants who have passed

NCLEX as further proof of their nursing capability. Since August 2007, the Philippines has been an official testing site. This change came about as a result of intensive lobbying from the Philippines on the grounds that Filipinos had constituted the majority of foreign-born nurses taking NCLEX in Guam and Saipan.

23. The monthly earnings of a registered nurse in the Philippines ranges from 3,000 to 20,000 pesos ($60–$400) depending on years of experience, type of hospital, and expertise.

24. This is the service fee that they would collect from the nurse registry as payment for each nurse who was successfully processed for employment and deployed to the United States (field notes, November 18, 2001).

25. I thank Alejandra Elenes for this insight about the specificity of the "American dream" that brokers are selling to Filipinos.

26. *Palakasan* refers to a form of garnering favoritism or obtaining a favorable position in order to have a particular task or favor fulfilled. *Lakas* means "strength," so in this system of exchange, whoever has demonstrated a greater ability to finesse a particular relationship (such as through gift giving), will tend to experience a stronger likelihood of getting her or his favors fulfilled.

27. Agencies are allowed to collect a placement fee that is equivalent to only one month's salary.

28. Of course, such qualification does not translate into an increase in pay, since domestic workers in Hong Kong can earn only the state-mandated monthly salary of HK$3,670 (approximately $480 or 21,766 pesos).

CHAPTER 5 SELLING FILIPINAS' ADDED EXPORT VALUE

1. Although men serve as domestic workers and nurses and agencies claim to welcome applicants from both genders, the ways they market nursing and domestic work assumes that they are brokering women primarily and operates on the assumption that these occupations are women's work.

2. See Marije Meerman's documentary film (2001), *Chain of Love*, which documents the lives of Filipino migrant domestic workers in Italy and the Netherlands who leave their own children under the care of their parents, relatives, or another domestic worker.

3. See Bengwayan 2001.

4. The title of the conference was "Third International Nursing Conference: Sharing a Vision of a Healthy World"; it was held December 20–22, 2001 at the Hotel Intercontinental, Makati City, the Philippines.

5. The audience reacted with pride to this statement and agreed with its sentiments. I overheard one of the women express her amazement that "he knows so much about the characteristics of Filipinos."

6. Meanwhile, while the discursive construction of their patience, compliance, and loyalty can easily be interpreted as docility and passivity, it must be understood as inextricably linked to the economic realities that they face as nurses in the Philippines. As the Holodeck broker himself indicated, working overseas already promises much higher wages and better working conditions for Filipina nurses, who are underpaid and overworked in the Philippines, a fact that may help explain why they are less likely to challenge workplace norms or inequalities in ways that might jeopardize job security.

7. Following POEA regulations, agencies can use the print media to conduct two types of recruitment activities in order to generate a labor pool. One is

to post actual job vacancies and specific information about the job, skill categories, and place of employment. Another is to post prospective job orders and indicate that they are only doing "manpower pooling" at this time and that "no fees are to be collected" from applicants.

8. A biodata is equivalent to a résumé. But it also contains information that is most important to employers of domestic workers: age, education, marital status, religious background, height/weight, and prior work experience (in the Philippines and overseas).

9. This man could hardly stop giggling while explaining this situation to me. However, the fact that he wanted to go off the record for this one portion of our conversation indicated that he understood the gravity of the issue but simply did not want to be identified with it. First, it would ruin the "image" of the agency as a "caring" labor provider in the eyes of Filipino applicants. Second, he wanted to minimize further decreasing the marketability of the Saudi Arabian labor market by highlighting these kinds of cases. Or perhaps, this man just did not care about or did not take seriously these sexual advances committed against Filipino nurses.

10. This is the foreign labor broker with whom this domestic work agency is affiliated.

11. Constable's (1997a) ethnography of Filipino domestic workers in Hong Kong similarly discusses this point and the kinds of responsibilities and difficulties that domestic workers face in terms of proving such employer abuse, even when there is physical evidence (such as burn marks on workers' bodies).

12. A "sideline" business is any type of income-generating activity in which Filipinas engage in addition to working as domestics (selling Filipino food, clothing, and so on).

13. I thank Teresa Scherzer for this astute insight, which provides a richer conceptualization of the work that these agencies do.

CHAPTER 6   LIVING THE DREAM

1. Unless indicated otherwise, names are all pseudonyms. The names that are used were chosen by the participants.

2. MapQuest is an online database that provides maps and driving directions to and from a particular location.

3. The town's name is a pseudonym.

4. In the *Philippine Nurses Monitor* 1, no. 9, a Filipina cardiology nurse, Fleur Magbanua, was featured as a nurse "turned entrepreneur"; she had established a home health care service in Arizona called Valley Home Care.

5. I thank Alejandra Elenes for this insight.

6. Here I am thinking about the Filipino teachers recruited to work in Baltimore's school districts who, driven by depression, committed suicide last year.

7. This was an educational program sponsored by the U.S. colonial government that allowed Filipino men and women from elite families to study in U.S. colleges and universities.

8. Numerous health care organizations have mobilized to identify strategic long-term solutions to this shortage that involve reevaluating the state of the profession (see AHA 2002; American Nurses Association 2002; Daffron and Hart 2001; Joint Commission 2002) or developing initiatives to address the shortage through the formation of task forces, broad-based nurse coalitions,

or nurse workforce centers (see Brodeur and Laraway 2002; Cleary 2001; Cooksey et al. 2004).

9. See Goodin 2003.

10. See Aiken et al. 2002; Slomka, Fulton, and Fitzpatrick 2001; Sochalski 2002; United States General Accounting Office 2001; White 2001.

11. This is done by the employer through the PERM labor certification process, whereby U.S. companies must engage in advertising the position locally and provide a rationale for the foreign labor recruitment and why U.S. applicants cannot perform the job at hand before the labor request can be certified. Employers are also responsible for paying the recruited workers the prevailing wage.

12. This is for a thirty-six-hour workweek. The nurses I interviewed work twelve-hour shifts three days a week. Any time beyond this is considered overtime hours.

13. What is important to also note here is that the total expenses also acts as the employers' "surety bond" to the workers so that in the event that workers may decide to terminate relations with this particular agency, they are liable for this amount.

14. CGFNS: Commission on Graduates of Foreign Nursing Schools; NCLEX: National Council Licensure Examination; TSE: Test of Spoken English; TOEFL: Test of English as a Foreign Language.

CHAPTER 7 SECURING THEIR ADDED EXPORT VALUE

1. Filipino nurses use the terms "American" (*kano*) and "white" (*puti*) interchangeably to refer to any of their colleagues who are fair-skinned (or *puti*—as they say it in Tagalog—which literally translates to "the color white") or fit the stereotypical perception of the "white American." They do not make any racial or ethnic distinctions, so that someone may be of Canadian, Italian, or British descent, but because of their skin color, they label them as white or American. Although their units are not completely white, whenever they compare themselves to other nurses, they seem to always do so in relation to their white or American colleagues.

2. When Kitty made this point, she also alluded to the fact that her complaints were often much more frequent when they were directed to Filipino supervisors. From this, I assumed that she was not comfortable with voicing her grievance to her non-Filipino colleagues.

CHAPTER 8 CONCLUSION

1. See Waldman 2005.

References

Abella, Manolo I. 1979. *Export of Filipino Manpower*. Manila: Institute of Labor and Manpower Studies, Ministry of Labor.

Abu-Lughod, Lila. 1988. "Fieldwork of a Dutiful Daughter." In *Arab Women in the Field: Studying Your Own Society*, edited by Soraya Altorki and Camillia Fawzi El-Soh, 139–161. Syracuse: Syracuse University Press.

Acker, Joan. 2004. "Gender, Capitalism, and Globalization." *Critical Sociology* 30:17–41.

Agoncillo, Teodoro A. 1990. *History of the Filipino People*. 8th ed. Quezon City, Philippines: Garotech.

Aiken, Linda H., Sean P. Clarke, Douglas Sloane, Julie Sochalski, and Jeffrey Silber. 2002. "Hospital Nurse Staffing and Patient Mortality, Nurse Burnout, and Job Dissatisfaction." *JAMA: The Journal of the American Medical Association* 288:1987–1993.

American Hospital Association. 2002. *In Our Hands: How Hospital Leaders Can Build a Thriving Workforce*. Washington, D.C.: AHA Commission on Workforce for Hospital and Health Systems.

American Nurses Association. 2002. *Nursing's Agenda for the Future: A Call to the Nation*. Washington, D.C. : American Nurses Association.

Anderson, Bridget. 2002. *Doing the Dirty Work? The Global Politics of Domestic Labour*. London: Zed Books.

Appadurai, Arjun. 1996. *Modernity at Large: Cultural Dimensions of Globalization*. Minneapolis: University of Minnesota Press.

Arizona Governor's Task Force on the Nursing Shortage. 2004–2005. *Statewide Strategic Plan for Nursing in the State of Arizona*. Arizona: Governor's Task Force on the Nursing Shortage.

Arroyo, Gloria Macapagal. 2002. "Declaring the Year 2002 as the 'Year of the Overseas Employment Providers.'" *Proclamation No. 76*, July 30, 2001. Manila: Malacañan.

Asian Development Bank. 2004. *Enhancing the Efficiency of Overseas Filipino Workers Remittances: Final Report*. Mandaluyong City, Philippines: Asian Development Bank.

Asis, Maruja B. 1992. "The Overseas Employment Program Policy." In *Philippine Labor Migration: Impact and Policy*, edited by Graziano Battistella and Anthony Paganoni, 68–112. Quezon City, Philippines: Scalabrini Migration Center.

———. 2002. "From the Life Stories of Filipino Women: Personal and Family Agendas in Migration." *Asian and Pacific Migration Journal* 11 (1): 67–93.

———. 2004. "When Men and Women Migrate: Comparing Gendered Migration in Asia." Paper presented at "Migration and Mobility and How This Movement Affects Women: United Division for the Advancement of Women Conference," Malmo, Sweden, December 2–3, 2003.

———. 2006. "The Philippines' Culture of Migration." Washington, D.C.: Migration Policy Institute.

Asperilla, Purita Falgui. 1971. "The Mobility of Filipino Nurses." PhD diss., Columbia University, New York.

Baca Zinn, Maxine. 1979. "Field Research in Minority Communities: Ethical, Methodological, and Political Observations by an Insider." *Social Problems* 27 (2): 209–219.

Bakan, Abigail B., and Daiva K. Stasiulis. 1995. "Making the Match: Domestic Placement Agencies and the Racialization of Women's Household Work." *Signs: Journal of Women in Culture and Society* 20 (2): 303–335.

———, eds. 1997. *Not One of the Family: Foreign Domestic Workers in Canada.* Toronto: University of Toronto Press.

Ball, Rochelle E. 1996. "A Nation-Building or Dissolution: The Globalization of Nursing: The Case of the Philippines." *Pilipinas* 27:66–91.

———. 2000. "The Individual and Global Processes: Labour Migration Decision-Making and Filipino Nurses." *Pilipinas* 34: 83–92.

Barry, Andrew, Thomas Osborne, and Nikolas Rose. 1996. *Foucault and Political Reason: Liberalism, Neo-liberalism, and Rationalities of Government.* Chicago: University of Chicago Press.

Basch, Linda, Nina Glick Schiller, and Cristina Szanton Blanc. 1994. *Nations Unbound: Transnational Projects, Postcolonial Predicaments, and Deterritorialized Nation-States.* New York: Gordon and Breach.

Bello, Walden, David Kinley, and Elaine Elinson. 1982. *Development Debacle: The World Bank in the Philippines.* San Francisco: Institute for Food and Development Policy.

Bengwayan, Michael A. 2001. "When Filipino Maids Return Home in Coffins." *New Straits Times*, March 7, 2001.

Beoku-Betts, Josephine. 1994. "When Black Is Not Enough: Doing Field Research among Gullah Women." *NWSA Journal* 6 (3): 413–433.

Bergamini, Marie Carmen. 1964. "An Assessment of International Nursing Students in the United States: A Case Study of the Philippine Experience." PhD diss., University of California, Berkeley.

Bourdieu, Pierre. 1980/1990. *The Logic of Practice.* Stanford: Stanford University Press.

———. 1984. *Distinction: A Social Critique of the Judgement of Taste.* London: Routledge and Kegan Paul.

Brodeur, Melissa A., and Alisha S. Laraway. 2002. "States Respond to Nursing Shortage." *Policy, Politics, and Nursing Practice* 3: 228–234.

Buerhaus, Peter I., David O. Staiger, and Douglas Auerbach. 2000. "The Implications of an Aging Registered Nurse Workforce." *JAMA: The Journal of the American Medical Association* 283 (22): 2498–2954.

Burchell, Graham. 1996. "Liberal Government and Techniques of the Self." In *Foucault and Political Reason: Liberalism, Neoliberalism, and Rationalities of Government,* edited by Andrew Barry, Thomas Osborne and Nikolas Rose, 19–36. Chicago: Chicago University Press.

Burchell, Graham, Colin Gordon, and Peter Miller. 1991. *The Foucault Effect: Studies in Governmentality*. Chicago: Chicago University Press.

Canlas, Mamerto, Mariano Miranda, and James Putzel. 1988. *Land, Poverty, and Politics in the Philippines*. London: Catholic Institute for International Relations.

Commission on Filipinos Overseas. 1995. *Handbook for Filipinos Overseas*. 3rd ed. Manila: Philippine Commission on Filipinos Overseas, Department of Foreign Affairs.

———. 2007. "Stock Estimates of Overseas Filipinos." www.cfo.gov.ph.

Chang, Grace. 2000. *Disposable Domestics: Immigrant Women in the Global Economy*. Cambridge, U.K.: South End Press.

Chang, Kimberly A., and Julian M. Groves. 2000. "Neither "Saints" nor "Prostitutes": Sexual Discourse in the Filipina Domestic Workers Community in Hong Kong." *Women's Studies International Forum* 23 (1): 73–87.

Chant, Sylvia, and Cathy McIlwaine. 1995. *Women of a Lesser Cost: Female Labour, Foreign Exchange and Philippine Development*. East Haven, Conn.: Pluto Press.

Chin, Christine B. N. 1998. *In Service and Servitude: Foreign Female Domestic Workers and the Malaysian "Modernity" Project*. New York: Columbia University Press.

Choy, Catherine Ceniza. 2003. *Empire of Care: Nursing and Migration in Filipino American History*. Durham: Duke University Press.

Clarke, Adele E, and Theresa Montini. 1993. "The Many Faces of RU486: Tales of Situated Knowledges and Technological Contestations." *Science, Technology, and Human Values* 18 (1): 42–78.

Cleary, Brenda L. 2001. "The North Carolina Center for Nursing: A Pioneering State Nurse Workforce Policy Initiative." *Policy, Politics, and Nursing Practice* 2 (3): 210–215.

Constable, Nicole. 1997a. *Maid to Order in Hong Kong: Stories of Filipina Workers*. Ithaca: Cornell University.

———. 1997b. "Sexuality and Discipline among Filipina Domestic Workers in Hong Kong." *American Ethnologist* 24 (3): 539–558.

———. 1999. "At Home but Not at Home: Filipina Narratives of Ambivalent Returns." *Cultural Anthropology* 14 (2): 203–228.

Cooksey, Judith A., Wendy McLaughlin, Hollis Russinof, Louise Martinez, and Cynthia Gordon. 2004. "Active State-level Engagement with the Nursing Shortage: A Study of Five Midwestern States." *Policy, Politics, and Nursing Practice* 5 (2): 102–112.

Cordova, Fred. 1983. *Filipinos: Forgotten Asian Americans: A Pictorial Essay, 1763–circa 1963*. Seattle: Demonstration Project for Asian Americans.

Cortes, Rosario M., Celestina P. Boncan, and Ricardo T. Jose. 2000. *The Filipino Saga: History as Social Change*. Quezon City, Philippines: New Day.

Cruz, Victoria Paz. 1987. *Seasonal Orphans and Solo Parents: The Impacts of Overseas Migration*. Quezon City, Philippines: Scalabrini Migration Center.

Daffron, Jeannie M., and Sara E. Hart. 2001. "The American Hospital Association Responds to the Nursing Shortage." *Policy, Politics, and Nursing Practice* 2 (3): 206–209.

Department of Labor and Employment. 1995. *The Overseas Employment Programme*. Manila: Philippine Department of Labor and Employment.

Ehrenreich, Barbara, and Arlie Hochschild, eds. 2002. *Global Woman: Nannies, Maids, and Sex Workers in the New Economy*. New York: Henry Holt.

Ericta, Carmelita, Mercedita E. Tia, Amalia S. Sevilla, and Teodoro M. Orteza. 2003. Profile of Overseas Workers (Results from the 2000 Census of Population and Housing, NSO). Paper presented to Statistical Research Center (SRTC) Annual Conference, October 2003. In Quezon City, Philippines.

Espiritu, Yen Le. 2007. "Gender, Migration, and Work: Filipina Health Care Professionals in the United States." In *Contemporary Asian America: A Multidisciplinary Reader* 2nd ed, edited by Min Zhou and James V. Gatewood, 259–278. New York: New York University Press.

Eviota, Elizabeth U. 1992. *The Political Economy of Gender: Women and the Sexual Division of Labour in the Philippines*. London: Zed Books.

Fernandez-Kelly, Maria Patricia. 1983. *For We Are Sold, I and My People: Women and Industry in Mexico's Mexican Border Industrialization, Female Labor Force Participation, and Migration Frontier*. Albany: State University New York Press.

———. 2001. "Mexican Border Industrialization, Female Labor Force Participation, and Migration." In *Women, Men, and the International Division of Labor*, edited by June Nash and María Patricia Fernández-Kelly, 205–223. Albany: State University of New York.

Foucault, Michel. 1972. *The Archaeology of Knowledge and the Discourse on Language*. New York: Pantheon Books.

———. 1979. *Discipline and Punish: The Birth of the Prison*. New York: Vintage Books.

———. 1990/1978. *The History of Sexuality: An Introduction*. Vol. 1. New York: Vintage Books.

———. 1991. "Governmentality." In *The Foucault Effect: Studies in Governmentality*, edited by Graham Burchell, Colin Gordon and Peter Miller, 87–104. Chicago: Chicago University Press.

Freeman, Carla. 1993. "Designing Women: Corporate Discipline and Barbados' Off-Shore Pink Collar Sector." *Cultural Anthropology* 8 (2): 169–186.

———. 2000. *High Tech and High Heels in the Global Economy: Women, Work, and Pink-Collar Identities in the Caribbean*. Durham: Duke University Press.

Gancayco, Emilio A. 1996. "Response from the Bureaucracy: The Gancayco Commission Report." In *Filipino Women Migrant Workers: At the Crossroads and Beyond Beijing*, edited by Ruby Palma-Beltran and Gloria Rodriguez, 69–80. Quezon City, Philippines: Giraffe Books.

George, Sheba Mariam. 2005. *When Women Come First: Gender and Class in Transnational Migration*. Berkeley and Los Angeles: University California Press.

Go, Stella, and Leticia T. Postrado. 1986. "Filipino Overseas Contract Workers: Their Families and Communities." In *Asian Labor Migration: Pipeline to Middle East*, edited by Fred Arnold and Nasra Shah, 125–144. Boulder, Colo.: Westview Press.

Goldring, Luin. 2002. "The Mexican State and Transmigrant Organizations: Negotiating the Boundaries of Membership and Participation." *Latin American Research Review* 37 (3): 55–99.

Gonzalez, Joaquin L, III. 1998. *Philippine Labour Migration: Critical Dimensions of Public Policy*. Manila: De La Salle University Press.

Gonzaga, Ruth. 2006. *Overseas Filipino Workers' Remittances: Compilation Practices and*

Future Challenges. http://www.iaos2006conf.ca/pps/presentations/Gonzaga_ ru.pps.

Goodin, Heather Janiszewski. 2003. "The Nursing Shortage in the United States of America: An Integrative Review of the Literature." *Journal of Advanced Nursing* 43 (4): 335–350.

Grewal, Inderpal. 2005. *Transnational America: Feminisms, Diasporas, Neoliberalism.* Durham: Duke University Press.

Guarnizo, Luis E. 1998. "The Rise of Transnational Social Formations: Mexican and Dominican State Responses to Transnational Migration." *Political Power and Social Theory* 12: 45–94.

Guevarra, Anna Romina. 2003. *Manufacturing the "Ideal" Workforce: The Transnational Labor Brokering of Nurses and Domestic Workers from the Philippines.* PhD diss., Department of Social and Behavioral Sciences, University of California, San Francisco.

———. 2006a. "The Balikbayan Researcher: Negotiating Vulnerability in Fieldwork with Filipino Labor Brokers." *Journal of Contemporary Ethnography* 35 (5): 526–551.

———. 2006b. "Managing 'Vulnerabilities' and 'Empowering' Migrant Filipina Workers: The Philippines' Overseas Employment Program." *Journal for the Study of Race, Nation, and Culture* 12 (5): 523–541.

Hochschild, Arlie. 1983. *The Managed Heart: Commercialization of Human Feeling.* Berkeley and Los Angeles: University of California Press.

———. 2002. "Love and Gold." In *Global Woman: Nannies, Maids, and Sex Workers in the New Economy,* edited by Barbara Ehrenreich and Arlie Hochschild, 15–30. New York: Henry Holt.

Hondagneu-Sotelo, Pierrette. 2001. *Domestica: Immigrant Workers Cleaning and Caring in the Shadow of Affluence.* Berkeley and Los Angeles: University of California Press.

Hossfeld, Karen J. 1990. "Their Logic against Them: Contradictions in Sex, Race, and Class in the Silicon Valley." In *Women Workers and Global Restructuring,* edited by Kathryn Ward, 149–178. Ithaca: Cornell University Press.

Ileto, Reynaldo. 1979. *Pasyon and Revolution: Popular Movements in the Philippines, 1840–1910.* Quezon City, Philippines: Ateneo de Manila University Press.

Imson, Manuel. n.d. "The Philippine Experience in Marketing Overseas Employment: Sharing Best Practices." Philippine Department of Labor and Employment, Manila.

International Organization for Migration. 2005. *World Migration Report 2005: Costs and Benefits of International Migration.* IOM World Migration Report Series. Geneva: International Organization Migration.

Ishi, Tomoji. 1987. "Class Conflict, the State, and Linkage: The International Migration of Nurses from the Philippines." *Berkeley Journal of Sociology* 32: 281–312.

Jameson, Fredric. 1991. *Postmodernism, or The Cultural Logic of Late Capitalism.* Durham: Duke University Press.

Joint Commission on Accreditation of Health Care Organizations. 2002. *Health Care at the Crossroads: Strategies for Addressing the Evolving Nursing Crisis.* Washington, D.C.: Joint Commission on Accreditation of Health Care Organizations.

Kang, Laura Hyun. 2002. *Compositional Subjects: Enfiguring Asian/American Women.* Durham: Duke University Press.

Keely, Charles B. 1973. "Philippine Migration: Internal Movements and Emigration to the United States." *International Migration Review* 7 (2): 177–187.

Kelly, Phillip. 2002. *Landscapes of Globalization: Human Geographies of Economic Change in the Philippines.* London: Routledge.

Lan, Pei-Chia. 2003a. "Maid or Madam? Filipina Migrant Workers and the Continuity of Domestic Labor." *Gender and Society* 17 (2): 187–208.

———. 2003b. "'They Have More Money but I Speak Better English!' Transnational Encounters between Filipina Domestics and Taiwanese Employers." *Identities: Global Studies in Power and Culture* 10 (2): 133–161.

———. 2006. *Global Cinderellas: Migrant Domestics and Newly Rich Employers in Taiwan.* Durham: Duke University Press.

Lichauco, Alejandro A. 1982. "The International Economic Order and the Philippine Experience." In *Mortgaging the Future: The World Bank and IMF in the Philippines*, edited by Vivencio Jose, 12–48. Quezon City, Philippines: Foundation for Nationalist Studies.

Lindio-McGovern. 1997. *Filipino Peasant Women: Exploitation and Resistance.* Philadelphia: University of Pennsylvania Press.

Liu, John M. 1984. "Race, Ethnicity, and the Sugar Plantation System: Asian Labor in Hawaii, 1850–1900." In *Labor Immigration under Capitalism: Asian Workers in the United States before World War II*, edited by Lucie Cheng and Edna Bonacich, 186–210. Berkeley and Los Angeles: University of California Press.

Liu, John M., Paul Ong, and Carolyn Rosenstein. 1991. "Dual Chain Migration: Post-1965 Filipino Immigration to the United States." *International Migration Review* 25 (3): 487–513.

Marx, Karl. 1867/1978. "Capital, Volume 1." In *The Marx-Engels Reader*, 2nd ed., edited by Robert Tucker, 293–438. New York: W. W. Norton.

May, R. J. 1997. "The Domestic in Foreign Policy: The Flor Contemplacion Case and Philippine-Singapore Relations." *Pilipinas* 29: 63–75.

Mediavilla, Sam. 2006 "Displaced Domestic Help to Return as Supermaids." *Manila Times*, August 4, 2006, A1–A2.

Meerman, Marije. 2001. *Chain of Love* (Keten Van Liefde). Brooklyn, N.Y.: First Run/Icarus Films.

Mies, Maria. 1982. *The Lacemakers of Narsapur: Indian Housewives Produce for the World Market.* London: Zed Press.

Mohanty, Chandra Talpade. 1997. "Women Workers and Capitalist Scripts: Ideologies of Domination, Common Interests, and the Politics of Solidarity." In *Feminist Geneologies, Colonial Legacies, Democratic Futures*, edited by M. Jacqui Alexander and Chandra Talpade Mohanty, 3–29. New York: Routledge.

Mohanty, Chandra Talpade, Ann Russo, and Lourdes Torres, eds. 1991. *Third World Women and the Politics of Feminism.* Bloomington: Indiana University Press.

Momsen, Janet Henshall, ed. 1999. *Gender, Migration, and Domestic Service.* New York: Routledge.

Moselina, Leopoldo M. 1979. "Olongapo's Rest and Recreation Industry: A Sociological Analysis of Institutionalized Prostitution with Implications for a Grassroots Oriented Sociology." *Philippines Sociological Review* 27 (3): 181–193.

Narayan, Kirin. 1997. "How Native Is a "Native" Anthropologist?" In *Situated Lives: Gender and Culture in Everyday Life*, edited by Louise Lamphere, Helena Ragone, and Patricia Zavella, 23–41. New York: Routledge.

Nash, June, and Maria Patricia Fernandez-Kelly, eds. 2001. *Women, Men, and the International Division of Labor.* Albany: State University of New York.

National Economic Development Authority. 2002. *The Medium-Term Philippine Development Plan of 2001–2004.* http://www.neda.gov.ph.

———. 2005. *The Medium-Term Philippine Development Plan of 2004–2010.* http://www.neda.gov.ph.

National Statistical Coordination Board. 2004. "A View of the Philippines." National Statistical Coordination Board. http://www.nscb.gov.ph/view/people.asp.

———. 2008. "Poverty Statistics, 2006." National Statistical Coordination Board. http://www.nscb.gov.ph.

Nolledo, Jose N., ed. 1992. *The Labor Code of the Philippines.* Revised edition. Caloocan City, Philippines: Philippine Graphic Arts.

Ong, Aihwa. 1987. *Spirits of Resistance and Capitalist Discipline: Factory Women in Malaysia.* Albany: State University of New York Press.

———. 1991. "The Gender and Labor Politics of Postmodernity." *Annual Review of Anthropology* 20:279–309.

———. 1995. "Women out of China: Traveling Tales and Traveling Theories in Postcolonial Feminism." In *Women Writing Culture,* edited by Ruth Behar and Deborah Gordon, 350–372. Berkeley and Los Angeles: University of California Press.

———. 1999. *Flexible Citizenship: The Cultural Logics of Transnationality.* Durham: Duke University Press.

———. 2006. *Neoliberalism as Exception: Mutations in Citizenship and Sovereignty.* Durham: Duke University Press.

Ong, Paul, and Tania Azores. 1994. "The Migration and Incorporation of Filipino Nurses." In *The New Asian Immigration in Los Angeles and Global Restructuring,* edited by Paul Ong, Edna Bonacich and Lucie Cheng, 164–195. Philadelphia: Temple University Press.

Parreñas, Rhacel. 2001a. "Mothering from a Distance: Emotions, Gender, and Intergenerational Relations in Filipino Transnational Families." *Feminist Studies* 27 (2): 361–390.

———. 2001b. *Servants of Globalization: Women, Migration, and Domestic Work.* Stanford: Stanford University Press.

———. 2002. "The Care Crisis in the Philippines." In *Global Woman: Nannies, Maids, and Sex Workers in the New Economy,* edited by Barbara Ehrenreich and Arlie Hochschild, 39–54. New York: Henry Holt.

———. 2005. *Children of Global Migration: Transnational Families and Gendered Woes.* Stanford: Stanford University Press.

———. 2008. *The Force of Domesticity: Filipina Migrants and Globalization.* New York: New York University.

Pellow, David N., and Lisa Sun-Hee Park. 2002. *The Silicon Valley of Dreams: Environmental Injustice, Immigrant Workers, and the High Tech Global Economy.* New York: New York University Press.

Philippines Overseas Employment Administration. 1995. *Migrant Workers and Overseas Filipinos Act of 1995 (Republic Act No. 8042 and Its Implementing Rules and Regulations).* Mandaluyong City, Philippines: Philippine Overseas Employment Administration.

———. 2002a. *Philippine Overseas Employment Administration 2001 Annual Report.* Mandaluyong City, Philippines: Philippine Overseas Employment Administration.

———. 2002b. *Revised Rules and Regulations Governing Overseas Employment of Landbased Workers.* Mandaluyong City, Philippines: Philippine Overseas Employment Administration.

———. 2003. *Philippine Overseas Employment Administration 2002 Annual Report.* Mandaluyong City, Philippines: Philippine Overseas Employment Administration.

———. 2004. *Philippine Overseas Employment Administration 2003 Annual Report.* Mandaluyong City, Philippines: Philippine Overseas Employment Administration.

———. 2005. *Philippine Overseas Employment Administration 2004 Annual Report.* Mandaluyong City, Philippines: Philippine Overseas Employment Administration.

———. 2006a. *OFW Global Presence: A Compendium of Employment Statistics.* Mandaluyong City, Philippines: Philippine Overseas Employment Administration.

———. 2006b. *Philippine Overseas Employment Administration 2005 Annual Report.* Mandaluyong City, Philippines: Philippine Overseas Employment Administration.

———. 2007. *Philippine Overseas Employment Administration 2006 Annual Report.* Mandaluyong City, Philippines: Philippine Overseas Employment Administration.

———. 2008. *Philippine Overseas Employment Administration 2007 Annual Report.* Mandaluyong City, Philippines: Philippine Overseas Employment Administration.

Pratt, Geraldine. 1997. "Stereotypes and Ambivalence: The Construction of Domestic Workers in Vancouver, British Columbia." *Gender, Place, and Culture: A Journal of Feminist Geography* 4 (2): 159–177.

———. 1998. "Inscribing Domestic Work on Filipina Bodies." In *Places Through the Body*, edited by Heidi Nast and Steve Pile, 283–304. London and New York: Routledge.

———. 1999. "From Registered Nurses to Registered Nanny: Discursive Geographies of Filipina Domestic Workers in Vancouver, B.C." *Economic Geography* 75:215–236.

Racelis, Mary, and Judy C. Ick, eds. 2001. *Bearers of Benevolence: The Thomasites and Public Education in the Philippines.* Pasig City, Philippines: Anvil.

Rafael, Vicente L. 1988. *Contracting Colonialism: Translation and Christian Conversion in Tagalog Society Under Spanish Rule.* Quezon City, Philippines: Ateneo de Manila University Press.

———. 1995 (Fall). "Mimetic Subjects: Engendering Race at the Edge of Empire." *Differences: A Journal of Feminist Cultural Studies* 7 (2): 127–149.

———. 1997. "'Your Grief Is Our Gossip:' Overseas Filipinos and Other Spectral Presences." *Public Culture* 9 (2): 267–291.

Rocamora, Joel, and D. O'Connor. 1977. "The U.S., Land Reform, and Rural Development in the Philippines." In *The Logistics of Repression: The Role of U.S. Assistance in Consolidating the Martial Law Regime in the Philippines*, edited by

Walden Bello and Severina Rivera, 63–92. Washington, D.C.: Friends of the Filipino People.

Rodriguez, Robyn. 2002. "Migrant Heroes: Nationalism, Citizenship, and the Politics of Filipino Migrant Labor." *Citizenship Studies* 6 (3): 341–356.

———. 2005. *The Labor Brokering State: The Philippine State and the Globalization of Philippine Citizen-Workers.* PhD diss., University of California Berkeley.

———. Forthcoming. *Brokering Bodies: The Philippine State and the Globalization of Migrant Workers.* Minneapolis: University of Minnesota Press.

Romero, Mary. 1992. *Maid in the U.S.A.* New York: Routledge.

Rose, Nikolas. 1999. *Powers of Freedom: Reframing Political Thought.* Cambridge: Cambridge University Press.

Rose, Nikolas, and Paul Miller. 1992. "Political Power beyond the State: Problematics of Government." *British Journal of Sociology* 43 (2): 173–205.

Rudnyckyj, Daromir. 2004. "Technologies of Servitude: Governmentality and Indonesian Transnational Labor Migration." *Anthropology Quarterly* 77: 407–434.

Safa, Helen I. 1995. *The Myth of the Male Breadwinner: Women and Industrialization in the Caribbean.* Boulder, Colo.: Westview Press.

Salzinger, Leslie. 2003. *Genders in Production: Making Workers in Mexico's Global Factories.* Berkeley and Los Angeles: University of California Press.

———. 2004 (April). "From Gender as Object to Gender as Verb: Rethinking How Global Restructuring Happens." *Critical Sociology* 30 (1): 43–62.

Samper, Maria Luz. 1997. "An International Division of Labor and the Information Technology Industry." *International Journal of Politics, Culture, and Society* 10 (4): 635–658.

Sassen, Saskia. 1996. *Losing Control? Sovereignty in an Age of Globalization.* New York: Columbia University Press.

———. 2002. "Global Cities and Survival Circuits." In *Global Woman: Nannies, Maids, and Sex Workers in the New Economy*, edited by Barbara Ehrenreich and Arlie Hochschild, 254–274. New York: Henry Holt.

Scott, James. 1976. *The Moral Economy of the Peasant: Rebellion and Subsistence in Southeast Asia.* New Haven: Yale University Press.

Sharma, Miriam. 1984. "Labor Migration and Class Formation among the Filipinos in Hawaii, 1906–1946." In *Labor immigration under Capitalism: Asian Workers in the United States before World War II*, edited by Lucie Cheng and Edna Bonacich, 579–615. Berkeley and Los Angeles: University of California Press.

Slomka, Jacquelyn, Jane Fulton, and Joyce Fitzpatrick. 2001. "The Nursing Shortage: Not Just a Problem for Nursing." *Policy, Politics, and Nursing Practice* 2 (3): 187–190.

Sochalski, Julie. 2002. "Nursing Shortage Redux." *Health Affairs* 21 (5): 157–164.

Stasiulis, Daiva K., and Abigail B. Bakan. 2003. *Negotiating Citizenship.* New York: Palgrave Macmillan.

Stiell, Bernadette, and Kim England. 1999. "Jamaican Domestics, Filipina Housekeepers, and English Nannies: Representations of Toronto's Foreign Domestic Workers." In *Gender, Migration, and Domestic Service*, edited by Janet Henshall Momsen, 44–62. New York: Routledge.

Sto. Tomas, Patricia. 1984. "Overseas Employment in the Philippines: Policies and

Program." In *Migration from the Philippines*, edited by Anthony Paganoni, 101–121. Quezon City: Scalabrini Migration Center.

Sturdevant, Saudra Pollock, and Brenda Stoltzfus. 1992. *Let the Good Times Roll: Prostitution and the U.S. Military in Asia.* New York: The New Press.

Tadiar, Neferti. 2004. *Fantasy-Production: Sexual Economies and Other Philippine Consequences for the New World Order.* Hong Kong University Press.

Takaki, Ronald. 1998. *A History of Asian Americans: Strangers from a Different Shore.* Updated and revised edition. Boston: Little, Brown.

Taylor, Frederick. 1911. *Principles of Scientific Management.* New York: Harper and Brothers.

Thai, Hung Cam. 2008. *For Better or for Worse: Vietnamese International Marriages in the New Global Economy.* New Brunswick: Rutgers University Press.

Tyner, James. 1996. "The Gendering of Philippine International Labor Migration." *Professional Geographer* 48 (4): 405–416.

———. 2000. "Global Cities and Circuits of Labor: The Case of Manila, Philippines." *Professional Geographer* 52 (1): 61–74.

Tung, Charlene. 1999. *The Social Reproductive Labor of Filipina Transmigrant Workers in Southern California.* PhD diss., University of California, Irvine.

United States Adjutant General of the Army. 1902. *Correspondence Relating to the War with Spain.* Vols. 1 and 2. Washington, D.C.: Government Printing Office.

United States General Accounting Office. 2001. *Nursing Workforce: Emerging Nurse Shortages Due to Multiple Factors.* Washington D.C.: United States General Accounting Office.

Villegas, Edberto M. 1988. *The Political Economy of Philippine Labor Laws.* Manila: Foundation of Nationalist Studies.

Villenas, Sofia. 1996. "The Colonizer/Colonized Chicana Ethnographer: Identity, Marginalization, and Co-optation in the Field." *Harvard Educational Review* 66 (4): 711–731.

Visayan Forum Foundation. 2006. *Clarifying the Batas Kasambahay: Q&A on the Bill for Domestic Workers in the Philippines.* http://www.visayanforum.org/article.php?mode_id=721.

Waldman, Amy. 2005. "Sri Lankan Maids' High Price for Foreign Jobs." *New York Times*, May 8, 2005.

Ward, Kathryn ed. 1990. *Women Workers and Global Restructuring.* Ithaca: Cornell University Press.

White, Kathleen. 2001. "A New and Very Real Nursing Shortage." *Policy, Politics, and Nursing Practice* 2 (3): 200–205.

Wolf, Diane L. 1992. *Factory Daughters: Gender, Household Dynamics, and Rural Industrialization in Java.* Berkeley and Los Angeles: University of California Press.

Woodward, Peter N. 1988. *Oil and Labor in the Middle East: Saudi Arabia and the Oil Boom.* New York: Praeger.

Zavella, Patricia. 1997. "Feminist Insider Dilemmas: Constructing Ethnic Identity with "Chicana" Informants." In *Situated Lives: Gender and Culture in Everyday Life*, edited by Louise Lamphere, Helena Ragone and Patricia Zavella, 42–61. New York: Routledge.

Index

accents, 196
accountability, 83, 100
accreditation, 212n19; of employers, 92, 220n10; of Philippine Embassy, 35
adaptability, 23, 153
added export value, 11, 123–154, 178–203, 206–207; disparate work responsibilities and, 185–191; of education, 143, 153, 181; Filipino nursing care and, 180–185; flexibility as, 135–136, 179, 182–183, 194–198; gendered, 153; manpower sourcing/pooling and, 139–153; marketing perceptions and, 126–139; medical culture of fear and, 191–194; overqualification and, 137–139, 153–154; racialization of, 134–135, 153; specifications of, 132–133. *See also* comparative advantage
adventure, 114, 128
advertisements, 139; for Baylor, 116–117; in classified section, 2, 142; for Filipino workers, 213n2; for PEAs, 113
agencies. *See* private employment agencies (PEAs)
agriculture, 27–29, 214n12, 214n16
Alberto (nurse migrant), 172–173
all-around workers, 150–153
ambassadors of goodwill, 149; dishonoring, 52–58; responsibility for, 206

American dream, 155–177; Americanized nursing subjects and, 158–159; education and, 171–173; families of overseas workers and, 168–170; Filipino communities and, 163–165; Filipinos as "born to have," 165–168; the good life and, 173–177; hiring packages and, 161–163, 164–165; nurse shortage and, 159–161
Americanized consumerism, 115, 156–157, 166–168; ready-to-leave Filipinos and, 130–131. *See also* consumption
Americanized nursing subjects, 158–159
American nurses. *See* white nurses
Angelo, Virgilio, 74–75
Ansel (nurse migrant), 184–185, 191–192, 193
application process for U.S. work, 172
appropriate femininity, 133
Aquino, Corazon, 32, 33, 34, 52, 54, 211n1
Arizona, 155
Arroyo, Gloria Macapagal, ix, 3, 4, 21–22, 45–46, 156; audience of, 218n23; cultural ambassadors and, 176; new aristocracy and, 72; PEOs and, 59; policy changes by, 88; Supermaid training program and, 70
Artist Record Book system, 35
Asian Development Bank (ADB), 34
Asis, Maruja, 211n2

class, 16–17, 115, 154

classified ads, 2, 142

Client Referral Assistance
program, 93

coaching applicants, 144–153; added
export value and, 154; gendered
dynamics of, 149

college graduates, 143

colonial history of Philippines, 4, 10,
23, 24–27, 132; trope of productive
femininity and, 135; U.S. relations,
25–27, 32, 158, 166, 180

combativeness, 61, 199

"comfort zones," 174–175

Commission on Filipinos Overseas
(CFO), 13; Education Modules
and, 61–63

commodification, 51; of "ideal labor,"
206; of OFWs, 55, 204

comparative advantage, 2, 11;
discipline and, 124–125, 154; ethos
of labor migration and, 49; MTPDP
and, 46; of overqualification, 138;
PDOSs and, 51; racialization and,
134; ready-to-leave Filipinos and,
131; sustainability of, 103. *See also*
added export value

competence, image of, 197–198

Competency-Based Curriculum
Exemplar, 68–69

competition: economic, 51; for
Philippines, 102–103, 137;
among private employment
agencies, 90–94

complaints, 104–105, 147, 179,
187, 189, 199–200; disparate work
responsibilities and, 199; Filipino
nurse migrants and, 181, 188,
193–194, 224n2; image of
competence and, 197; patients',
193; vs. subservience, 137

conduct of Filipino workers, 47, 52

conflict resolution, 145

Constable, Nicole, 131, 223n11

consumerism, 115, 130–131,
156–157, 166–168

consumption, 157, 172–173, 176;
cars and, 166, 169; ready-to-leave
Filipinos and, 130–131. *See also*
Americanized consumerism

Contemplacion, Flor, 35–39, 62,
217n14

continuing education, 193

contracts: buying out, 178, 200;
completion of, 134; negotiations of,
58–59; visas and, 213n3

cosmopolitanism, 115, 167

counseling, 147

cultural ambassadors, 69–70, 176

cultural crimes, 69, 70

cultural logic, 4

culturally essentialist claims , 48, 184

culture: of dependency, 79; of
employment, 73; of
entrepreneurship, 73; of fear,
191–194; of migration, 23, 205,
211n2; of sacrifice, 131

currency conversion: British pound,
171; U.S. dollar, 162, 167, 169, 187

days off, 150; Eureka Incognito and,
183; rarity of, 155; sacrificing, 169,
186, 219n29

debt, 4, 73–74; of Philippines, 27–32

De La Salle University, 15, 16

denationalization of territory,
6, 211n4

Department of Foreign Affairs (DFA),
69, 90, 219n4

Department of Labor and
Employment (DOLE), 39, 219n4;
deregulation and, 98; in labor-
building landscape, 90; PEAs and,
90–91; protest marchers at, 87–88;
RA 8042 and, 36

Department of Tourism, 2

deploying underage workers, 96–97, 120–121

deregulation, 98–99. *See also* regulation

DFA. *See* Department of Foreign Affairs (DFA)

Diana (nurse migrant), 183, 185–187, 194–195, 196

"difficult to enter" aspect of policy change, 95–96, 97

Dimapilis-Baldoz, Rosalinda, 204

Dimzon, Carmelita, 48, 58–59, 80; deregulation and, 98; overseas resource centers and, 71; on PEOSs, 60

direct hiring, 31

disciplinary power, 5, 50–86, 124, 143, 199; ambassadors of goodwill and, 52–58; entrepreneurship and, 72–78; gendered, 8–9; productive women workers and, 78–84; professionalization and, 65–72; well-informed workers and, 58–65

discipline, 217n12; comparative advantage and, 124–125, 154; gendered, 149; self-imposed, 146–147

discourse, 180; of benevolence, 25–26; of responsibility, 80; of suffering, 131

disempowerment, 6, 9, 199. *See also* empowerment

docility, 10, 11, 202–203; vs. complaints, 179; determination and, 150; discipline and, 199; enduring difficult situations with, 146; job security and, 195–196; videos and, 143

DOLE. *See* Department of Labor and Employment (DOLE)

domestic work: employers of, 69; Indonesia and, 103; naturalized, 136; overqualification for, 119–120;

physical demands of, 136; professionalizing, 67–72; recruitment for, 142; trope of productive femininity and, 124; videos and, 124

domestic workers, 5; as all-around workers, 152–153; ban on overseas deployment of, 34; "basic" value of Filipina, 137; brokering of, 11–12; earnings of in Philippines, 40; education and, 218n19; gender and, 136, 222n1; in Hong Kong, 40, 47, 64, 131, 215n23; increase in deployment of, 33; marketing perceptions and, 127; men as, 136; nurses working as, 138; PDOSs and, 50, 63; potential "unruliness" of Filipina, 150; as property, 147, 150; remarketing, 127; women's family finances and, 79

downward economic mobility, 30–32

earnings: buying power and, 167; complaints and, 187; of domestic workers, 40, 215n23, 216n30; empowerment and, 177; Eureka Incognito and, 190; expenditures and, 173; guarantees of, 107; living wages and, 106, 130, 191–194; management of, 75; misuse of, 83; as motivation, 170; of nurses in Philippines, 40, 141, 192, 222n23; of nurses in U.S., 158, 161–162; race and, 221n19; ready-to-leave Filipinos and, 130; taxes and, 171. *See also* overtime hours

"easy to go" aspect of policy change, 96–97

"easy to operate" aspect of policy change, 95–96, 97

EB-3 visas, 112, 161, 188, 213n3

economic logic, 205

economy of Philippines, 28

Ilocos, 214n12
image building, 209
image: of ideal worker, 63–64;
of Philippines, 122, 136; of private
employment agencies, 95–96,
97, 113
immigration: categories of, 30, 213n3,
214n17; fees for, 162–163; visas for,
112–113, 159, 161, 188, 213n3
Immigration Act (1965), 158–159
import substitution, 213n8
in-bound marketing activity, 44–45
Incognito, Eureka (nurse migrant),
165, 169, 178–179, 203; challenges
by, 199–200; disparate work
responsibilities of, 197–198;
overtime hours and, 183, 186,
190, 198, 199; relocation of, 202
indebtedness, 73–74
India, 3, 207, 208
Indonesia, 3, 103, 141
intelligence, 172–173
International Labor Organization
(ILO), 22
International Monetary Fund (IMF),
28, 30
Intramuros (Manila), 219n1
investments, 6, 72–78, 156, 206;
overseas workers as families',
173–174
Ishi, Tomoji, 159
Israel, 153

Jamaican women, 10
Jan (nurse migrant), 164, 175,
191–192
Japan, 35, 115
Jesus Christ, 24
job security, 153, 180, 191, 194–195,
195–196
jobs fairs, 45, 93
Joen (nurse migrant), 170, 173–174,
181; complaints and, 188; relocation

of, 202; on responsibility, 185; on
self-sufficiency, 182
joint and solidarity liability clause,
103–104
Josue, Noel, 36–38, 138
Justin (nurse migrant), 165–166, 167,
170, 176, 181–182, 195, 198
juvenile delinquency, 128
J visas, 159

kababayan (compatriot), 16
Kaibigan ng OCW (Friends of
Overseas Contract Workers), 13, 36,
138, 218n17
Kang, Laura Hyun, 125
Kelly, Phillip, 215n20
Kit (nurse migrant), 167–168;
relocation of, 202
Kitty (nurse migrant), 155–158, 165,
169, 192; challenges by, 200–201
knowledge workers, 151

labor, 205; control of, 8, 85;
diplomacy and, 41, 45–49; global
division of, 5, 9–10, 33, 206;
specialization of, 93
labor-brokering process, 7–9, 204;
ethos of labor migration and, 4–5;
moral economy of Filipino
migrants and, 5; private sector and,
19–20; as racialized and gendered,
4–6; of state, 7; on unlevel playing
field, 97
labor brokers, 12, 17; as allies,
116–120; culture of migration and,
23; protest march of, 88
Labor Code of 1974, 31; amendment
(1978), 214n18
labor exploitation, 12, 34, 188–189,
191; Contemplacion as, 36
labor export policy, 3, 205; Labor
Code of 1974 and, 31; as stopgap
response, 22

overtime hours: complaints about, 179; definition of, 224n12; Eureka Incognito and, 183, 186, 190, 198, 199; Filipinos' readiness to work, 186; Kitty and, 155–156, 169; Mabolo and, 168; nurse shortage and, 160, 182–183, 186–187

OWWA. *See* Overseas Workers Welfare Administration (OWWA)

"padrino system," 188
palakasan system, 118, 222n26
Palmiery, Alfredo, 99, 100, 103
parity rights, 28, 188
Parreñas, Rhacel, 79–80, 211n3
PASEI. *See* Philippine Association of Service Exporters Inc. (PASEI)
patience, 134
patients, 190, 193, 195
PDOS. *See* pre-departure orientation seminars (PDOSs)
Pei-Chia, Lan, 47
pensionado, 158, 213n7
PEOSs. *See* preemployment orientation seminars (PEOSs)
PhD degree, 18
Philippine-American War (1898–1903), 25
Philippine Association of Service Exporters Inc. (PASEI), 102, 105, 221n14
Philippine Census of Population on Housing, 81
Philippine Daily Inquirer, 21
Philippine Department of Foreign Affairs (DFA), 69, 90, 219n4
Philippine Embassy, 35
Philippine Labor Code (1974), 40
Philippine Nurses Monitor, 156
Philippine Nursing Association, 129
Philippine Nursing Association of America, 129

Philippine Nursing Association of Arizona (PNAAZ), 15–16
Philippine Overseas Employment Administration (POEA), 13, 22, 204; accreditation and, 92, 212n19; awards from, 93, 117–118, 216n4, 216n6, 217n7, 220n6; BBA and, 52–54; cases filed to, 217n10; formation of, 32; Government Placement Branch of, 31, 57, 92; hiring process and, 92; in labor-building landscape, 90; liability and, 145; Marketing Division of, 42–45; on 1987 stats, 33; PEAs and, 90–91, 101–105; policy changes of, 67–68, 94–101, 141; power in, 97–98; PRAs and, 140; RA 8042 and, 36; as regulatory body, 95–96; role of, 41–42, 219n4
Philippine Overseas Labor Offices (POLOs), 43, 216n34; hiring process and, 92; in labor-building landscape, 90; qualification certification by, 67
Philippines: colonial history of, 4, 10, 23, 24–27, 132, 135; colonial relations between U.S. and, 25–27, 32, 158, 166, 180; constitution of, 212n8; as economically viable country, 63; life in, 157, 174–176; living-wage jobs in, 83; national identity of, 49; value of nursing work in, 188. *See also* governmentalized state
Philippines Department of Tourism, 22
Philippine stock exchange, 74
physical appearance, 82
physical transformations, 115–116
physical violence, 148, 217n10
physicians, 191–192
Pia (nurse migrant), 162, 167, 188–189, 191, 196

About the Author

ANNA ROMINA GUEVARRA is an assistant professor of sociology and Asian American studies and an affiliate faculty member in gender and women's studies at the University of Illinois at Chicago.

www.ingramcontent.com/pod-product-compliance
Lightning Source LLC
Chambersburg PA
CBHW021812270326
41932CB00007B/151

* 9 7 8 0 8 1 3 5 4 6 3 4 6 *